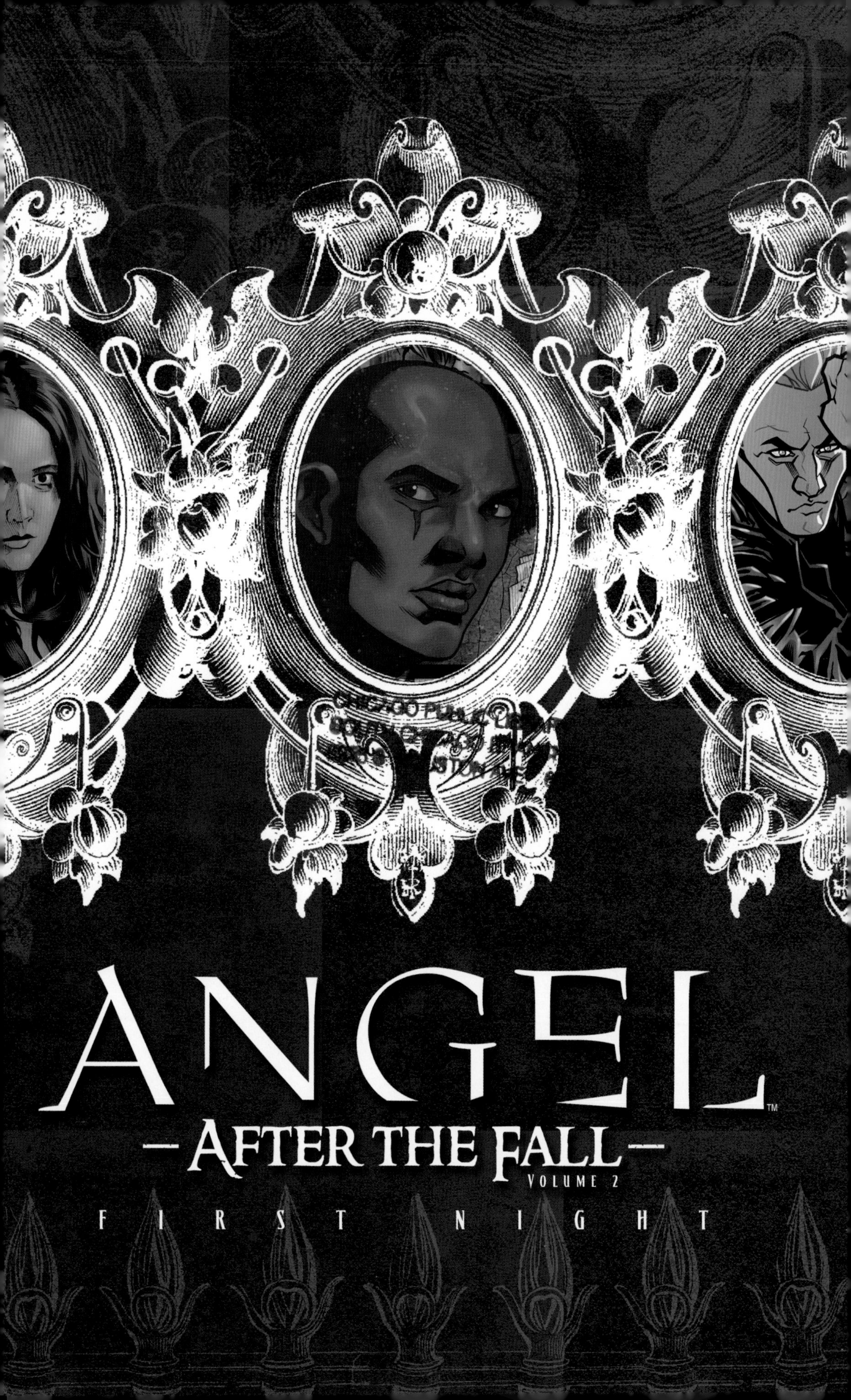
ANGEL™
—AFTER THE FALL—
VOLUME 2
FIRST NIGHT

PLOTTED BY
JOSS WHEDON AND BRIAN LYNCH
SCRIPTED BY BRIAN LYNCH

BETTA GEORGE · ILLUSTRATED BY TIM KANE, COLORS BY JEREMY TREEZE

SPIKE · ILLUSTRATED BY DAVID MESSINA, COLORS BY ILARIA TRAVERSI

CONNOR · ILLUSTRATED BY STEPHEN MOONEY, COLORS BY LISA JACKSON

LORNE · ILLUSTRATED BY JOHN BYRNE, COLORS BY LEONARD O'GRADY

WESLEY · ILLUSTRATED BY NICK RUNGE, COLORS BY JOHN RAUCH

KATE · ILLUSTRATED BY STEPHEN MOONEY, COLORS BY LISA JACKSON

GWEN · ILLUSTRATED BY FABIO MANTOVANI

CIVILIANS · ILLUSTRATED BY KEVYN SCHMIDT

GUNN · ILLUSTRATED BY MIRCO PIERFEDERICI,
COLORS BY FABIO MANTOVANI WITH MICHELE BUSCALFERRI

LETTERED BY ROBBIE ROBBINS
ORIGINAL SERIES EDITED BY CHRIS RYALL
COLLECTION EDITED BY JUSTIN EISINGER
COLLECTION DESIGNED BY ROBBIE ROBBINS

ISBN: 978-1-60010-231-8

11 10 09 08   02 03 04 05

www.IDWPUBLISHING.com

Angel created by Joss Whedon and David Greenwalt.
Special thanks to our Watcher, Joss Whedon, and Fox Worldwide Publishing's
Debbie Olshan for their invaluable assistance.

IDW Publishing
Operations:
Moshe Berger, Chairman
Ted Adams, President
Clifford Meth, EVP of Strategies
Matthew Ruzicka, CPA, Controller
Alan Payne, VP of Sales
Lorelei Bunjes, Dir. of Digital Services
Marci Kahn, Executive Assistant
Alonzo Simon, Shipping Manager

Editorial:
Chris Ryall, Publisher/Editor-in-Chief
Scott Dunbier, Editor, Special Projects
Justin Eisinger, Editor
Kris Oprisko, Editor/Foreign Lic.
Denton J. Tipton, Editor
Tom Waltz, Editor

Design:
Robbie Robbins, EVP/Sr. Graphic Artist
Ben Templesmith, Artist/Designer
Neil Uyetake, Art Director
Chris Mowry, Graphic Artist
Amauri Osorio, Graphic Artist

GROOSABLOG

07-17-08

Current Mood: Heroic yet recappish

Greetings, fair denizens of Cybre Space. It is Groosalugg, survivor of the Scum Pits of Ur, Champion of Pylea, proud originator of the 4,000,000,545th most popular weblog in all the land. Watch your back, BritneyFan2005, for I am rapidly gaining on your numbers, and soon you will be forced to redub yourself DefeatFan2008. So it is blogged, so it shall be.

I was updating my Wikipedia page (simple note, historians of the Web: it is "Groosalugg," not "Groosalog;" know it well) when I received a cyber parchment from man-woman Chris Ry-all of Eye Dee Double You apologizing on assumed knee for lack of inclusion in the main story of Volume the Seconde of ANGEL: AFTER THE FALL, and requesting that I recap all that has gone forth previously to help the confused reader.

I laughed to myself a hearty chuckle because apologies were not needed. Certainly my exclusion in this (you'll notice) much smaller volume (less Groosalugg translates to less mass and less excitement) was quite obviously so ladies and Ryall-esque men alike could recover from what is heretofore known as "Groo-induced-vapors." As for recapping? Of course! I shall recap in such a way that you believe this story has never been told UNTIL the recap. The recap shall replace actual events, and actual events shall now be known as "foreshadowing the recap." Brace yourself... for the recapping.

Lantern-Jawed Hero Angel and his band of not-even-close-resembling-merry men had incurred the wrath of evil law firm (AND SO MUCH MORE!) Wolfram & Hart. Wolfram & Hart had sent an army to throw down in glorious battle with them in an alleyway. There was much fighting and bloodshed. Soon after, Angel and his followers were tossed, along with all of Los Angeles, into hell itself. Much fighting and ghosting did occur, ending with the group being reunited. Only now Groosalugg is at their side, so they shall most certainly win the day (or night, as it may be).

But before you know where you're going, you must know where you've been. What of that first night in hell? How did Angel's cohorts react to a city gone straight to hell? How did they spend their FIRST NIGHT? BEHOLD! ANGEL: AFTER THE FALL: FIRST NIGHT has begun! And ended, in the very same book! That is convenience you can depend on!

I must take leave of you for now, for the Domino's Man is knock-knock-knocking at my door with promises of a great feast for an affordable price. He shall bring Cheesy Bread, lest he know what true vengeance means.

This blog is over and done with. You are welcome. Hopefully it has made you think, made you cry, and mostly, made you LOL (LONG-FOR-GROOSALUGG OUT LOUD). I am disabling comments for now because I tire of that awful Tyrannosaurus_Sex_69_4ever's disparaging remarks about my punctuation.

GROOSALUGG

Listening to: Cries of my enemies, squeals of lust from the local townswomen. Also Coldplay.

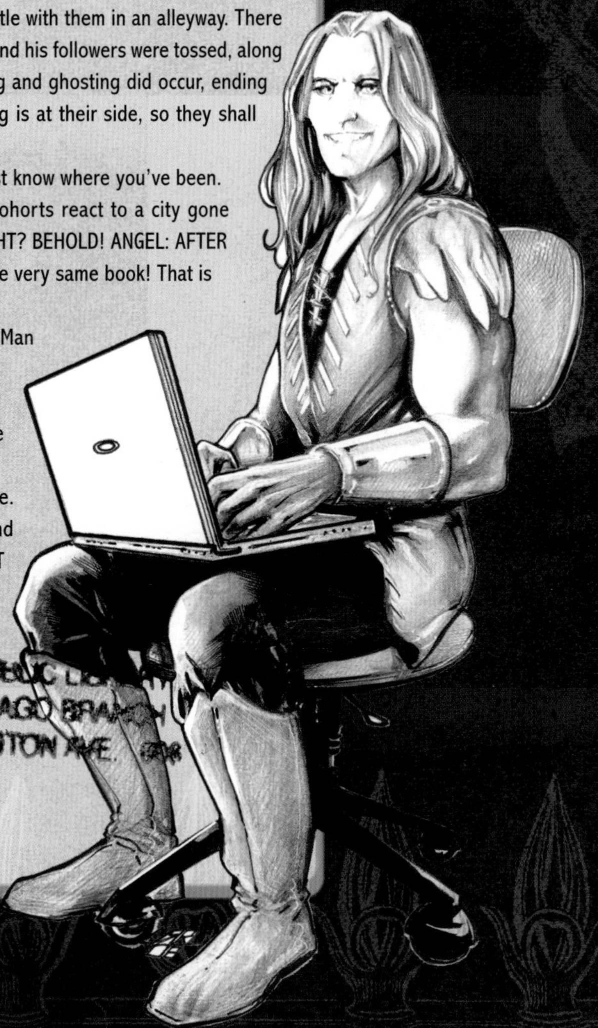

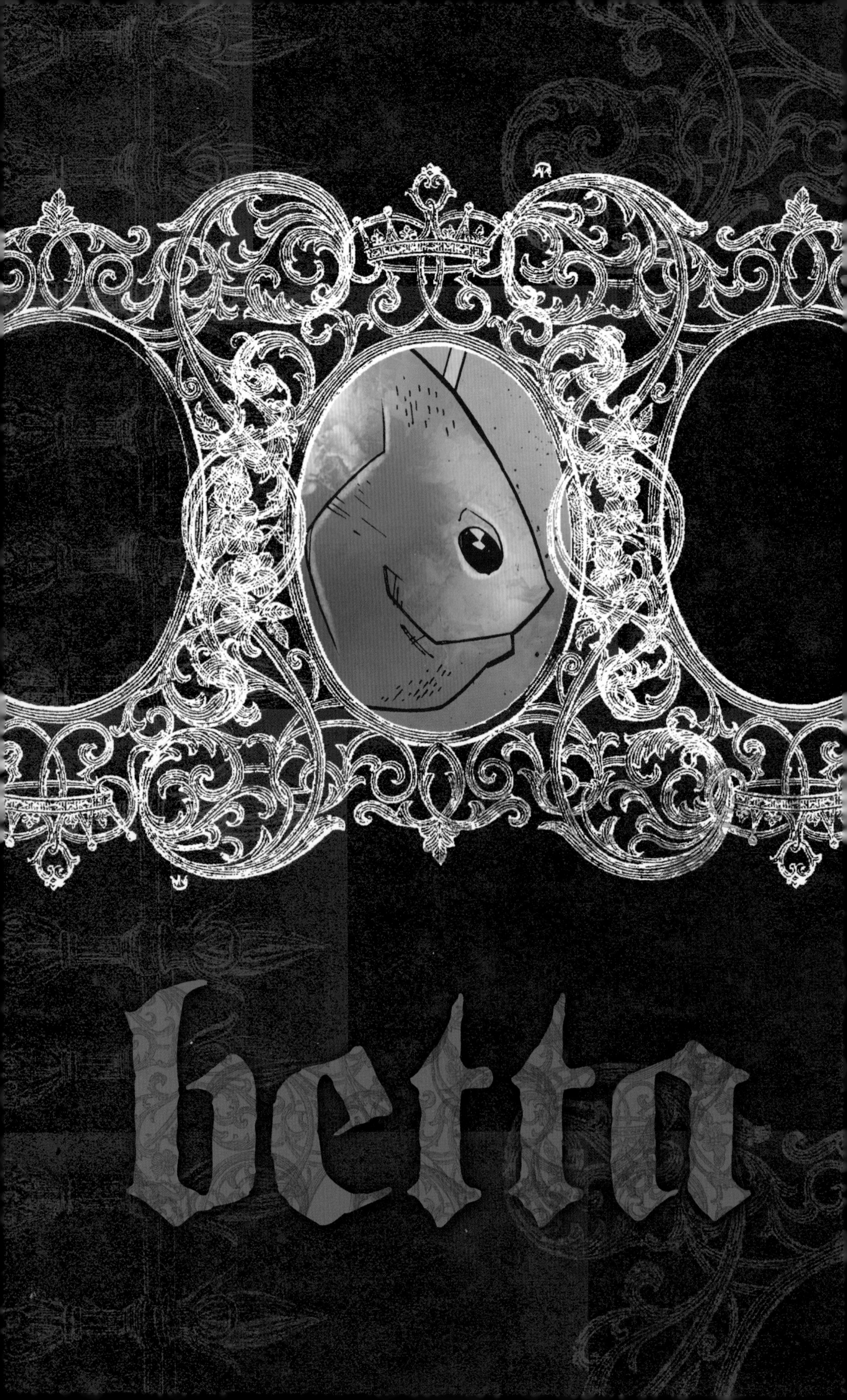
betta

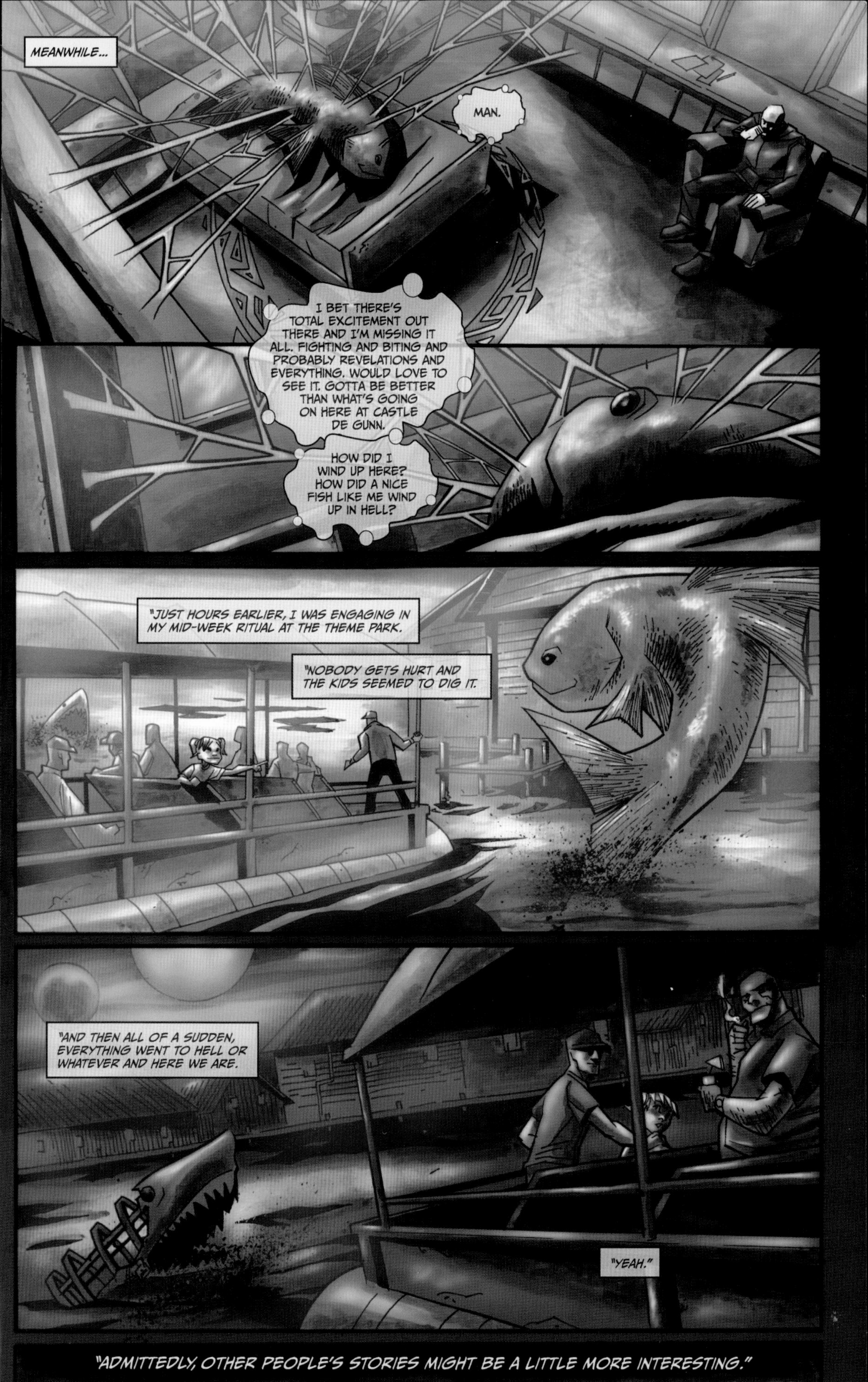
MEANWHILE...
MAN.
I BET THERE'S TOTAL EXCITEMENT OUT THERE AND I'M MISSING IT ALL. FIGHTING AND BITING AND PROBABLY REVELATIONS AND EVERYTHING. WOULD LOVE TO SEE IT. GOTTA BE BETTER THAN WHAT'S GOING ON HERE AT CASTLE DE GUNN.
HOW DID I WIND UP HERE? HOW DID A NICE FISH LIKE ME WIND UP IN HELL?
"JUST HOURS EARLIER, I WAS ENGAGING IN MY MID-WEEK RITUAL AT THE THEME PARK.
"NOBODY GETS HURT AND THE KIDS SEEMED TO DIG IT.
"AND THEN ALL OF A SUDDEN, EVERYTHING WENT TO HELL OR WHATEVER AND HERE WE ARE.
"YEAH."
"ADMITTEDLY, OTHER PEOPLE'S STORIES MIGHT BE A LITTLE MORE INTERESTING."

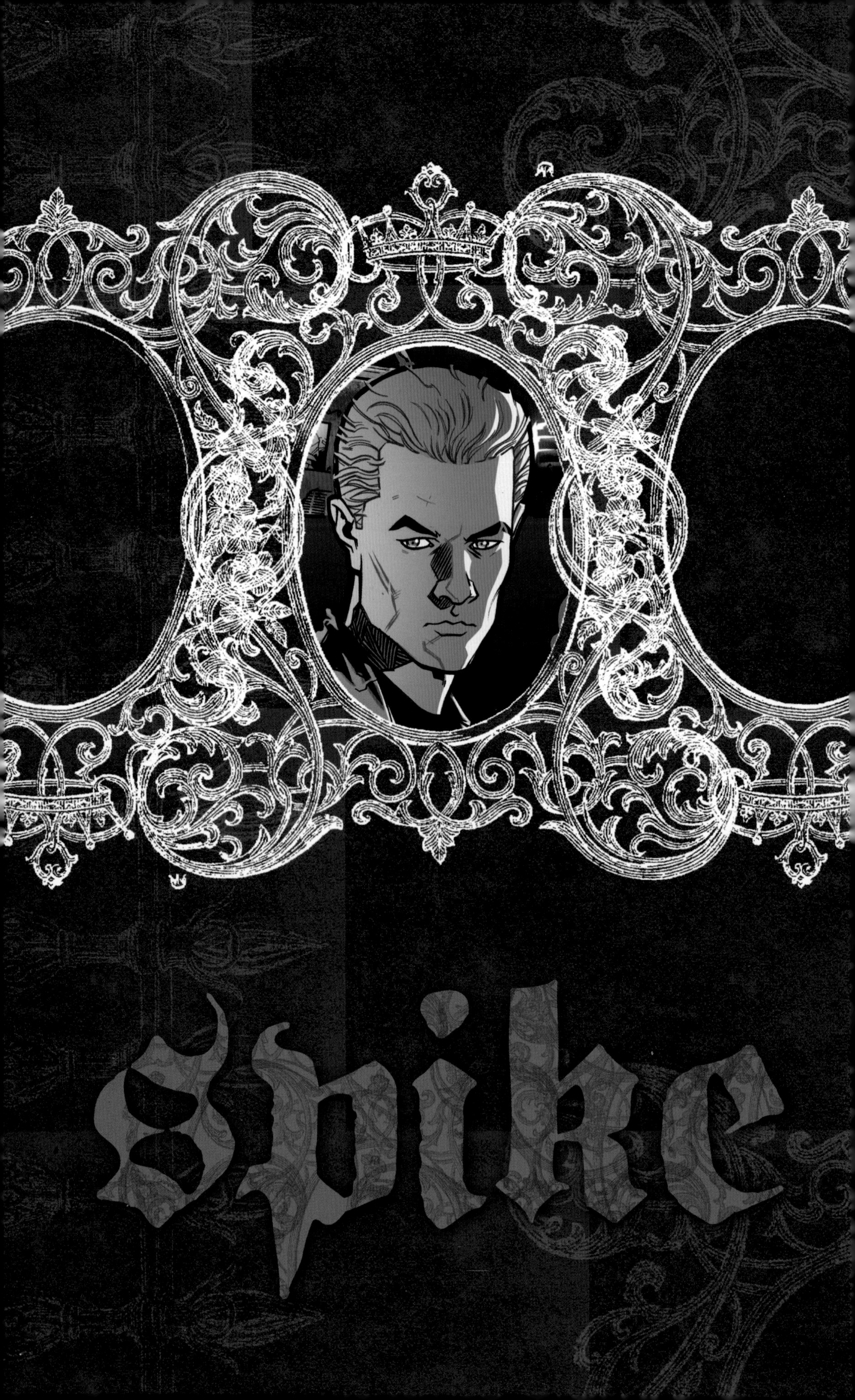
Spike

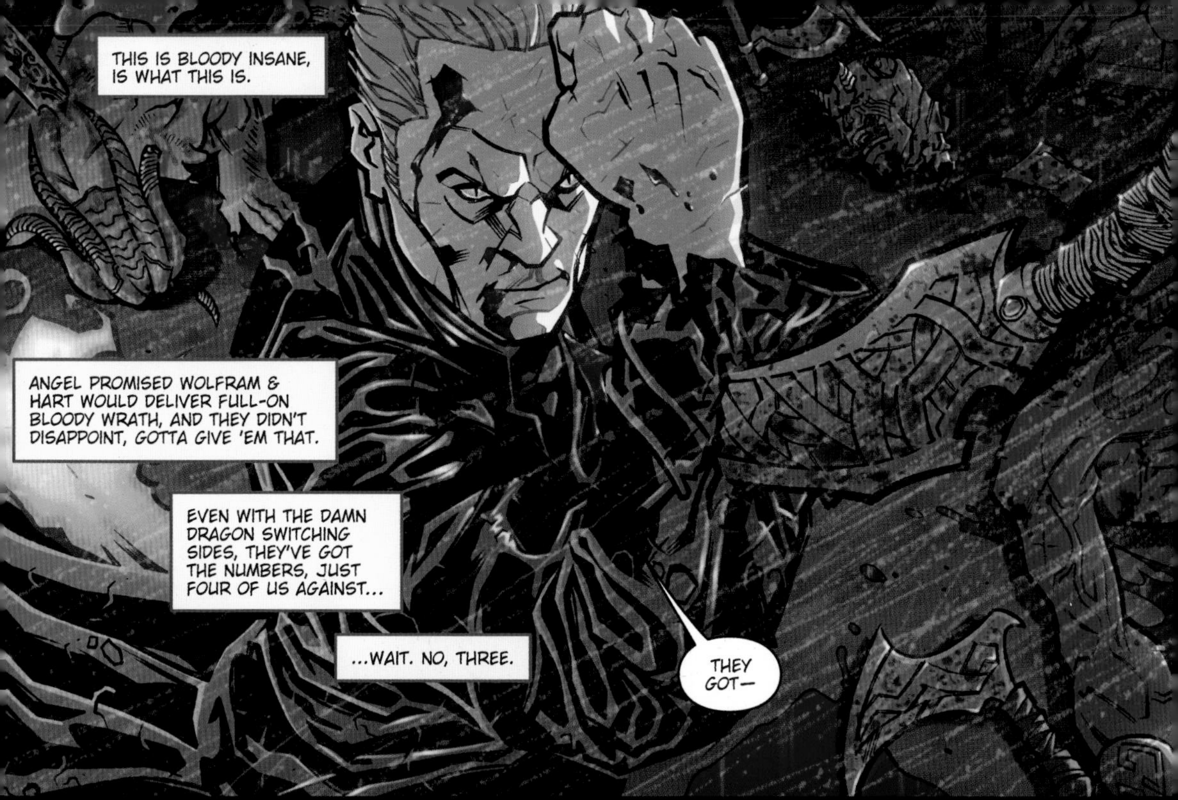
THIS IS BLOODY INSANE, IS WHAT THIS IS.
ANGEL PROMISED WOLFRAM & HART WOULD DELIVER FULL-ON BLOODY WRATH, AND THEY DIDN'T DISAPPOINT, GOTTA GIVE 'EM THAT.
EVEN WITH THE DAMN DRAGON SWITCHING SIDES, THEY'VE GOT THE NUMBERS, JUST FOUR OF US AGAINST...
...WAIT. NO, THREE.
THEY GOT—

SPIKE

written by brian lynch
art by david messina

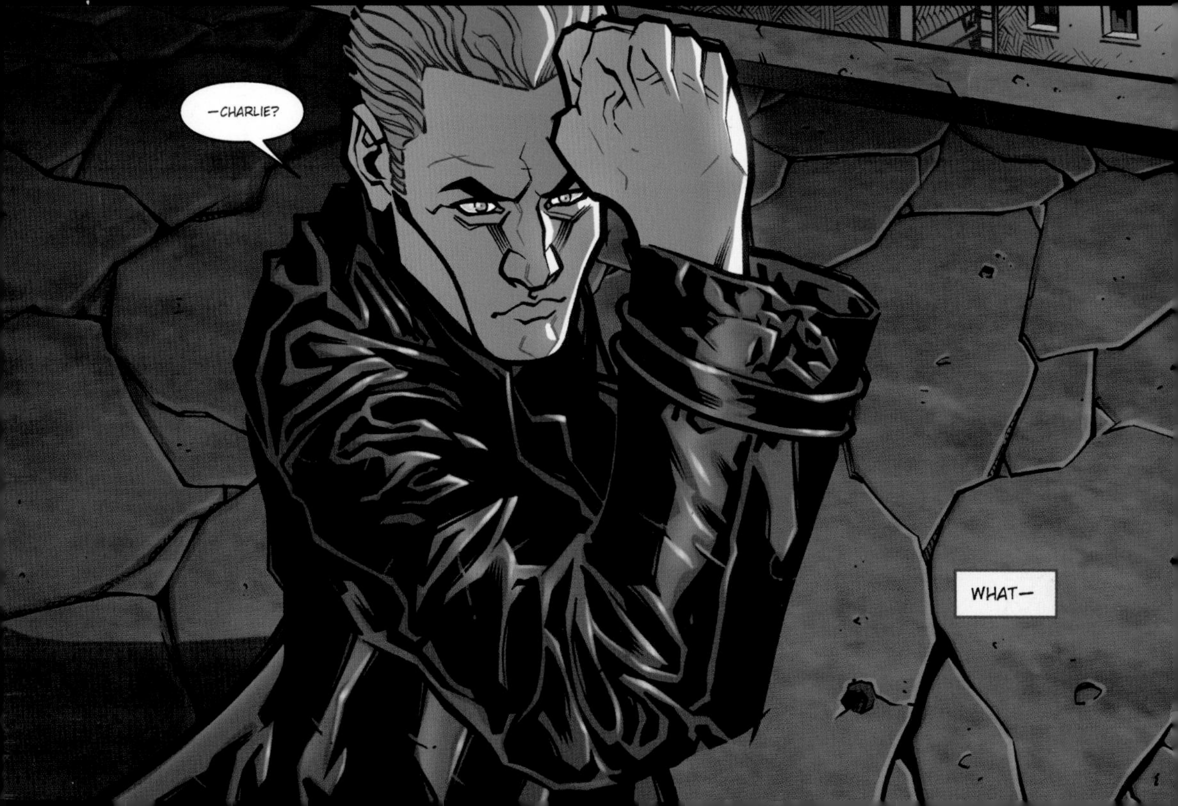
—CHARLIE?
WHAT—

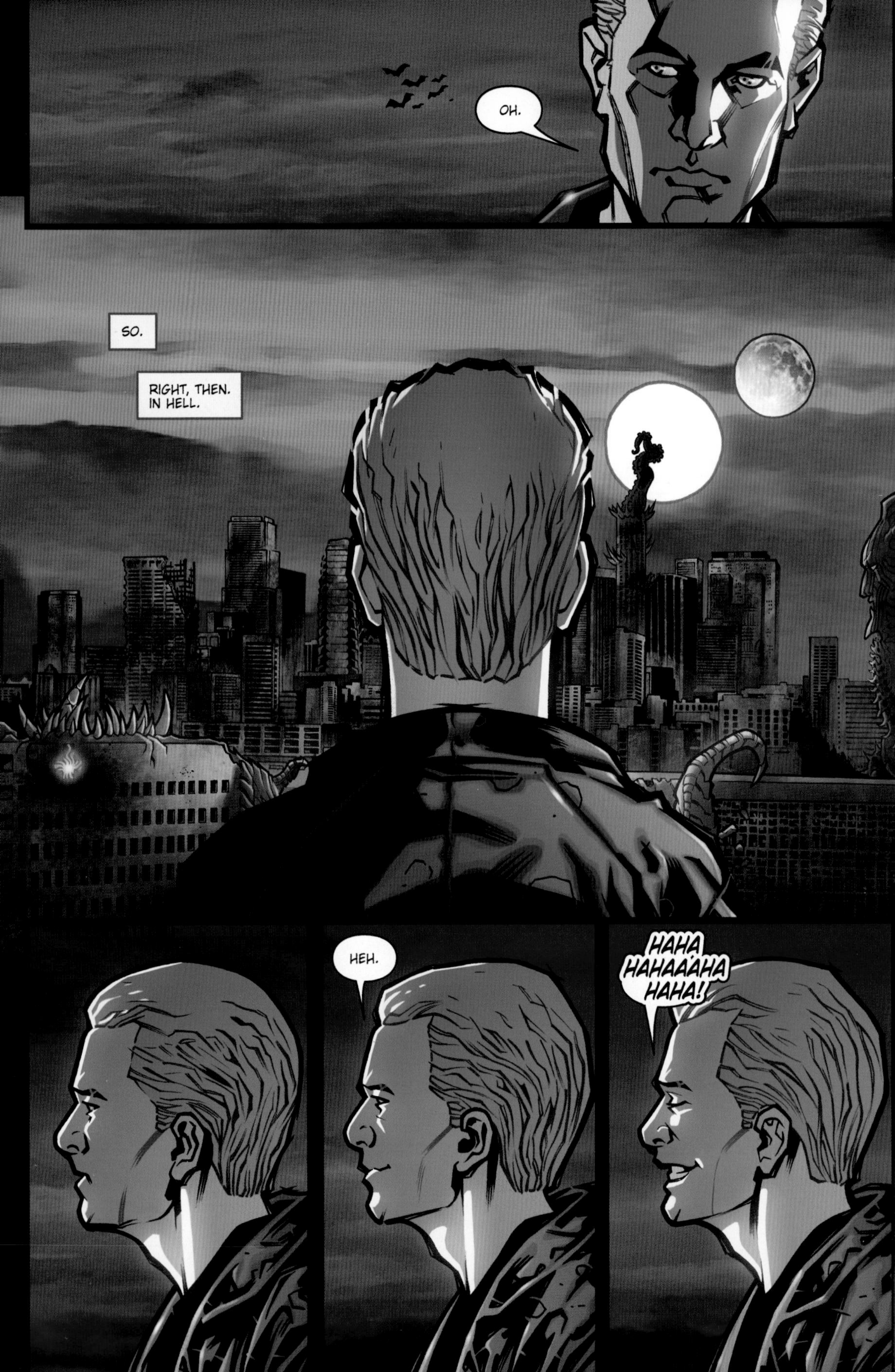
OH.
SO.
RIGHT, THEN.
IN HELL.
HEH.
HAHA
HAHAAAHA
HAHA!

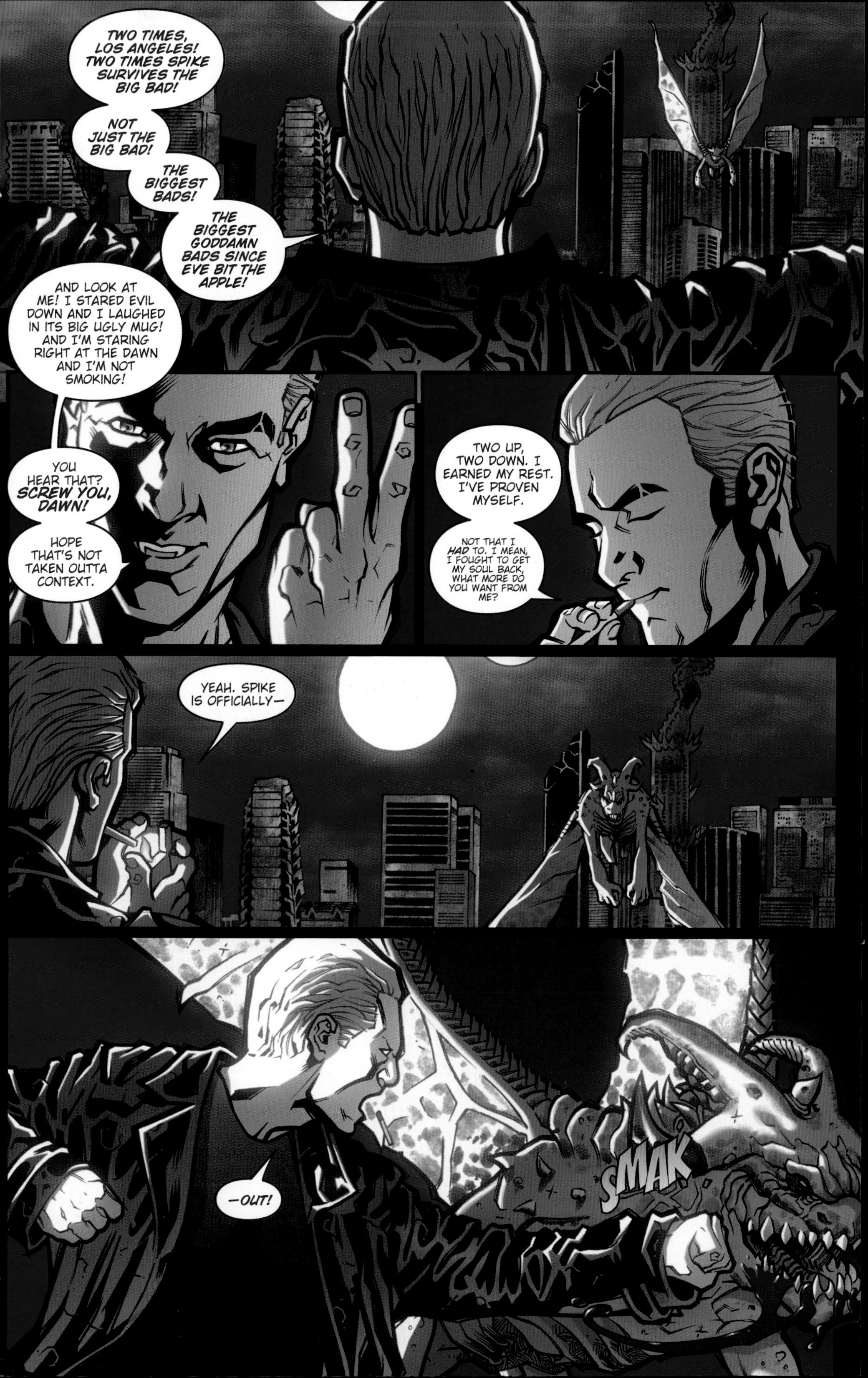
TWO TIMES, LOS ANGELES! TWO TIMES SPIKE SURVIVES THE BIG BAD!
NOT JUST THE BIG BAD!
THE BIGGEST BADS!
THE BIGGEST GODDAMN BADS SINCE EVE BIT THE APPLE!
AND LOOK AT ME! I STARED EVIL DOWN AND I LAUGHED IN ITS BIG UGLY MUG! AND I'M STARING RIGHT AT THE DAWN AND I'M NOT SMOKING!
YOU HEAR THAT? SCREW YOU, DAWN!
HOPE THAT'S NOT TAKEN OUTTA CONTEXT.
TWO UP, TWO DOWN. I EARNED MY REST. I'VE PROVEN MYSELF.
NOT THAT I HAD TO. I MEAN, I FOUGHT TO GET MY SOUL BACK, WHAT MORE DO YOU WANT FROM ME?
YEAH. SPIKE IS OFFICIALLY—
—OUT!
SMAK

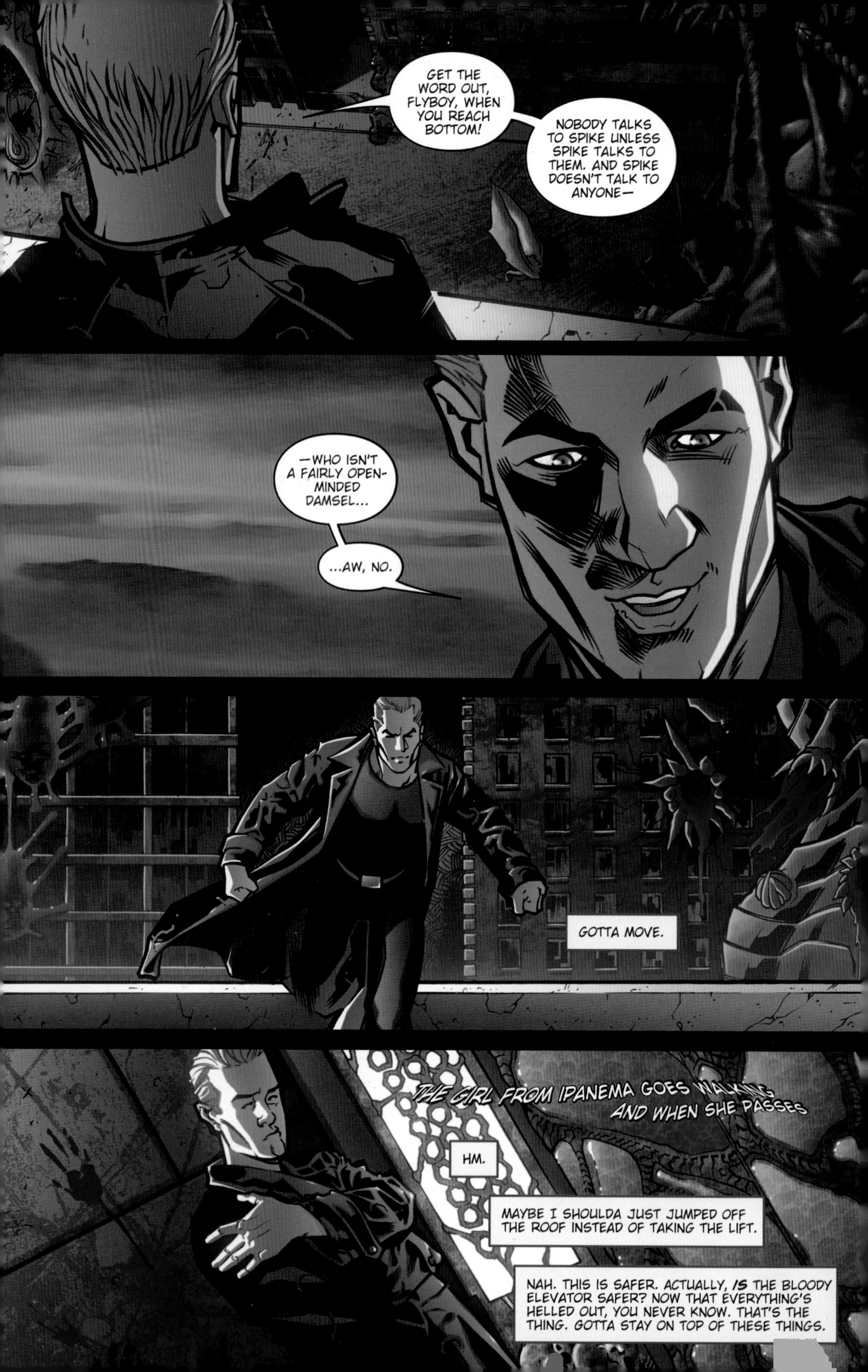
GET THE WORD OUT, FLYBOY, WHEN YOU REACH BOTTOM!
NOBODY TALKS TO SPIKE UNLESS SPIKE TALKS TO THEM. AND SPIKE DOESN'T TALK TO ANYONE—
—WHO ISN'T A FAIRLY OPEN-MINDED DAMSEL...
...AW, NO.
GOTTA MOVE.
THE GIRL FROM IPANEMA GOES WALKING
AND WHEN SHE PASSES
HM.
MAYBE I SHOULDA JUST JUMPED OFF THE ROOF INSTEAD OF TAKING THE LIFT.
NAH. THIS IS SAFER. ACTUALLY, IS THE BLOODY ELEVATOR SAFER? NOW THAT EVERYTHING'S HELLED OUT, YOU NEVER KNOW. THAT'S THE THING. GOTTA STAY ON TOP OF THESE THINGS.

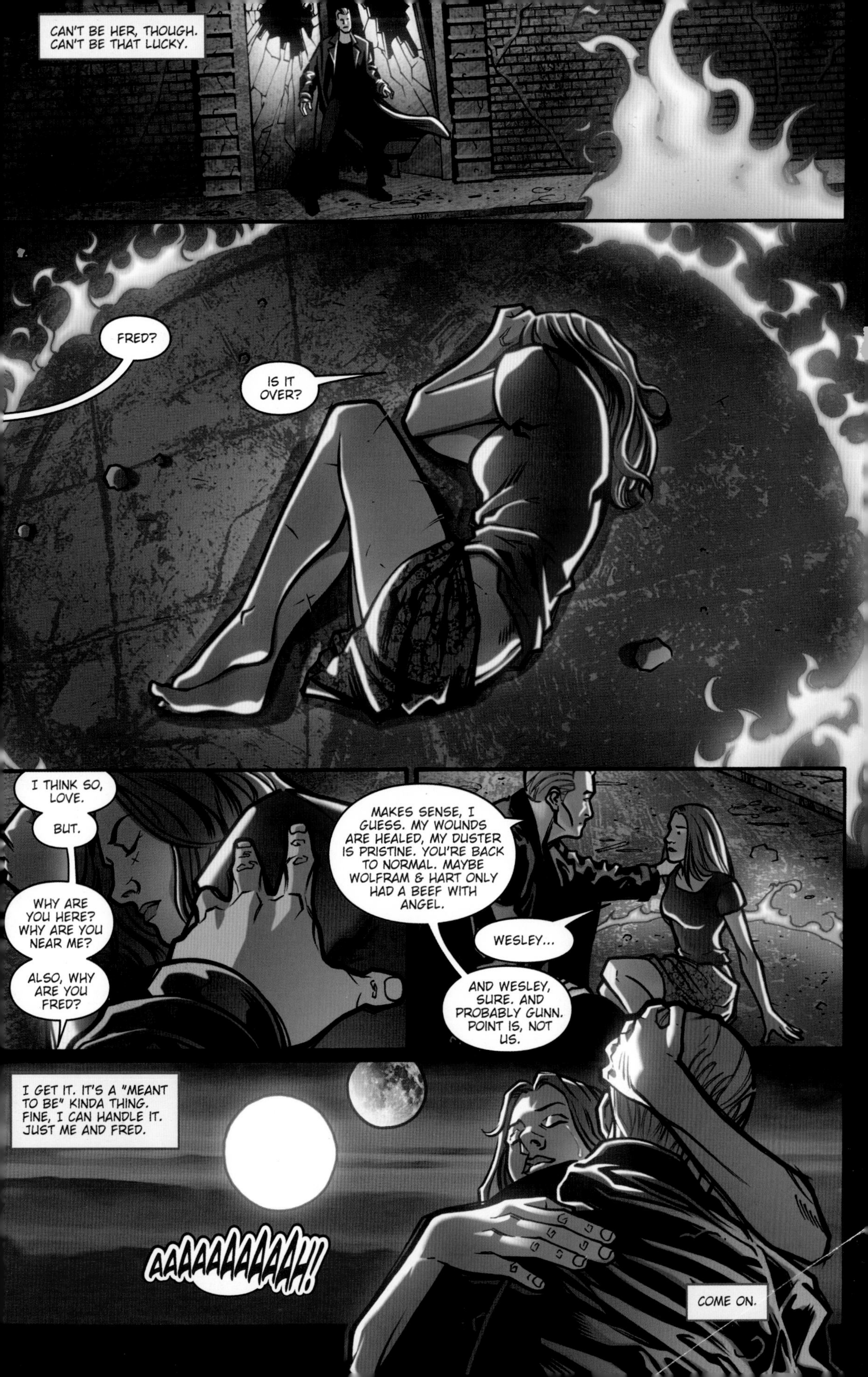
CAN'T BE HER, THOUGH. CAN'T BE THAT LUCKY.
FRED?
IS IT OVER?
I THINK SO, LOVE.
BUT.
WHY ARE YOU HERE? WHY ARE YOU NEAR ME?
ALSO, WHY ARE YOU FRED?
MAKES SENSE, I GUESS. MY WOUNDS ARE HEALED, MY DUSTER IS PRISTINE. YOU'RE BACK TO NORMAL. MAYBE WOLFRAM & HART ONLY HAD A BEEF WITH ANGEL.
WESLEY...
AND WESLEY, SURE. AND PROBABLY GUNN. POINT IS, NOT US.
I GET IT. IT'S A "MEANT TO BE" KINDA THING. FINE, I CAN HANDLE IT. JUST ME AND FRED.
AAAAAAAAAAH!!
COME ON.

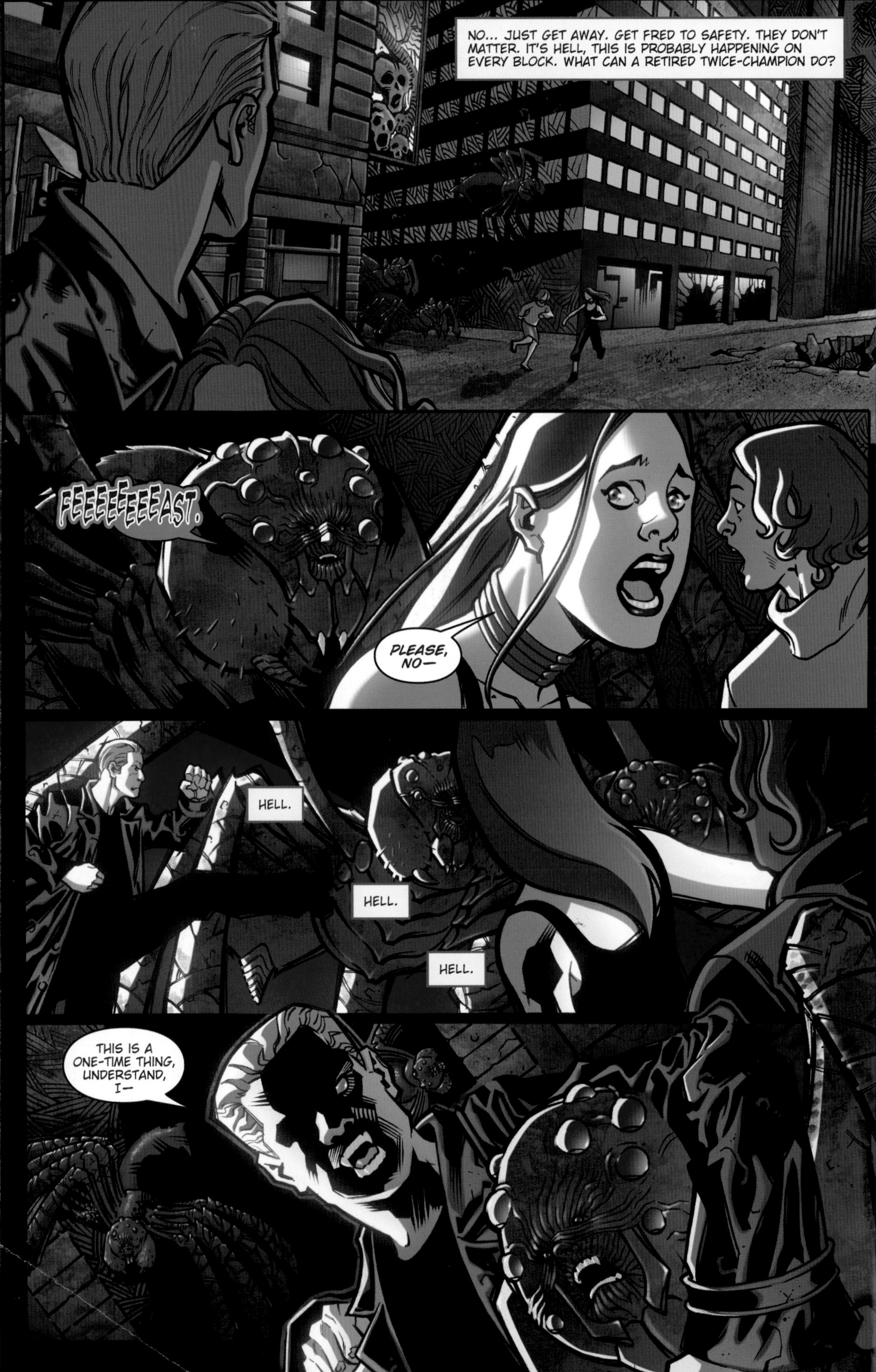
NO... JUST GET AWAY. GET FRED TO SAFETY. THEY DON'T MATTER. IT'S HELL, THIS IS PROBABLY HAPPENING ON EVERY BLOCK. WHAT CAN A RETIRED TWICE-CHAMPION DO?
FEEEEEEEEAST.
PLEASE, NO—
HELL.
HELL.
HELL.
THIS IS A ONE-TIME THING, UNDERSTAND, I—

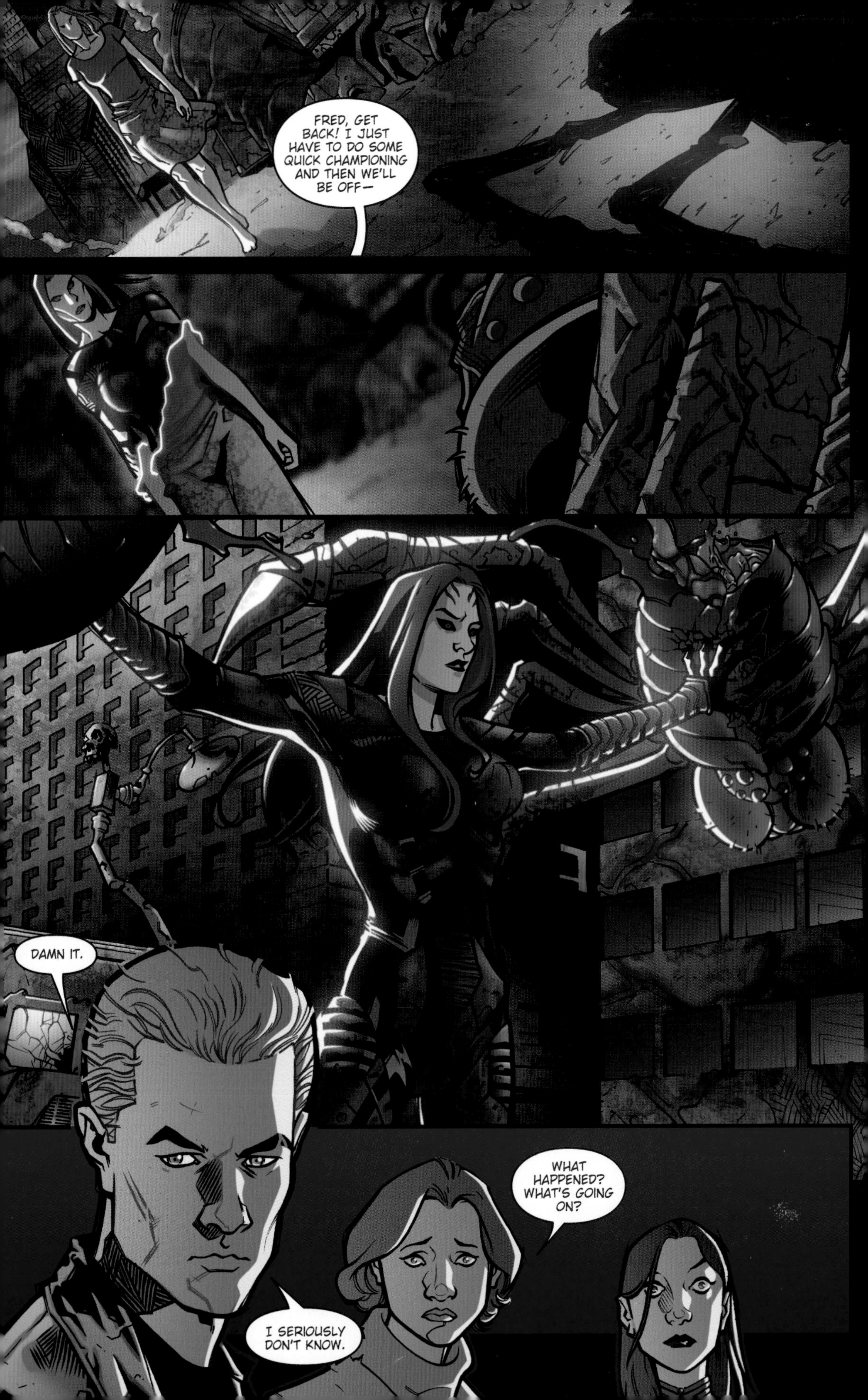
FRED, GET BACK! I JUST HAVE TO DO SOME QUICK CHAMPIONING AND THEN WE'LL BE OFF—
DAMN IT.
WHAT HAPPENED? WHAT'S GOING ON?
I SERIOUSLY DON'T KNOW.

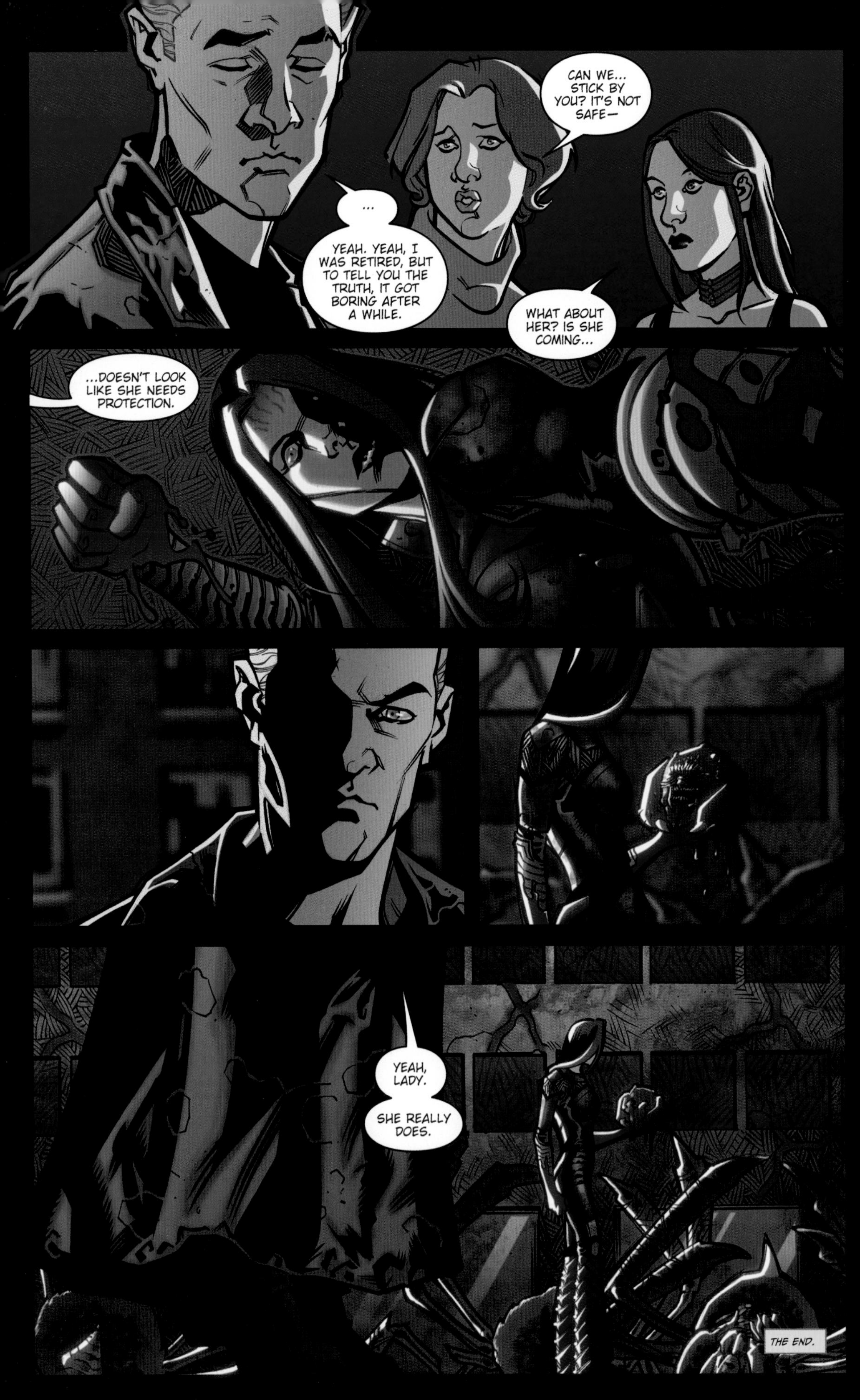
CAN WE... STICK BY YOU? IT'S NOT SAFE—
...
YEAH. YEAH, I WAS RETIRED, BUT TO TELL YOU THE TRUTH, IT GOT BORING AFTER A WHILE.
WHAT ABOUT HER? IS SHE COMING...
...DOESN'T LOOK LIKE SHE NEEDS PROTECTION.
YEAH, LADY.
SHE REALLY DOES.
THE END.

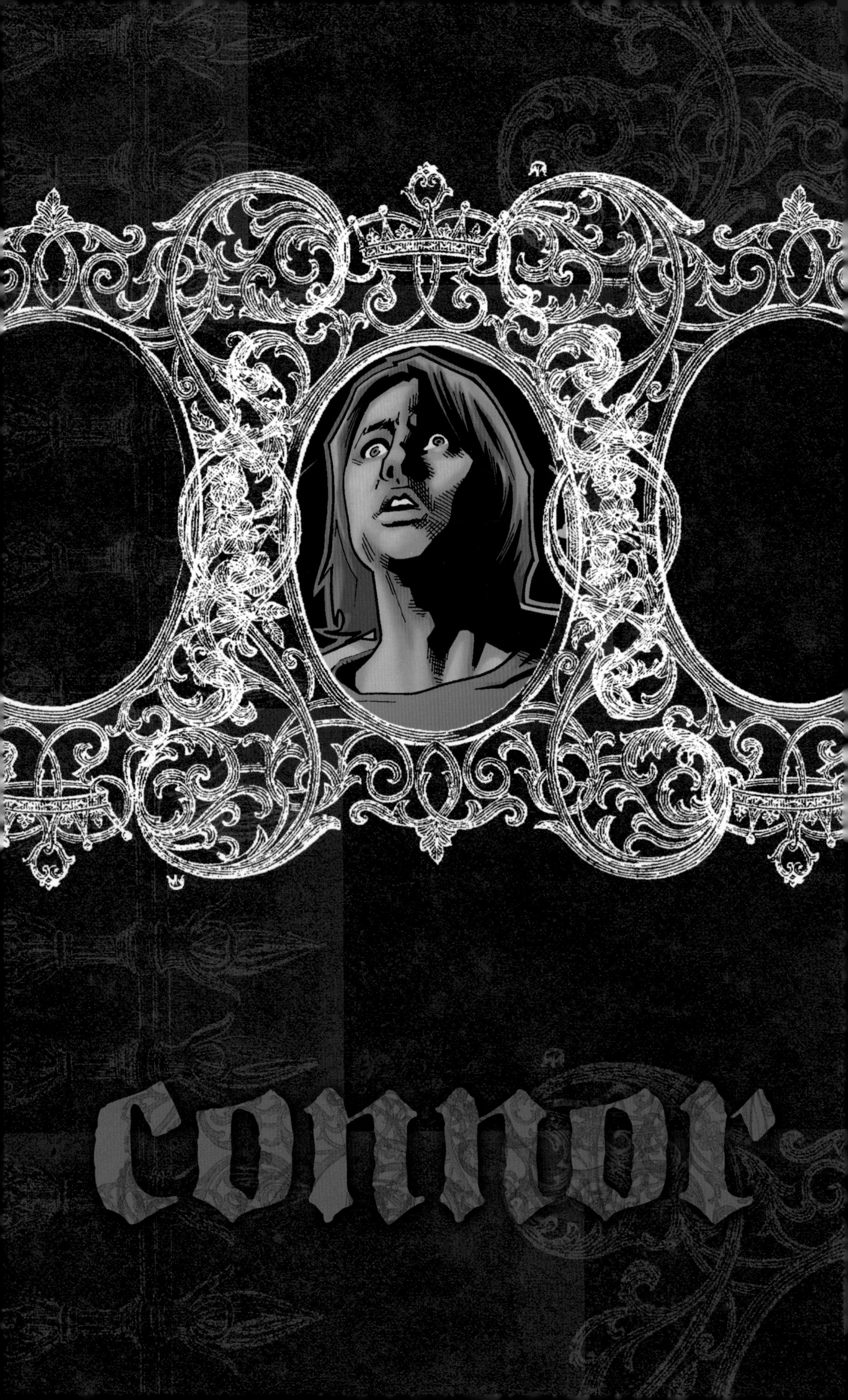

connor

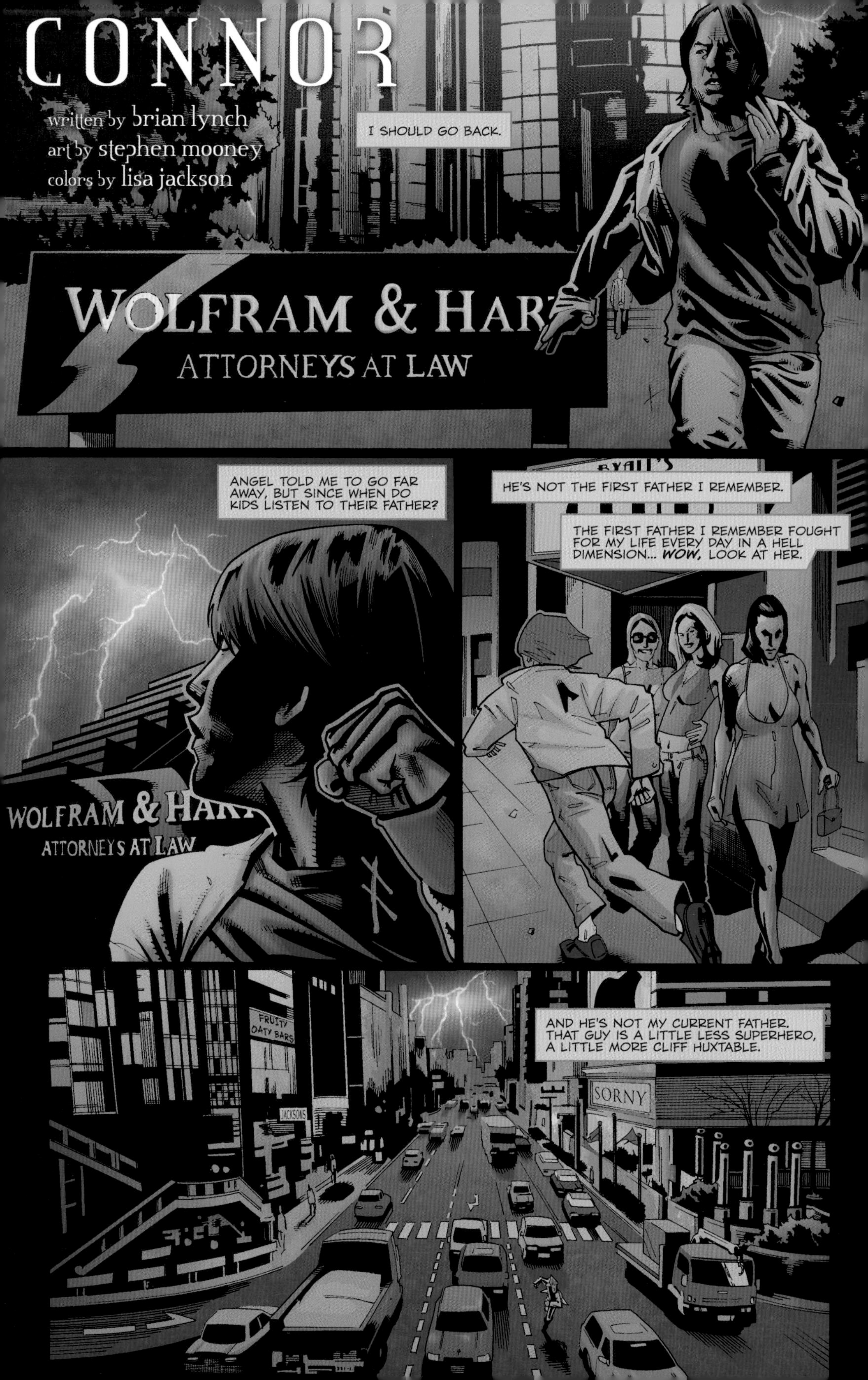
CONNOR
written by brian lynch
art by stephen mooney
colors by lisa jackson
I SHOULD GO BACK.
WOLFRAM & HART
ATTORNEYS AT LAW
ANGEL TOLD ME TO GO FAR AWAY, BUT SINCE WHEN DO KIDS LISTEN TO THEIR FATHER?
HE'S NOT THE FIRST FATHER I REMEMBER.
THE FIRST FATHER I REMEMBER FOUGHT FOR MY LIFE EVERY DAY IN A HELL DIMENSION... WOW, LOOK AT HER.
AND HE'S NOT MY CURRENT FATHER. THAT GUY IS A LITTLE LESS SUPERHERO, A LITTLE MORE CLIFF HUXTABLE.
FRUITY OATY BARS
JACKSONS
SORNY

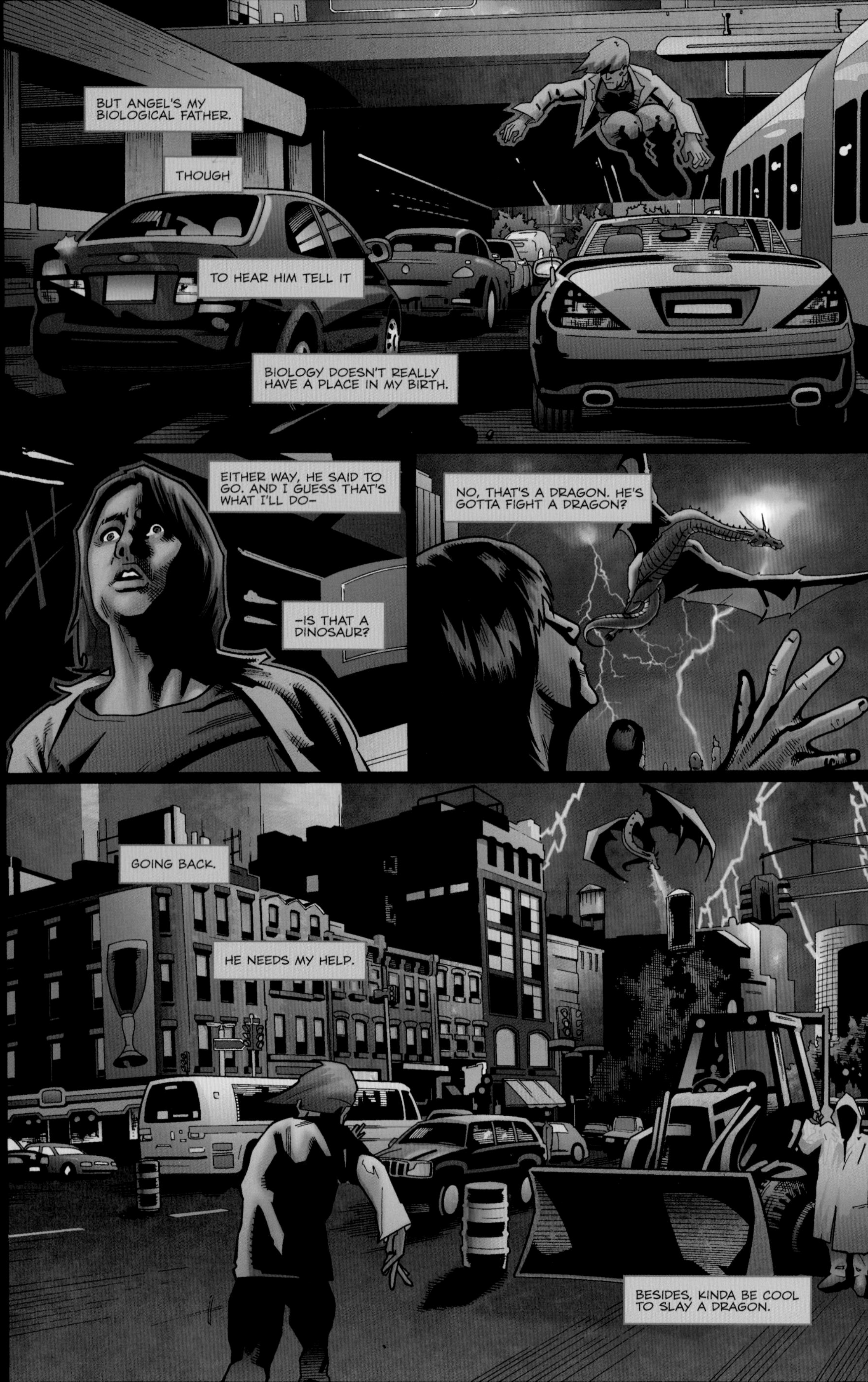

BUT ANGEL'S MY BIOLOGICAL FATHER.
THOUGH
TO HEAR HIM TELL IT
BIOLOGY DOESN'T REALLY HAVE A PLACE IN MY BIRTH.
EITHER WAY, HE SAID TO GO. AND I GUESS THAT'S WHAT I'LL DO–
–IS THAT A DINOSAUR?
NO, THAT'S A DRAGON. HE'S GOTTA FIGHT A DRAGON?
GOING BACK.
HE NEEDS MY HELP.
BESIDES, KINDA BE COOL TO SLAY A DRAGON.

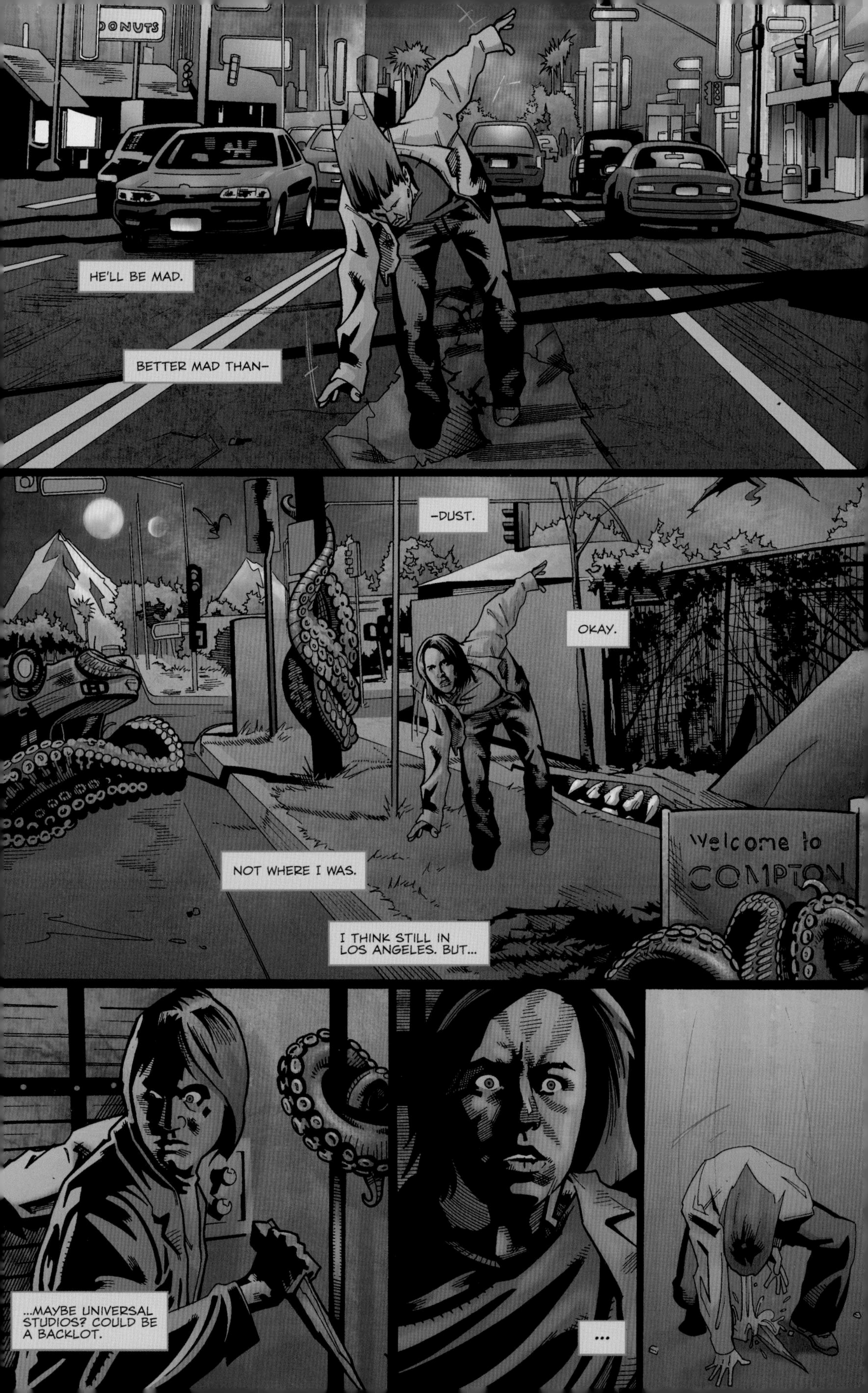
DONUTS
HE'LL BE MAD.
BETTER MAD THAN–
–DUST.
OKAY.
NOT WHERE I WAS.
I THINK STILL IN LOS ANGELES. BUT...
Welcome to COMPTON
...MAYBE UNIVERSAL STUDIOS? COULD BE A BACKLOT.
...

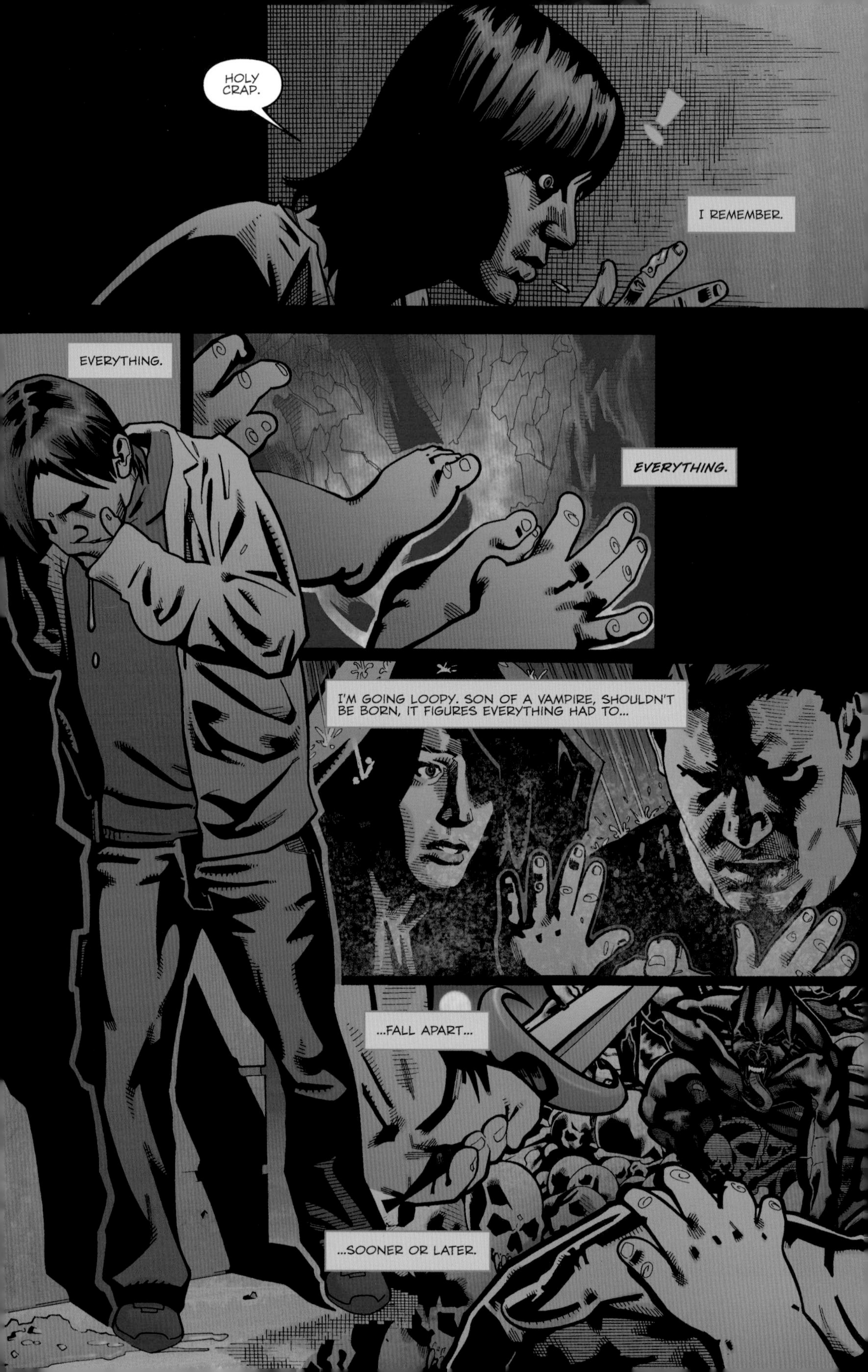
HOLY CRAP.
I REMEMBER.
EVERYTHING.
EVERYTHING.
I'M GOING LOOPY. SON OF A VAMPIRE, SHOULDN'T BE BORN, IT FIGURES EVERYTHING HAD TO...
...FALL APART...
...SOONER OR LATER.

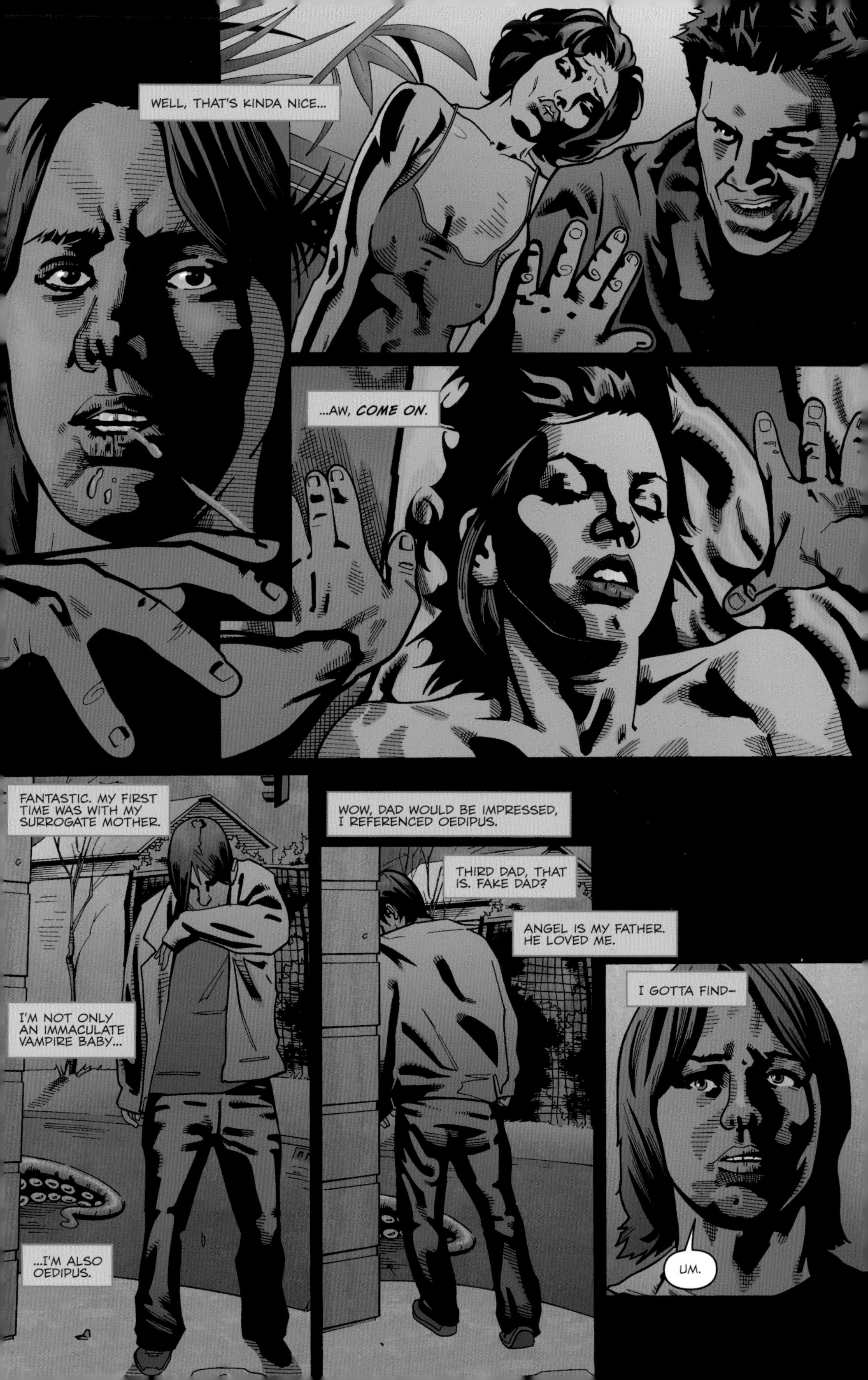
WELL, THAT'S KINDA NICE...
...AW, COME ON.
FANTASTIC. MY FIRST TIME WAS WITH MY SURROGATE MOTHER.
I'M NOT ONLY AN IMMACULATE VAMPIRE BABY...
...I'M ALSO OEDIPUS.
WOW, DAD WOULD BE IMPRESSED, I REFERENCED OEDIPUS.
THIRD DAD, THAT IS. FAKE DAD?
ANGEL IS MY FATHER. HE LOVED ME.
I GOTTA FIND-
UM.

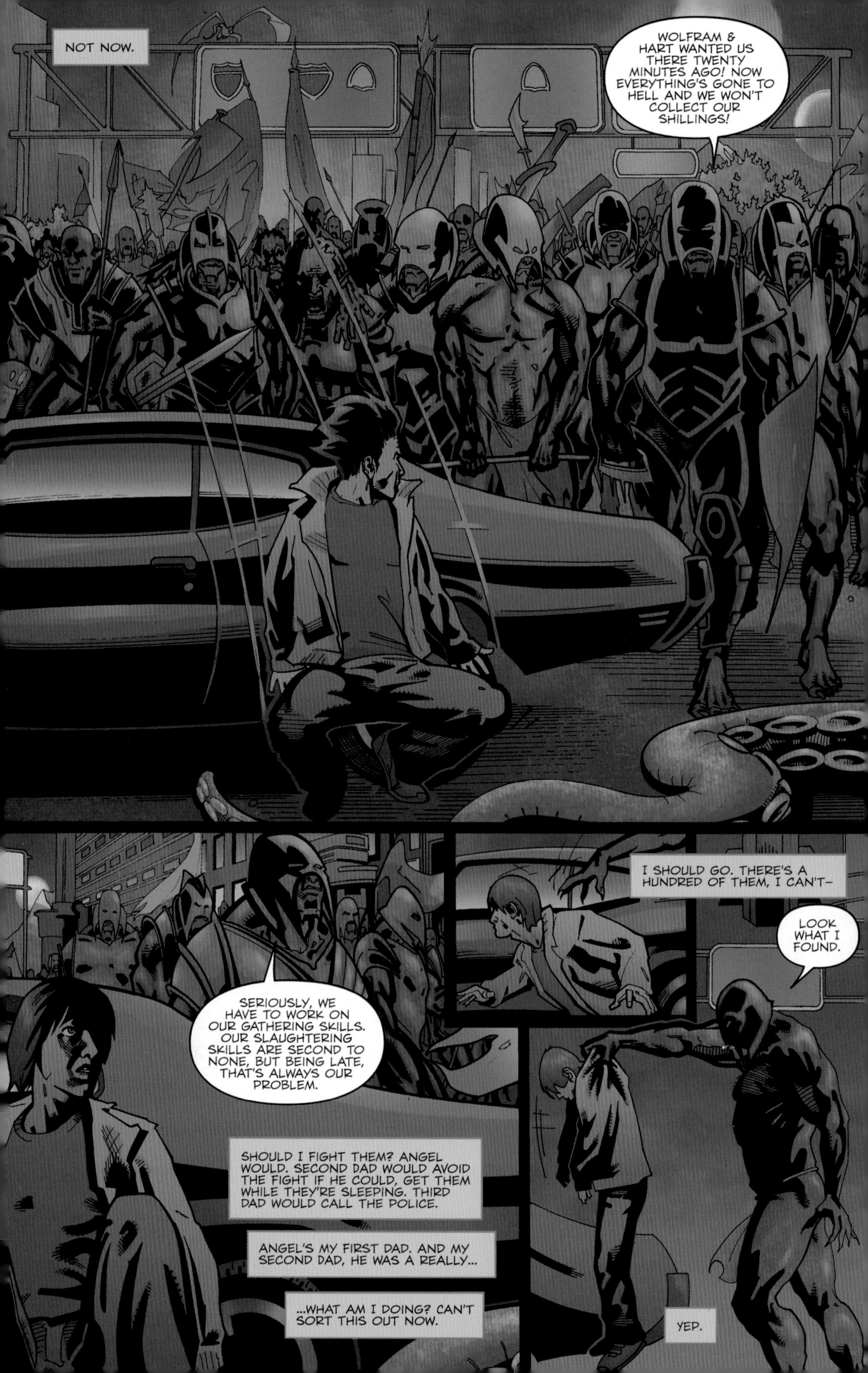
NOT NOW.
WOLFRAM & HART WANTED US THERE TWENTY MINUTES AGO! NOW EVERYTHING'S GONE TO HELL AND WE WON'T COLLECT OUR SHILLINGS!
SERIOUSLY, WE HAVE TO WORK ON OUR GATHERING SKILLS. OUR SLAUGHTERING SKILLS ARE SECOND TO NONE, BUT BEING LATE, THAT'S ALWAYS OUR PROBLEM.
SHOULD I FIGHT THEM? ANGEL WOULD. SECOND DAD WOULD AVOID THE FIGHT IF HE COULD, GET THEM WHILE THEY'RE SLEEPING. THIRD DAD WOULD CALL THE POLICE.
ANGEL'S MY FIRST DAD. AND MY SECOND DAD, HE WAS A REALLY...
...WHAT AM I DOING? CAN'T SORT THIS OUT NOW.
I SHOULD GO. THERE'S A HUNDRED OF THEM, I CAN'T–
LOOK WHAT I FOUND.
YEP.

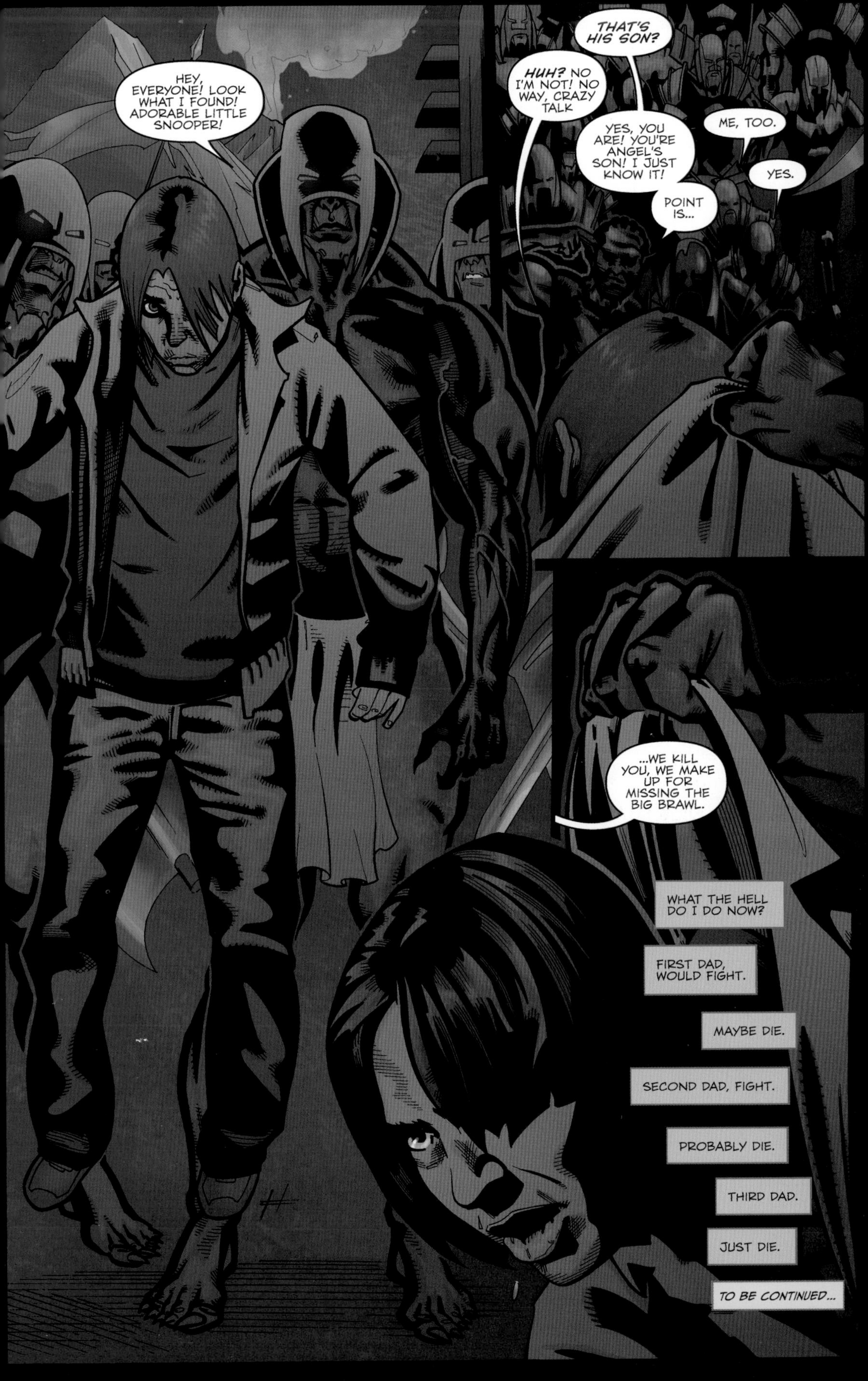
HEY, EVERYONE! LOOK WHAT I FOUND! ADORABLE LITTLE SNOOPER!
THAT'S HIS SON?
HUH? NO I'M NOT! NO WAY, CRAZY TALK
YES, YOU ARE! YOU'RE ANGEL'S SON! I JUST KNOW IT!
ME, TOO.
YES.
POINT IS...
...WE KILL YOU, WE MAKE UP FOR MISSING THE BIG BRAWL.
WHAT THE HELL DO I DO NOW?
FIRST DAD, WOULD FIGHT.
MAYBE DIE.
SECOND DAD, FIGHT.
PROBABLY DIE.
THIRD DAD.
JUST DIE.
TO BE CONTINUED...

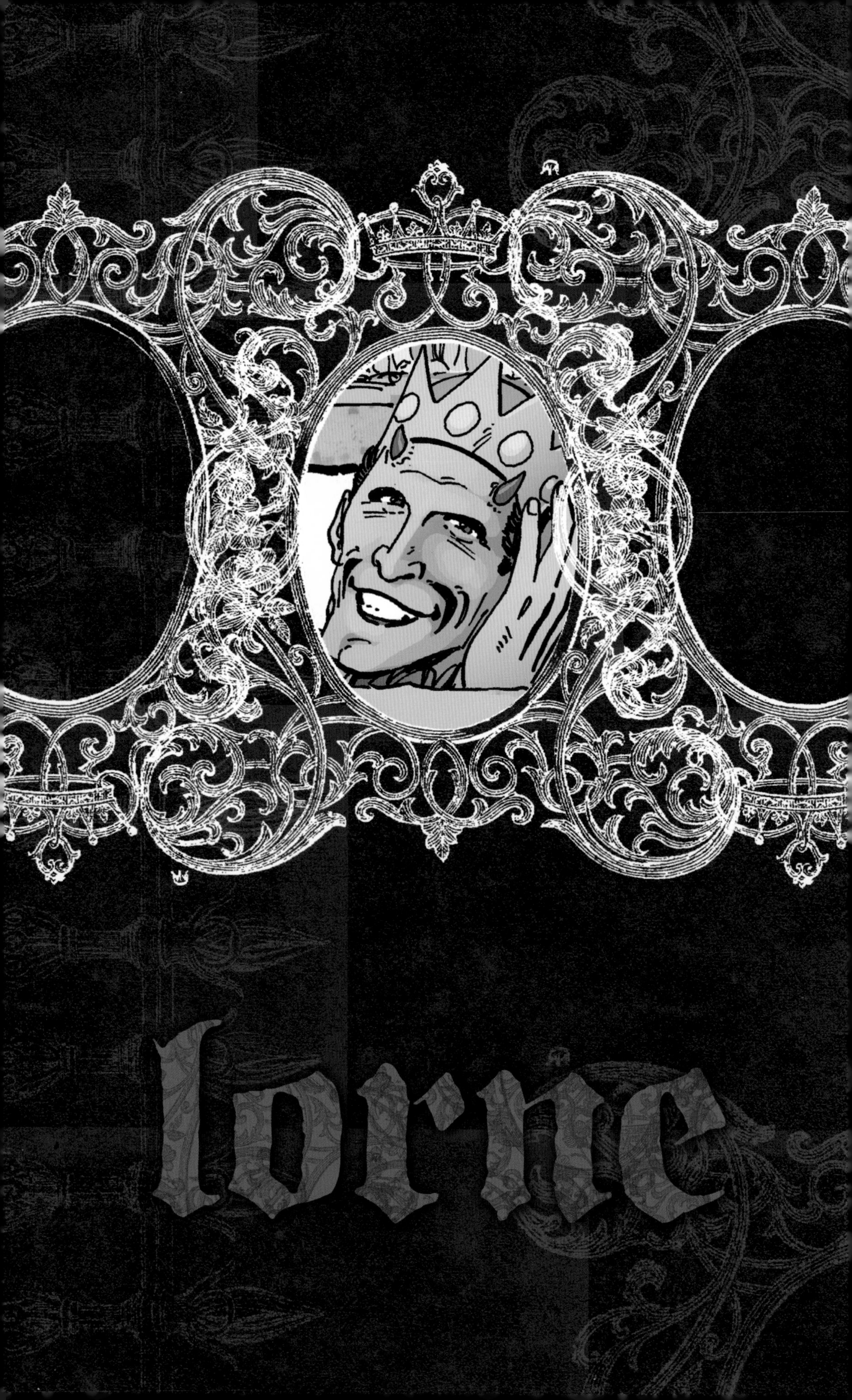
lorne

LORNE

written by brian lynch * art by john byrne * colors by art lyon

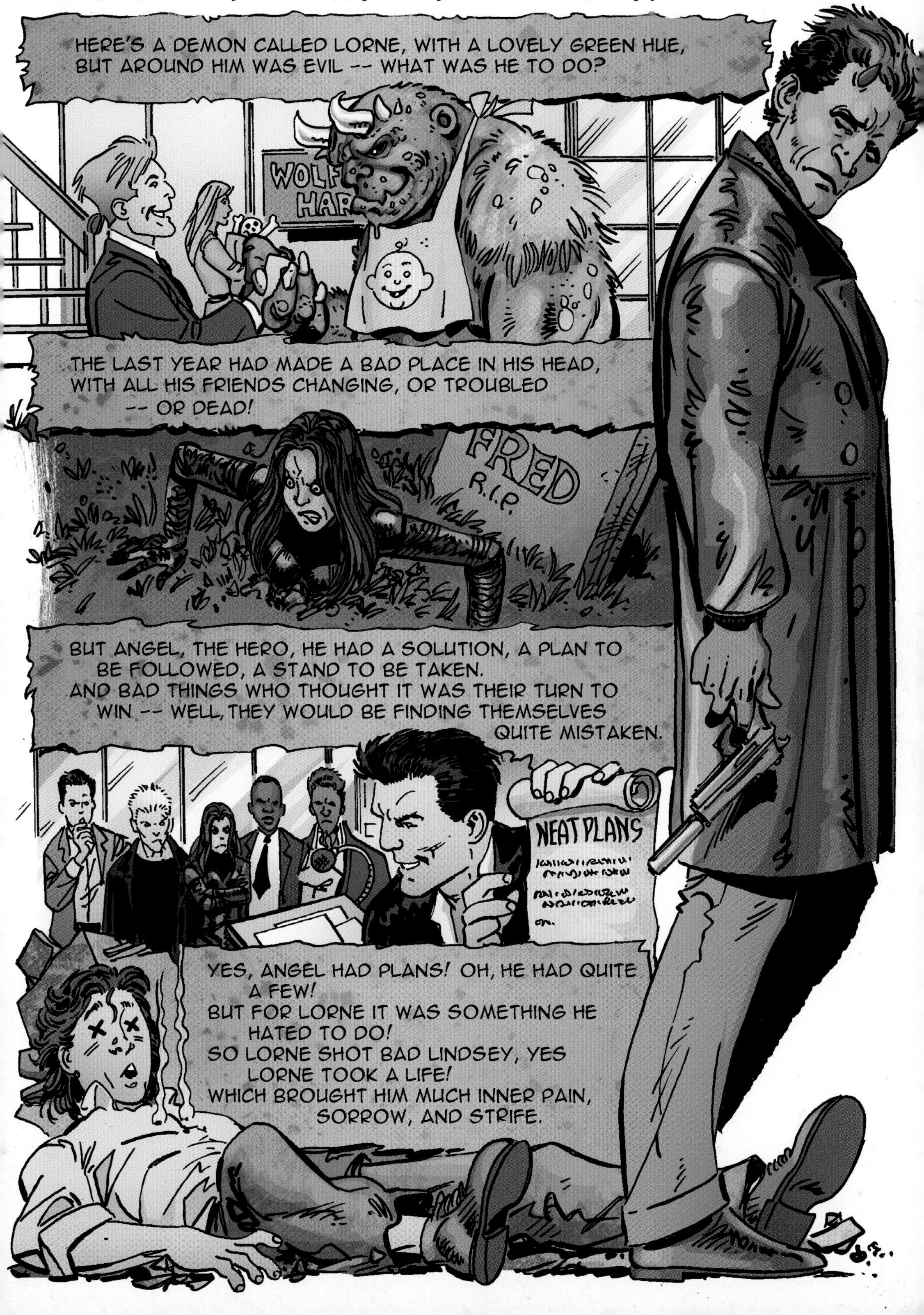

HERE'S A DEMON CALLED LORNE, WITH A LOVELY GREEN HUE, BUT AROUND HIM WAS EVIL -- WHAT WAS HE TO DO?
WOLF HAR
THE LAST YEAR HAD MADE A BAD PLACE IN HIS HEAD, WITH ALL HIS FRIENDS CHANGING, OR TROUBLED -- OR DEAD!
FRED R.I.P.
BUT ANGEL, THE HERO, HE HAD A SOLUTION, A PLAN TO BE FOLLOWED, A STAND TO BE TAKEN. AND BAD THINGS WHO THOUGHT IT WAS THEIR TURN TO WIN -- WELL, THEY WOULD BE FINDING THEMSELVES QUITE MISTAKEN.
NEAT PLANS
YES, ANGEL HAD PLANS! OH, HE HAD QUITE A FEW! BUT FOR LORNE IT WAS SOMETHING HE HATED TO DO! SO LORNE SHOT BAD LINDSEY, YES LORNE TOOK A LIFE! WHICH BROUGHT HIM MUCH INNER PAIN, SORROW, AND STRIFE.

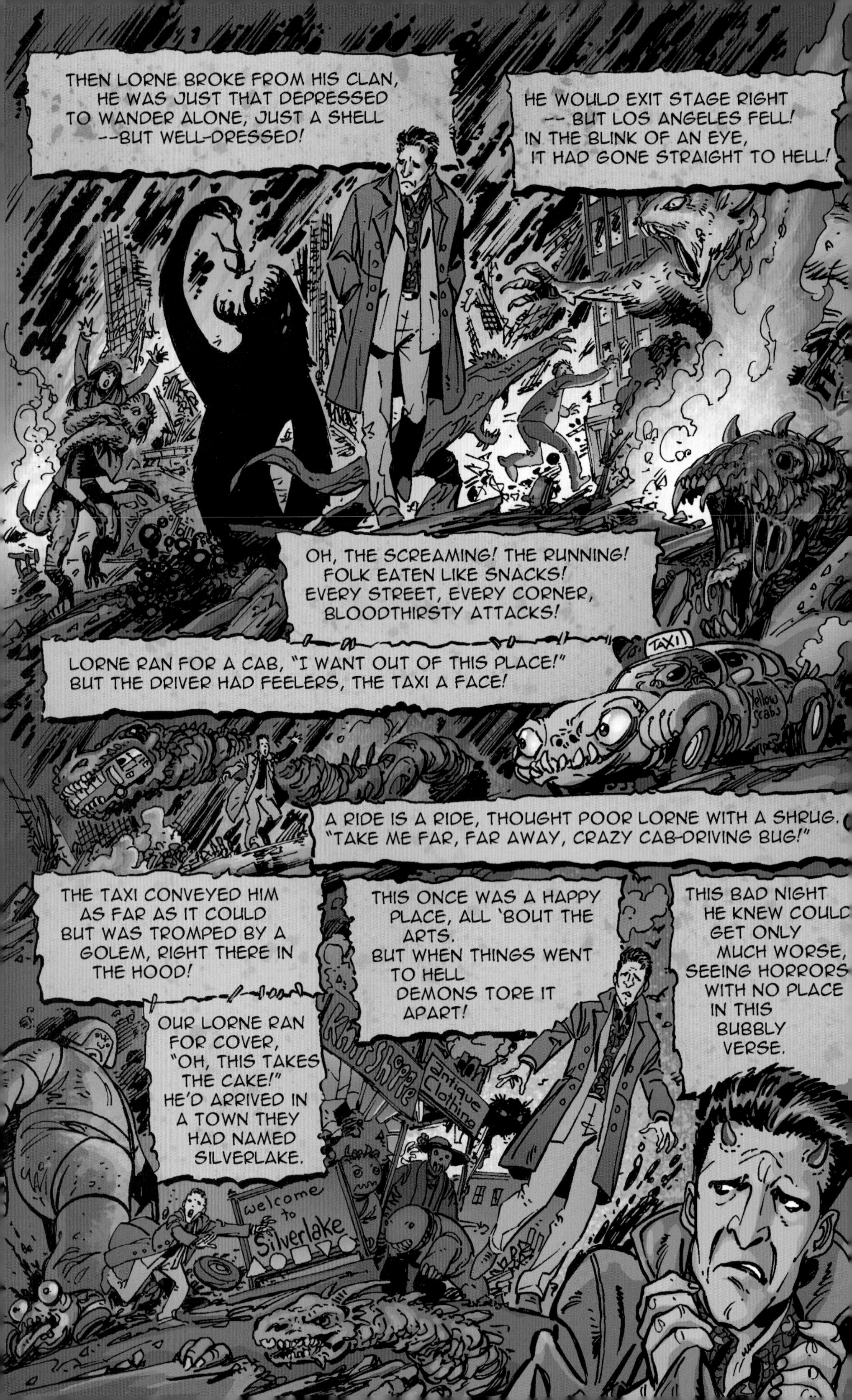
THEN LORNE BROKE FROM HIS CLAN, HE WAS JUST THAT DEPRESSED TO WANDER ALONE, JUST A SHELL --BUT WELL-DRESSED!
HE WOULD EXIT STAGE RIGHT -- BUT LOS ANGELES FELL! IN THE BLINK OF AN EYE, IT HAD GONE STRAIGHT TO HELL!
OH, THE SCREAMING! THE RUNNING! FOLK EATEN LIKE SNACKS! EVERY STREET, EVERY CORNER, BLOODTHIRSTY ATTACKS!
LORNE RAN FOR A CAB, "I WANT OUT OF THIS PLACE!" BUT THE DRIVER HAD FEELERS, THE TAXI A FACE!
TAXI
Yellow Scabs
A RIDE IS A RIDE, THOUGHT POOR LORNE WITH A SHRUG. "TAKE ME FAR, FAR AWAY, CRAZY CAB-DRIVING BUG!"
THE TAXI CONVEYED HIM AS FAR AS IT COULD BUT WAS TROMPED BY A GOLEM, RIGHT THERE IN THE HOOD!
OUR LORNE RAN FOR COVER, "OH, THIS TAKES THE CAKE!" HE'D ARRIVED IN A TOWN THEY HAD NAMED SILVERLAKE.
THIS ONCE WAS A HAPPY PLACE, ALL 'BOUT THE ARTS. BUT WHEN THINGS WENT TO HELL DEMONS TORE IT APART!
THIS BAD NIGHT HE KNEW COULD GET ONLY MUCH WORSE, SEEING HORRORS WITH NO PLACE IN THIS BUBBLY VERSE.
Antique Clothing
welcome to Silverlake

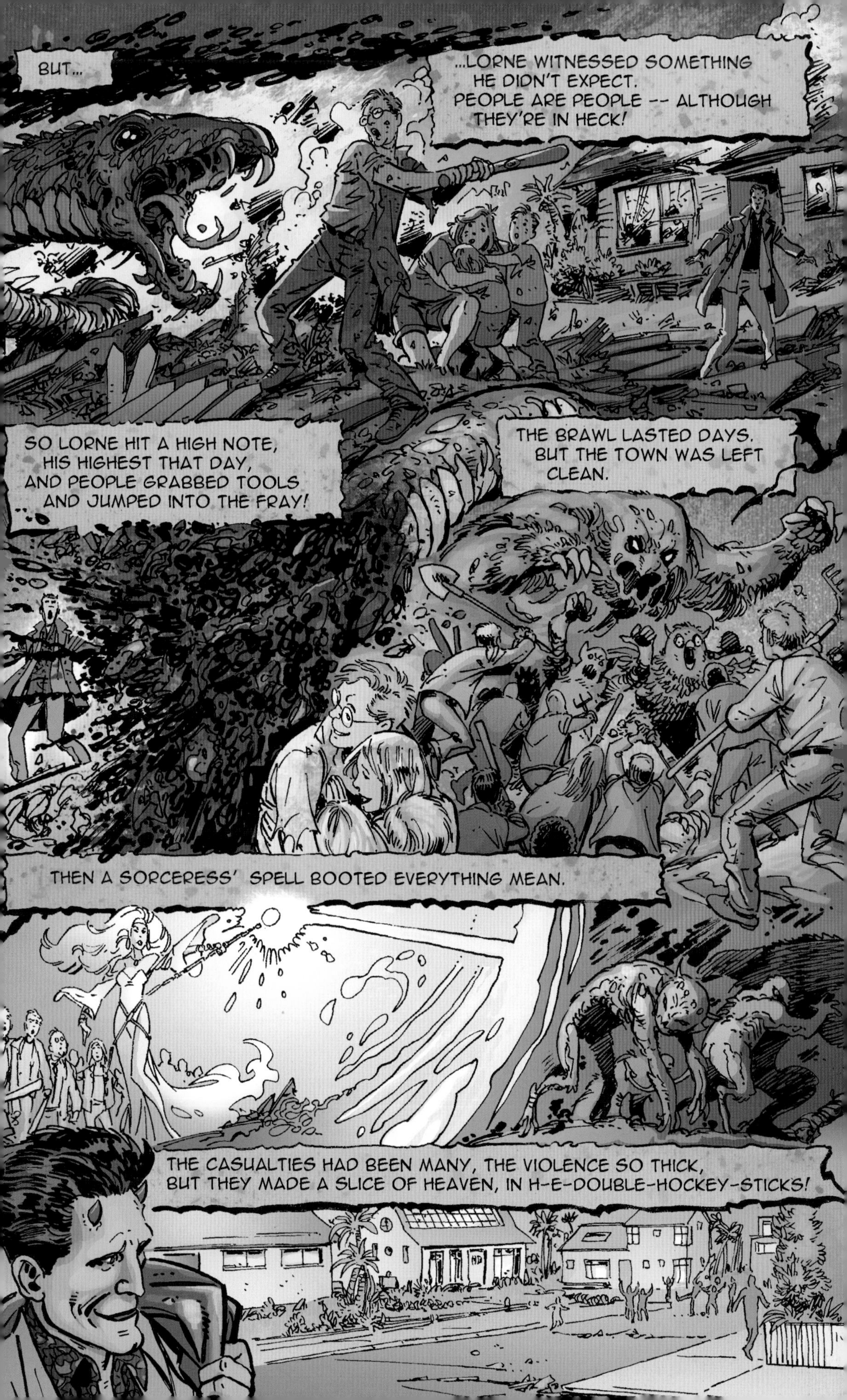
BUT...
...LORNE WITNESSED SOMETHING HE DIDN'T EXPECT. PEOPLE ARE PEOPLE -- ALTHOUGH THEY'RE IN HECK!
SO LORNE HIT A HIGH NOTE, HIS HIGHEST THAT DAY, AND PEOPLE GRABBED TOOLS AND JUMPED INTO THE FRAY!
THE BRAWL LASTED DAYS. BUT THE TOWN WAS LEFT CLEAN.
THEN A SORCERESS' SPELL BOOTED EVERYTHING MEAN.
THE CASUALTIES HAD BEEN MANY, THE VIOLENCE SO THICK, BUT THEY MADE A SLICE OF HEAVEN, IN H-E-DOUBLE-HOCKEY-STICKS!

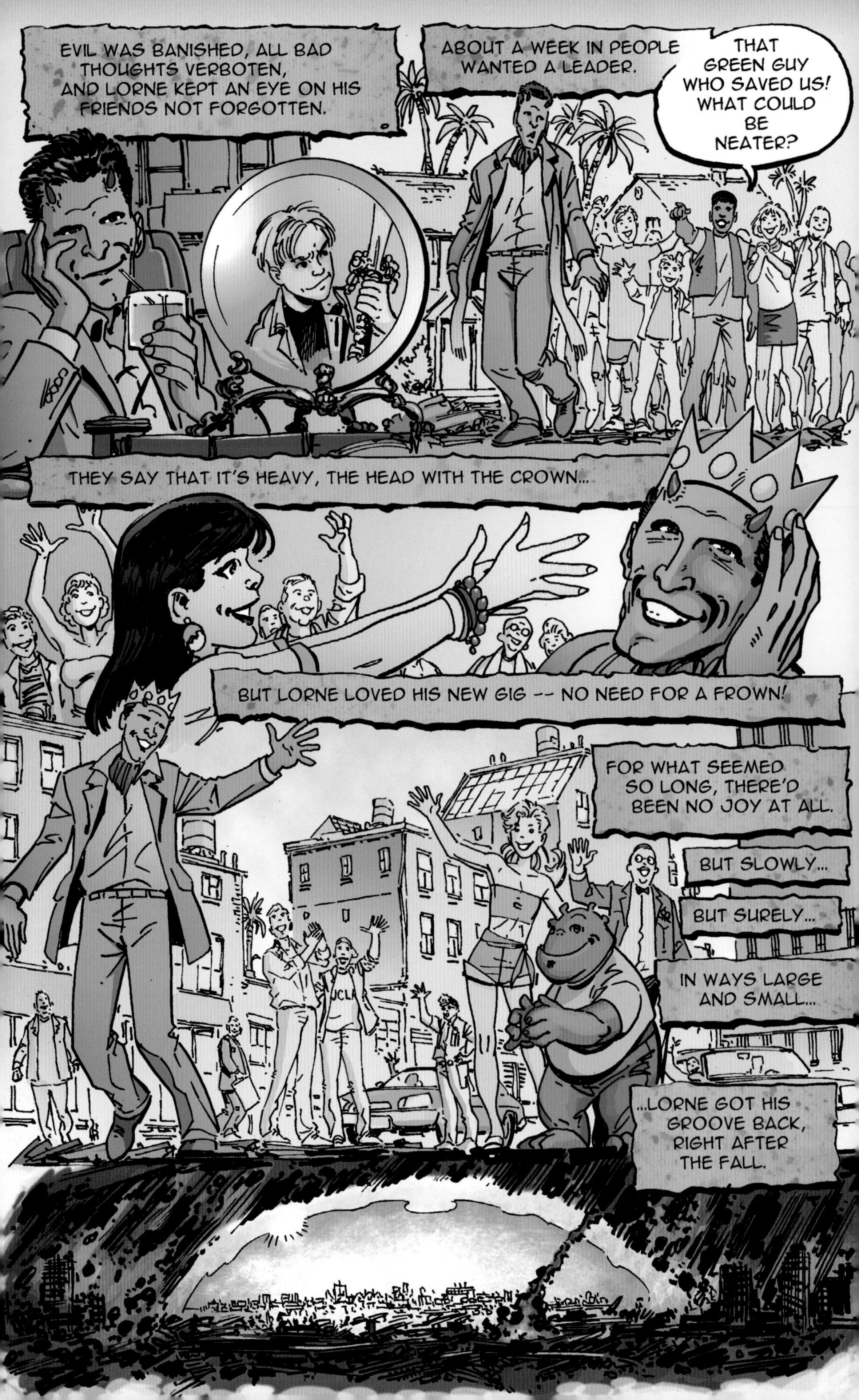
EVIL WAS BANISHED, ALL BAD THOUGHTS VERBOTEN, AND LORNE KEPT AN EYE ON HIS FRIENDS NOT FORGOTTEN.
ABOUT A WEEK IN PEOPLE WANTED A LEADER.
THAT GREEN GUY WHO SAVED US! WHAT COULD BE NEATER?
THEY SAY THAT IT'S HEAVY, THE HEAD WITH THE CROWN...
BUT LORNE LOVED HIS NEW GIG -- NO NEED FOR A FROWN!
FOR WHAT SEEMED SO LONG, THERE'D BEEN NO JOY AT ALL.
BUT SLOWLY...
BUT SURELY...
IN WAYS LARGE AND SMALL...
...LORNE GOT HIS GROOVE BACK, RIGHT AFTER THE FALL.
UCLA

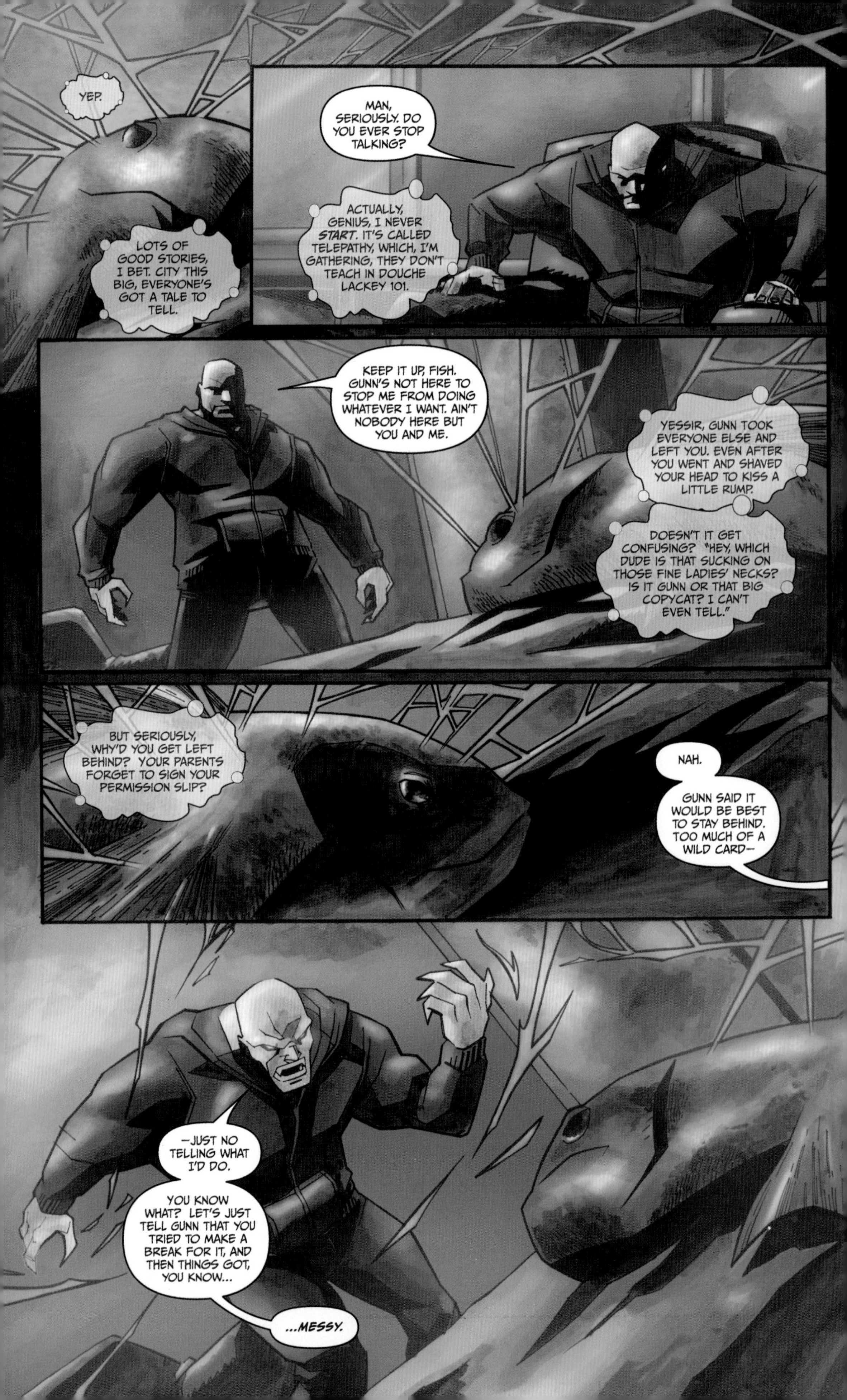
YEP.
MAN, SERIOUSLY. DO YOU EVER STOP TALKING?
LOTS OF GOOD STORIES, I BET. CITY THIS BIG, EVERYONE'S GOT A TALE TO TELL.
ACTUALLY, GENIUS, I NEVER START. IT'S CALLED TELEPATHY, WHICH, I'M GATHERING, THEY DON'T TEACH IN DOUCHE LACKEY 101.
KEEP IT UP, FISH. GUNN'S NOT HERE TO STOP ME FROM DOING WHATEVER I WANT. AIN'T NOBODY HERE BUT YOU AND ME.
YESSIR, GUNN TOOK EVERYONE ELSE AND LEFT YOU. EVEN AFTER YOU WENT AND SHAVED YOUR HEAD TO KISS A LITTLE RUMP.
DOESN'T IT GET CONFUSING? "HEY, WHICH DUDE IS THAT SUCKING ON THOSE FINE LADIES' NECKS? IS IT GUNN OR THAT BIG COPYCAT? I CAN'T EVEN TELL."
BUT SERIOUSLY, WHY'D YOU GET LEFT BEHIND? YOUR PARENTS FORGET TO SIGN YOUR PERMISSION SLIP?
NAH.
GUNN SAID IT WOULD BE BEST TO STAY BEHIND. TOO MUCH OF A WILD CARD—
—JUST NO TELLING WHAT I'D DO.
YOU KNOW WHAT? LET'S JUST TELL GUNN THAT YOU TRIED TO MAKE A BREAK FOR IT, AND THEN THINGS GOT, YOU KNOW...
...MESSY.

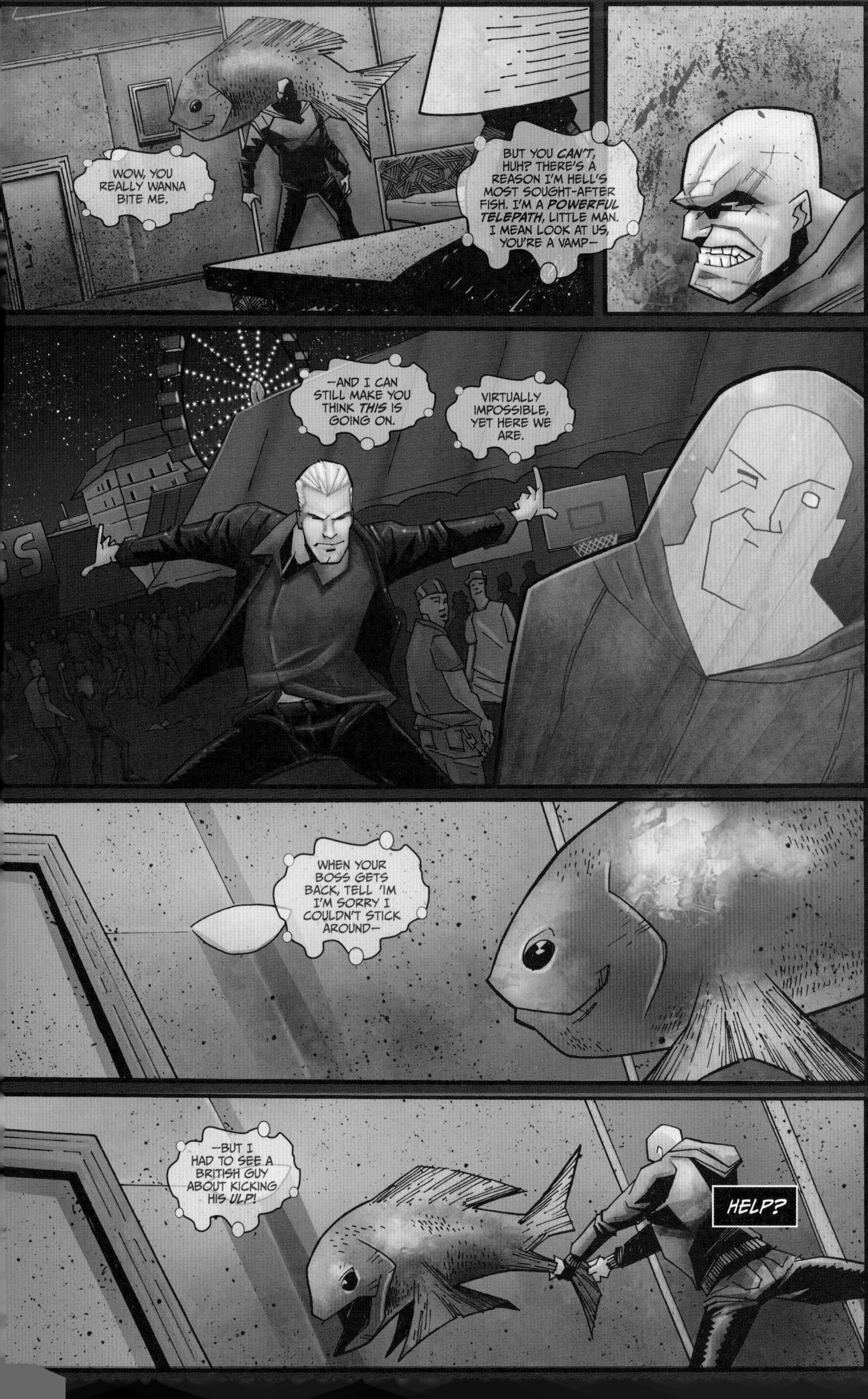
WOW, YOU REALLY WANNA BITE ME.
BUT YOU *CAN'T*, HUH? THERE'S A REASON I'M HELL'S MOST SOUGHT-AFTER FISH. I'M A ***POWERFUL TELEPATH***, LITTLE MAN. I MEAN LOOK AT US, YOU'RE A VAMP—
—AND I CAN STILL MAKE YOU THINK *THIS* IS GOING ON.
VIRTUALLY IMPOSSIBLE, YET HERE WE ARE.
WHEN YOUR BOSS GETS BACK, TELL 'IM I'M SORRY I COULDN'T STICK AROUND—
—BUT I HAD TO SEE A BRITISH GUY ABOUT KICKING HIS *ULP*!
HELP?

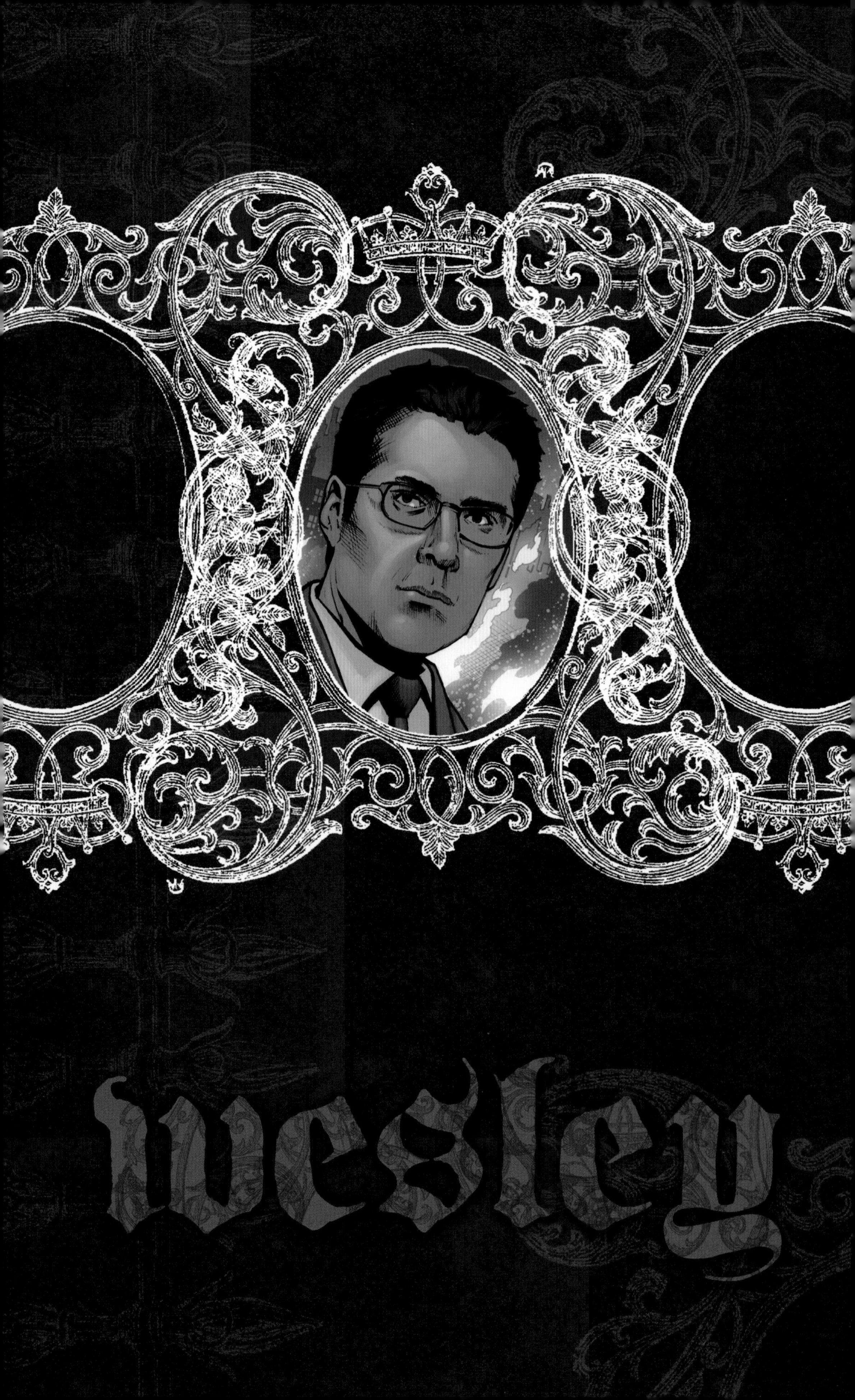
wesley

WESLEY

written by brian lynch · art by nick runge · colors by john rauch

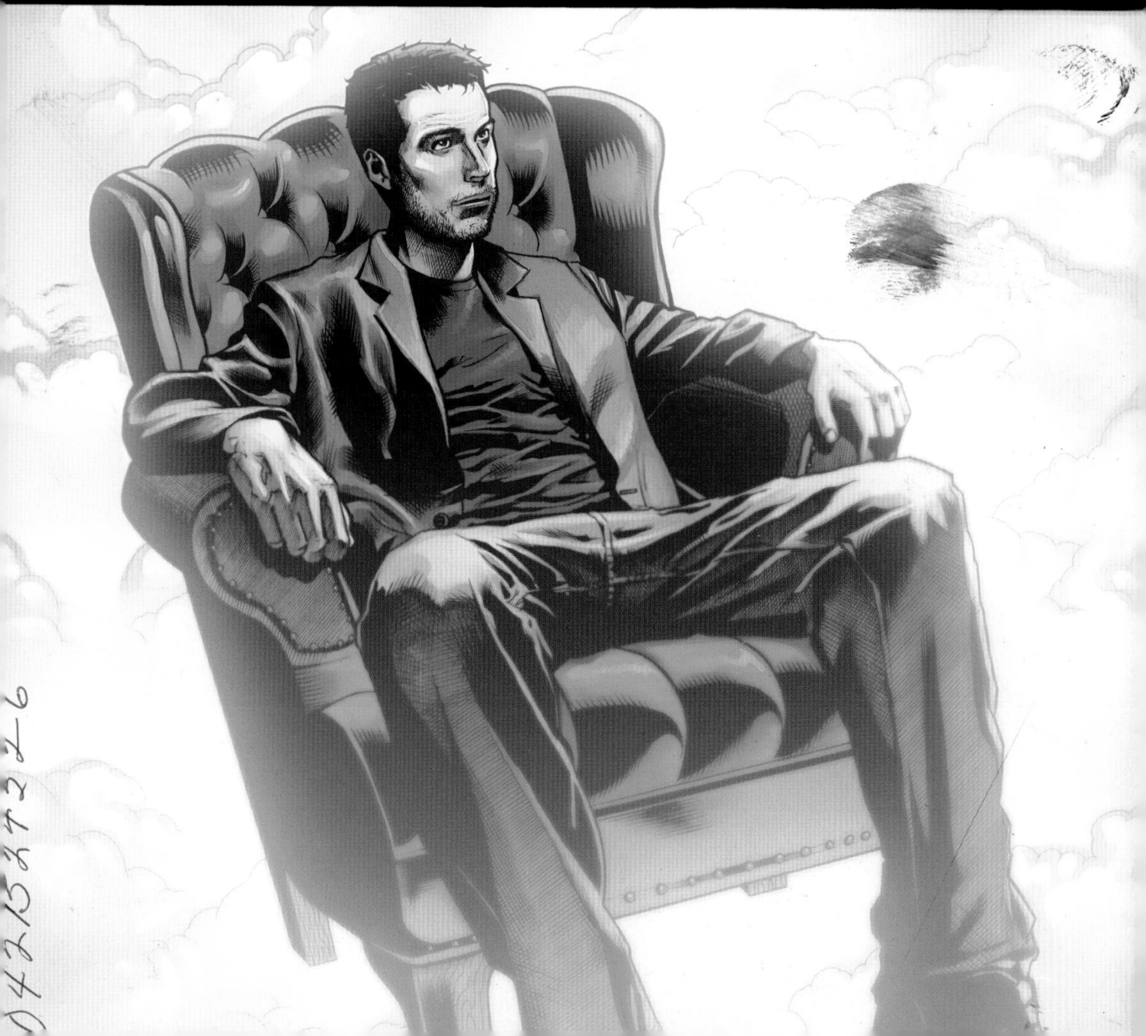

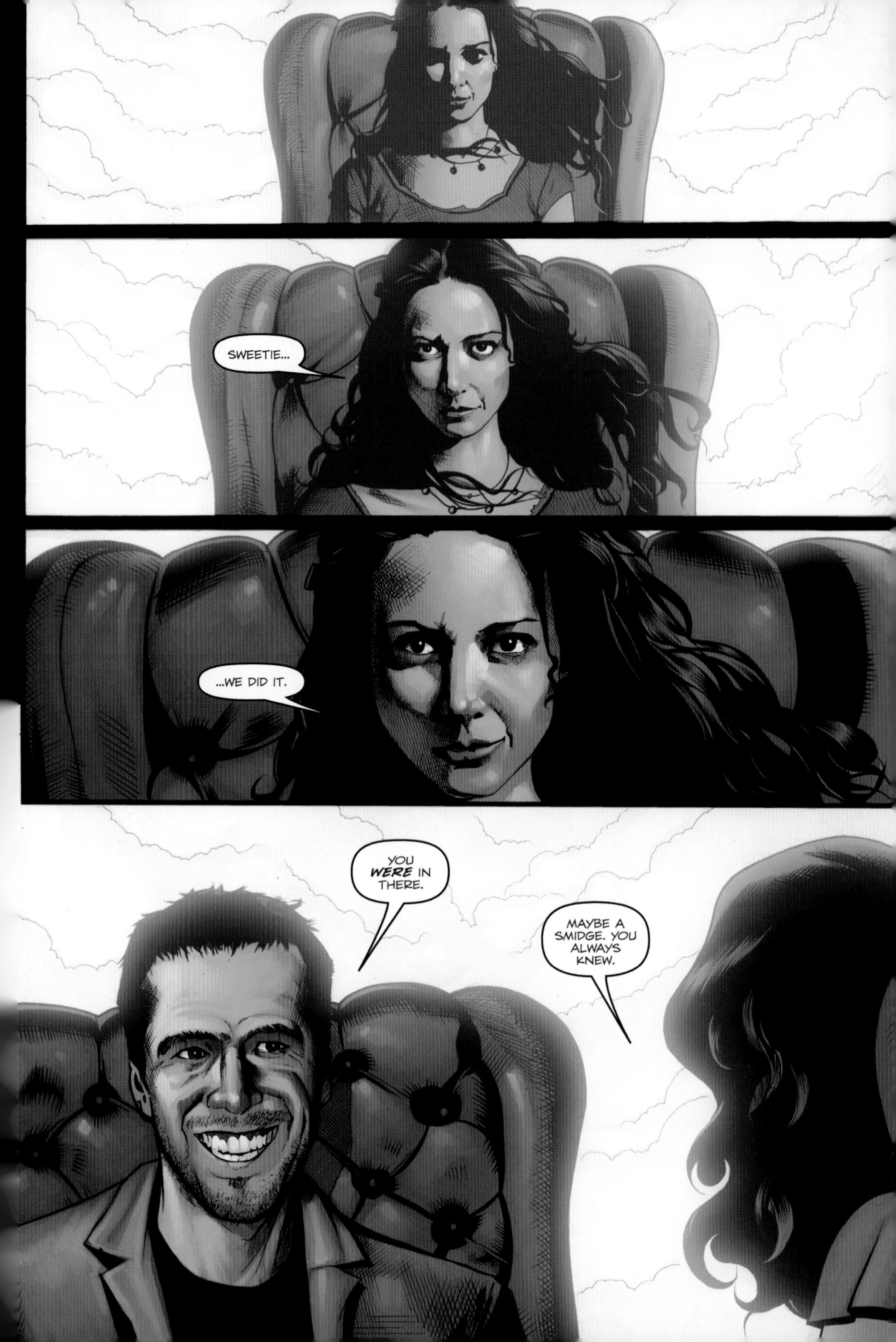
SWEETIE...
...WE DID IT.
YOU WERE IN THERE.
MAYBE A SMIDGE. YOU ALWAYS KNEW.

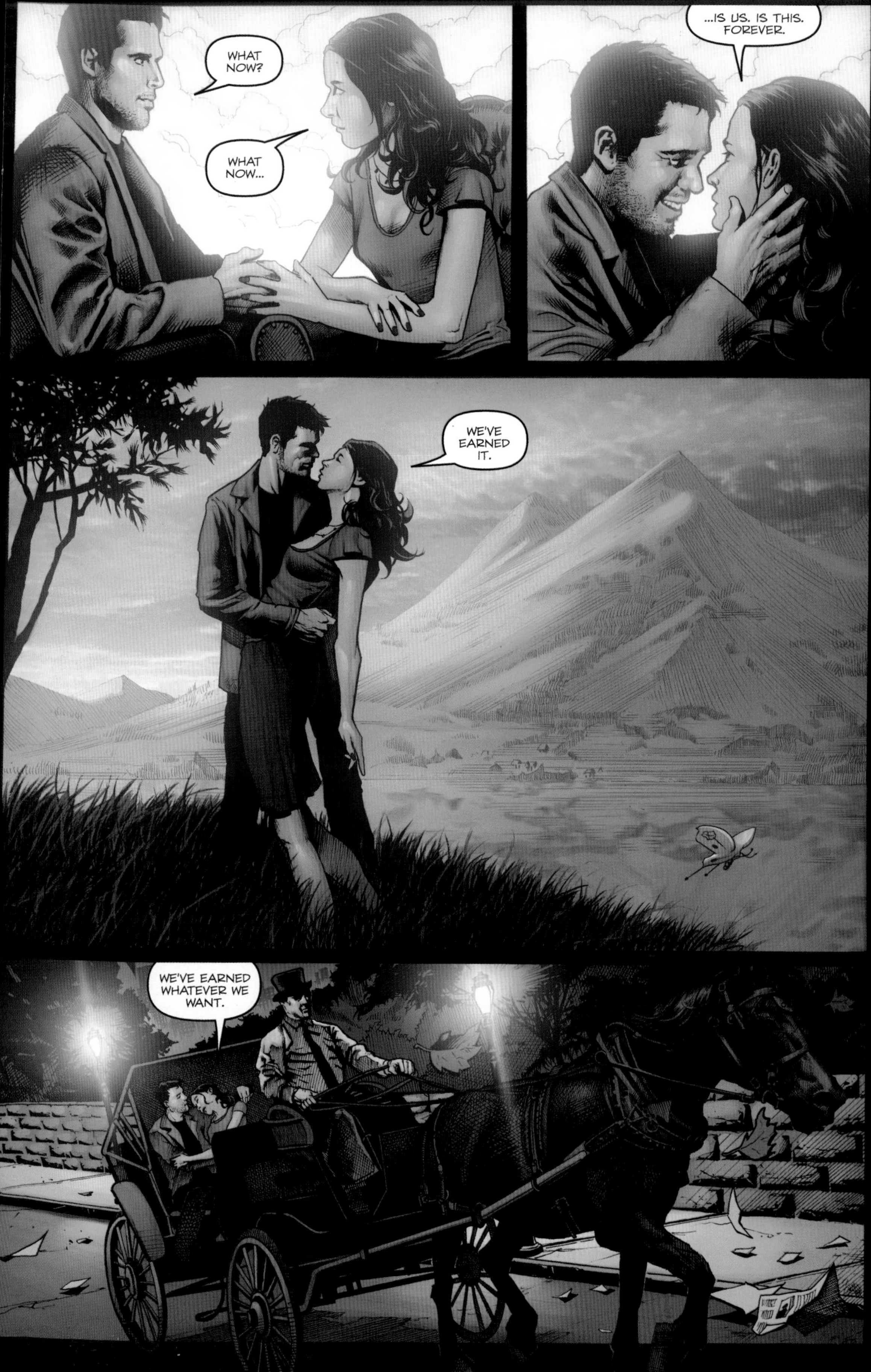
WHAT NOW?
WHAT NOW...
...IS US. IS THIS. FOREVER.
WE'VE EARNED IT.
WE'VE EARNED WHATEVER WE WANT.

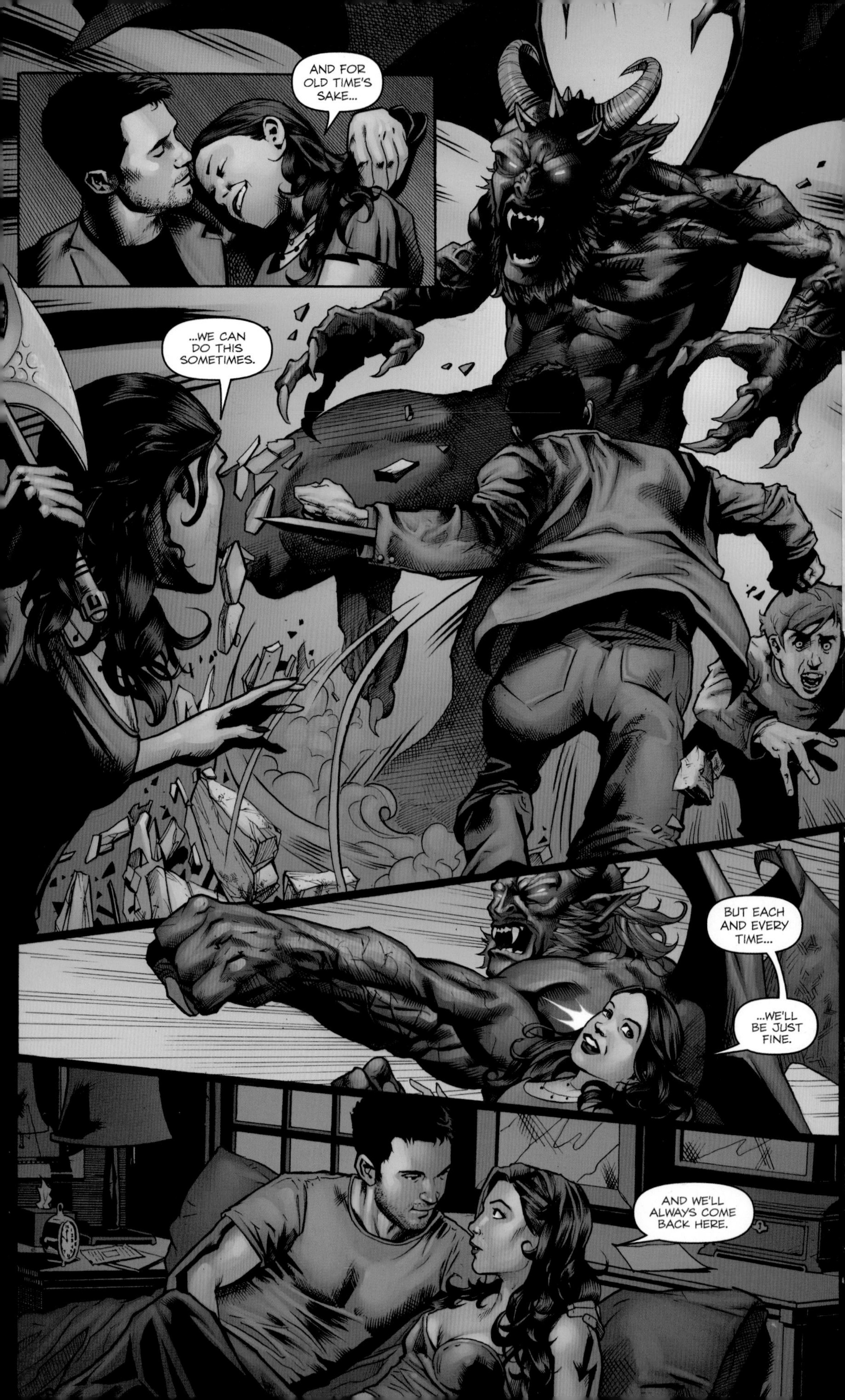
AND FOR OLD TIME'S SAKE...
...WE CAN DO THIS SOMETIMES.
BUT EACH AND EVERY TIME...
...WE'LL BE JUST FINE.
AND WE'LL ALWAYS COME BACK HERE.

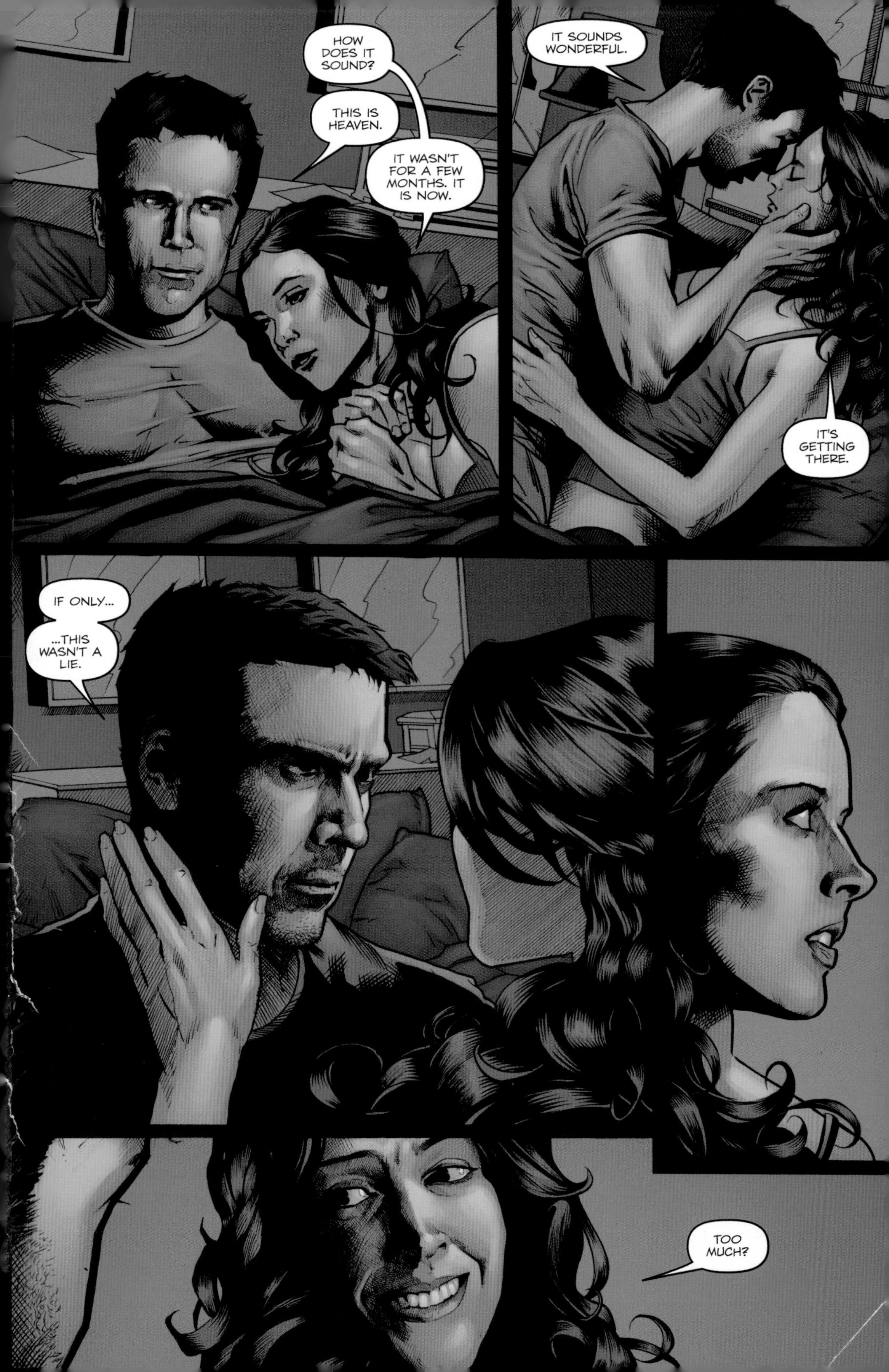
HOW DOES IT SOUND?
THIS IS HEAVEN.
IT WASN'T FOR A FEW MONTHS. IT IS NOW.
IT SOUNDS WONDERFUL.
IT'S GETTING THERE.
IF ONLY...
...THIS WASN'T A LIE.
TOO MUCH?

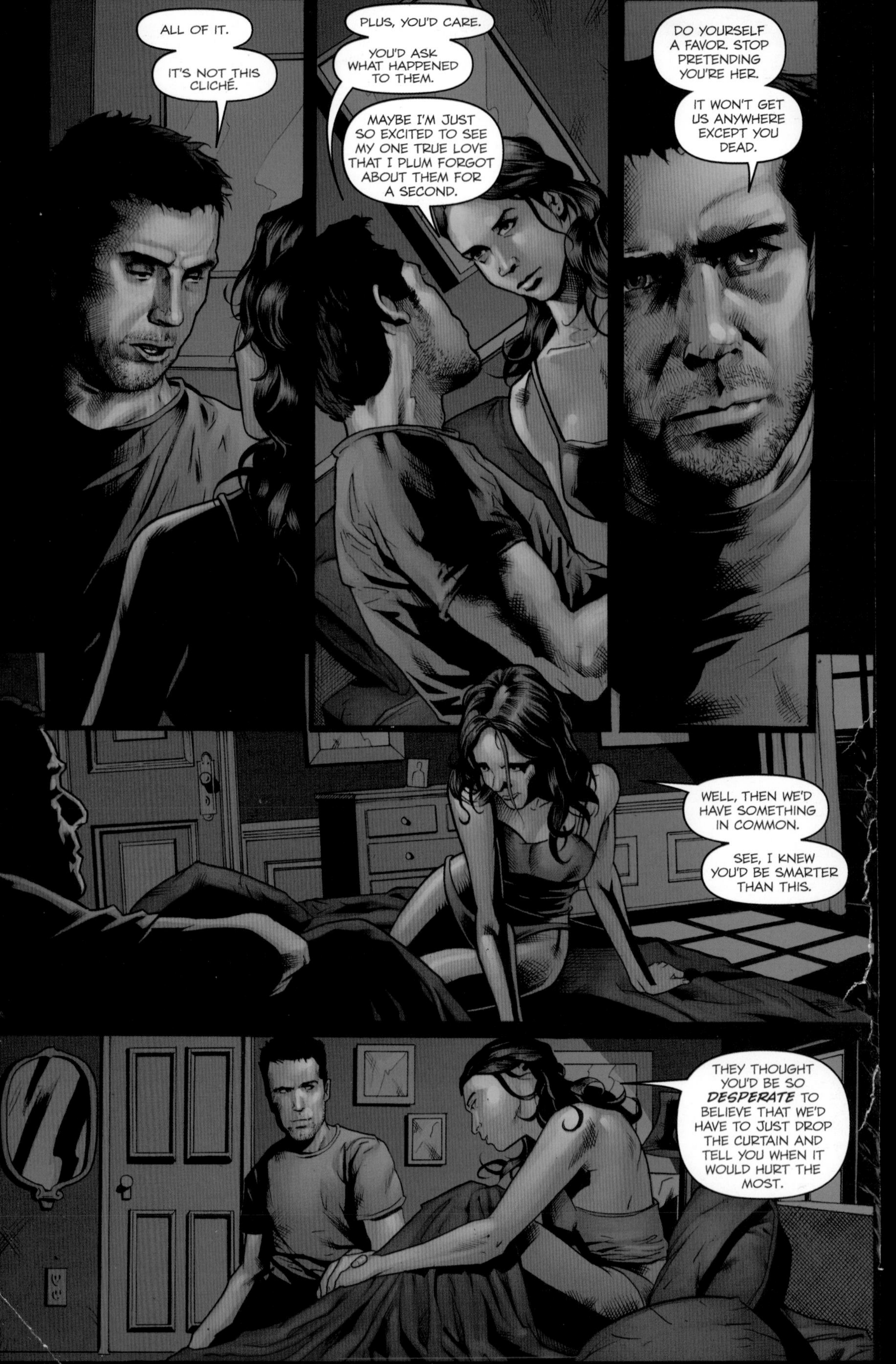
ALL OF IT.
IT'S NOT THIS CLICHÉ.
PLUS, YOU'D CARE.
YOU'D ASK WHAT HAPPENED TO THEM.
MAYBE I'M JUST SO EXCITED TO SEE MY ONE TRUE LOVE THAT I PLUM FORGOT ABOUT THEM FOR A SECOND.
DO YOURSELF A FAVOR. STOP PRETENDING YOU'RE HER.
IT WON'T GET US ANYWHERE EXCEPT YOU DEAD.
WELL, THEN WE'D HAVE SOMETHING IN COMMON.
SEE, I KNEW YOU'D BE SMARTER THAN THIS.
THEY THOUGHT YOU'D BE SO *DESPERATE* TO BELIEVE THAT WE'D HAVE TO JUST DROP THE CURTAIN AND TELL YOU WHEN IT WOULD HURT THE MOST.

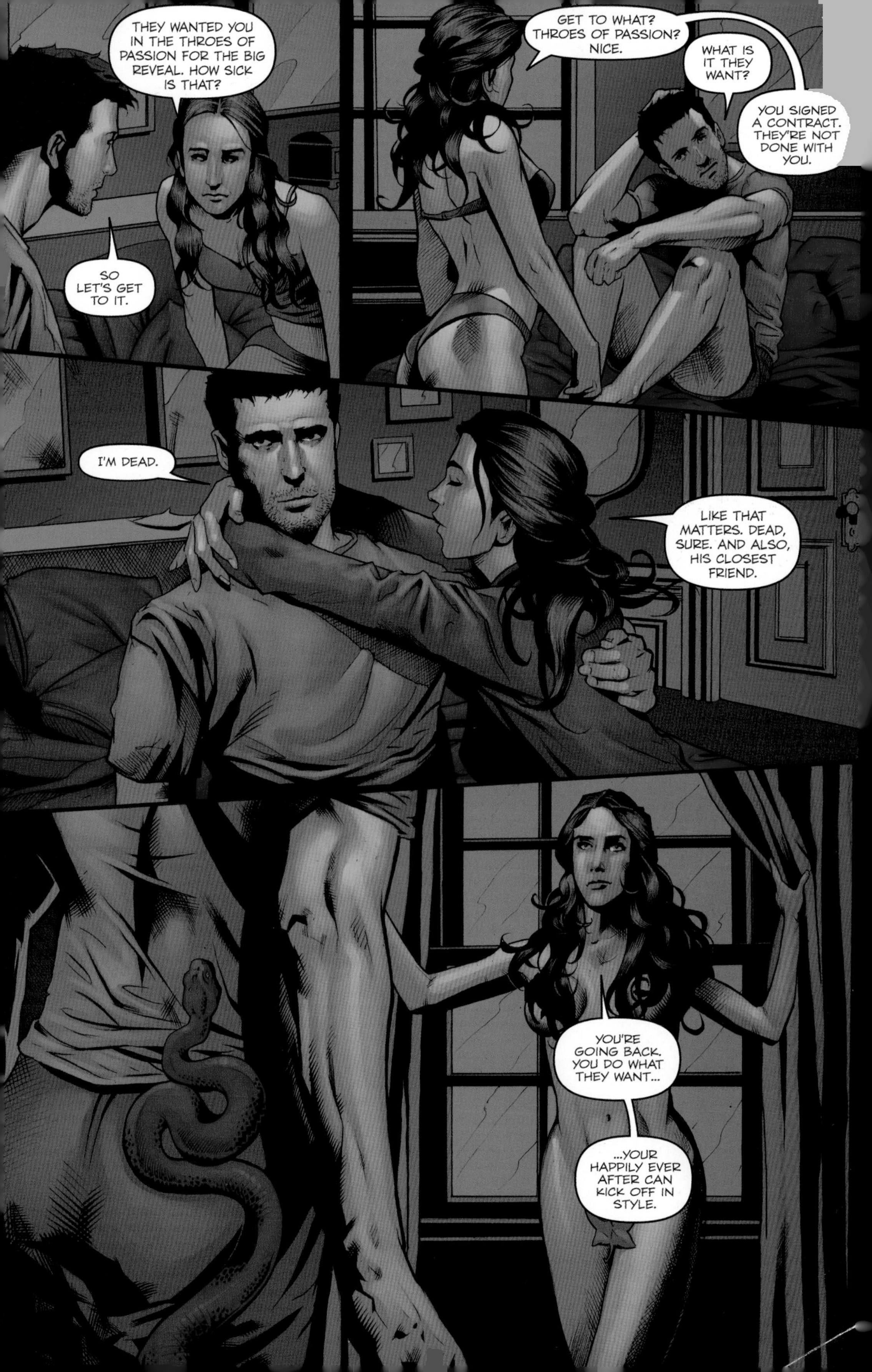
THEY WANTED YOU IN THE THROES OF PASSION FOR THE BIG REVEAL. HOW SICK IS THAT?
SO LET'S GET TO IT.
GET TO WHAT? THROES OF PASSION? NICE.
WHAT IS IT THEY WANT?
YOU SIGNED A CONTRACT. THEY'RE NOT DONE WITH YOU.
I'M DEAD.
LIKE THAT MATTERS. DEAD, SURE. AND ALSO, HIS CLOSEST FRIEND.
YOU'RE GOING BACK. YOU DO WHAT THEY WANT...
...YOUR HAPPILY EVER AFTER CAN KICK OFF IN STYLE.

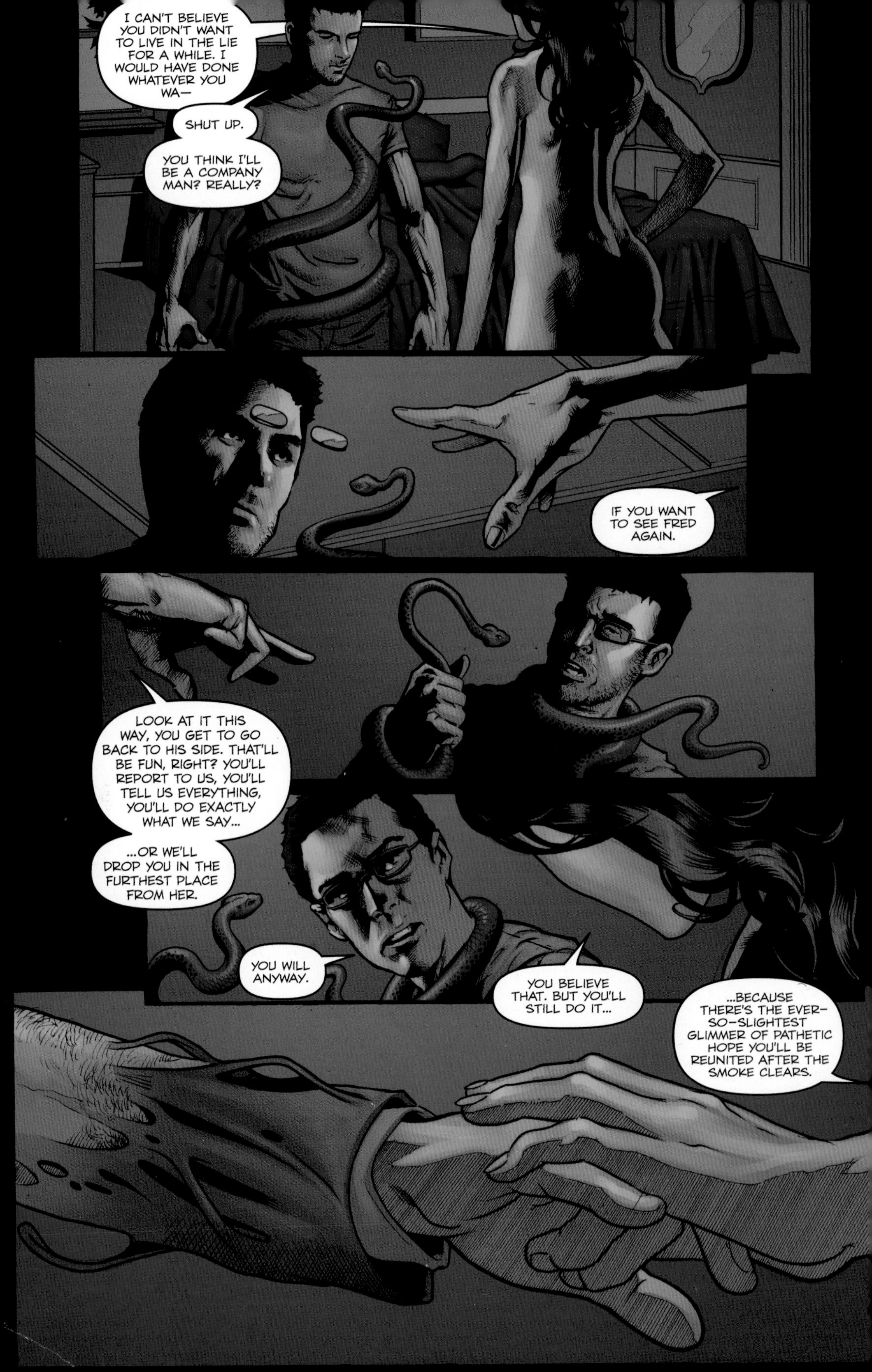
I CAN'T BELIEVE YOU DIDN'T WANT TO LIVE IN THE LIE FOR A WHILE. I WOULD HAVE DONE WHATEVER YOU WA—
SHUT UP.
YOU THINK I'LL BE A COMPANY MAN? REALLY?
IF YOU WANT TO SEE FRED AGAIN.
LOOK AT IT THIS WAY, YOU GET TO GO BACK TO HIS SIDE. THAT'LL BE FUN, RIGHT? YOU'LL REPORT TO US, YOU'LL TELL US EVERYTHING, YOU'LL DO EXACTLY WHAT WE SAY...
...OR WE'LL DROP YOU IN THE FURTHEST PLACE FROM HER.
YOU WILL ANYWAY.
YOU BELIEVE THAT. BUT YOU'LL STILL DO IT...
...BECAUSE THERE'S THE EVER-SO-SLIGHTEST GLIMMER OF PATHETIC HOPE YOU'LL BE REUNITED AFTER THE SMOKE CLEARS.

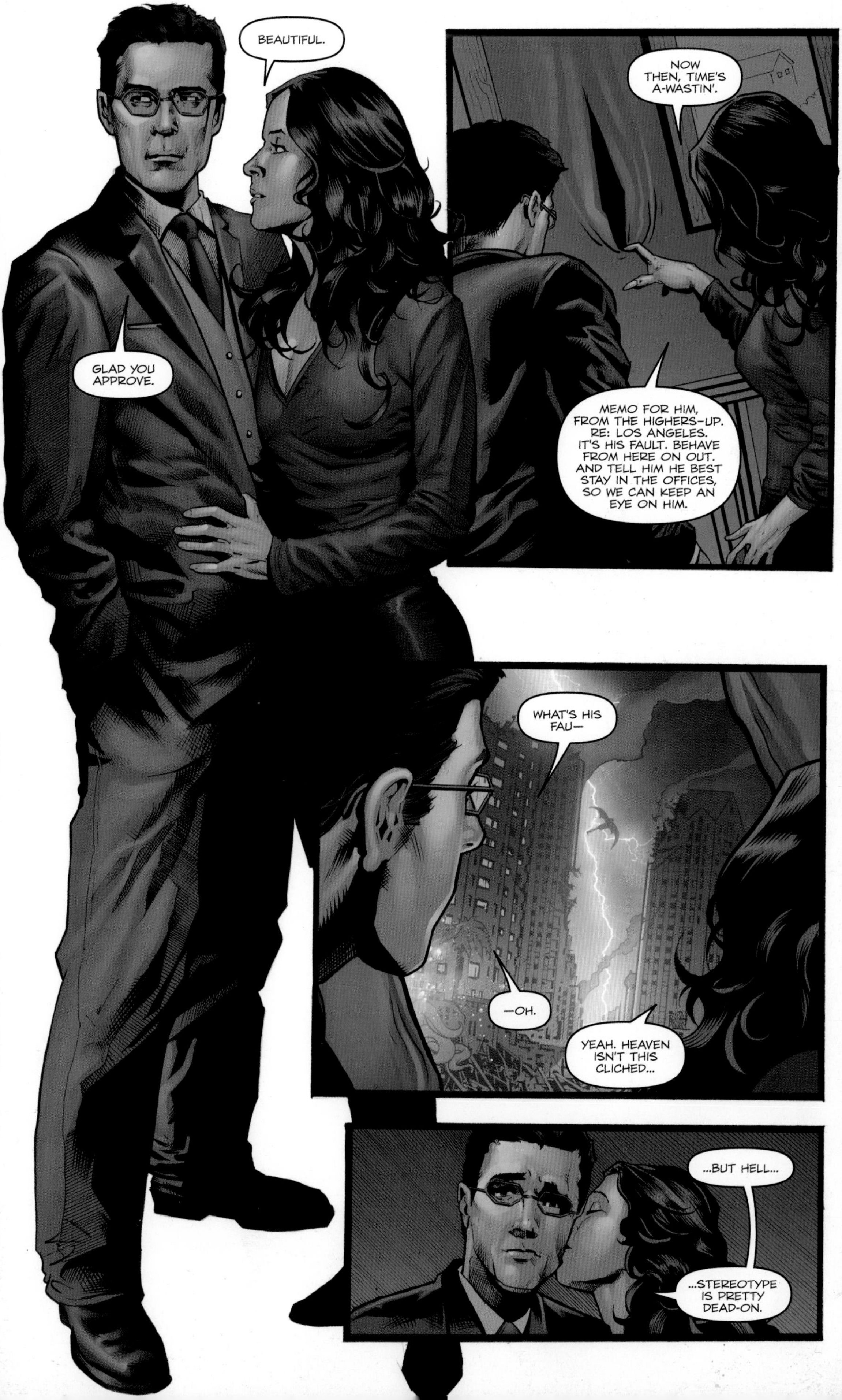
BEAUTIFUL.
GLAD YOU APPROVE.
NOW THEN, TIME'S A-WASTIN'.
MEMO FOR HIM, FROM THE HIGHERS-UP. RE: LOS ANGELES. IT'S HIS FAULT. BEHAVE FROM HERE ON OUT. AND TELL HIM HE BEST STAY IN THE OFFICES, SO WE CAN KEEP AN EYE ON HIM.
WHAT'S HIS FAU—
—OH.
YEAH. HEAVEN ISN'T THIS CLICHED...
...BUT HELL...
...STEREOTYPE IS PRETTY DEAD-ON.

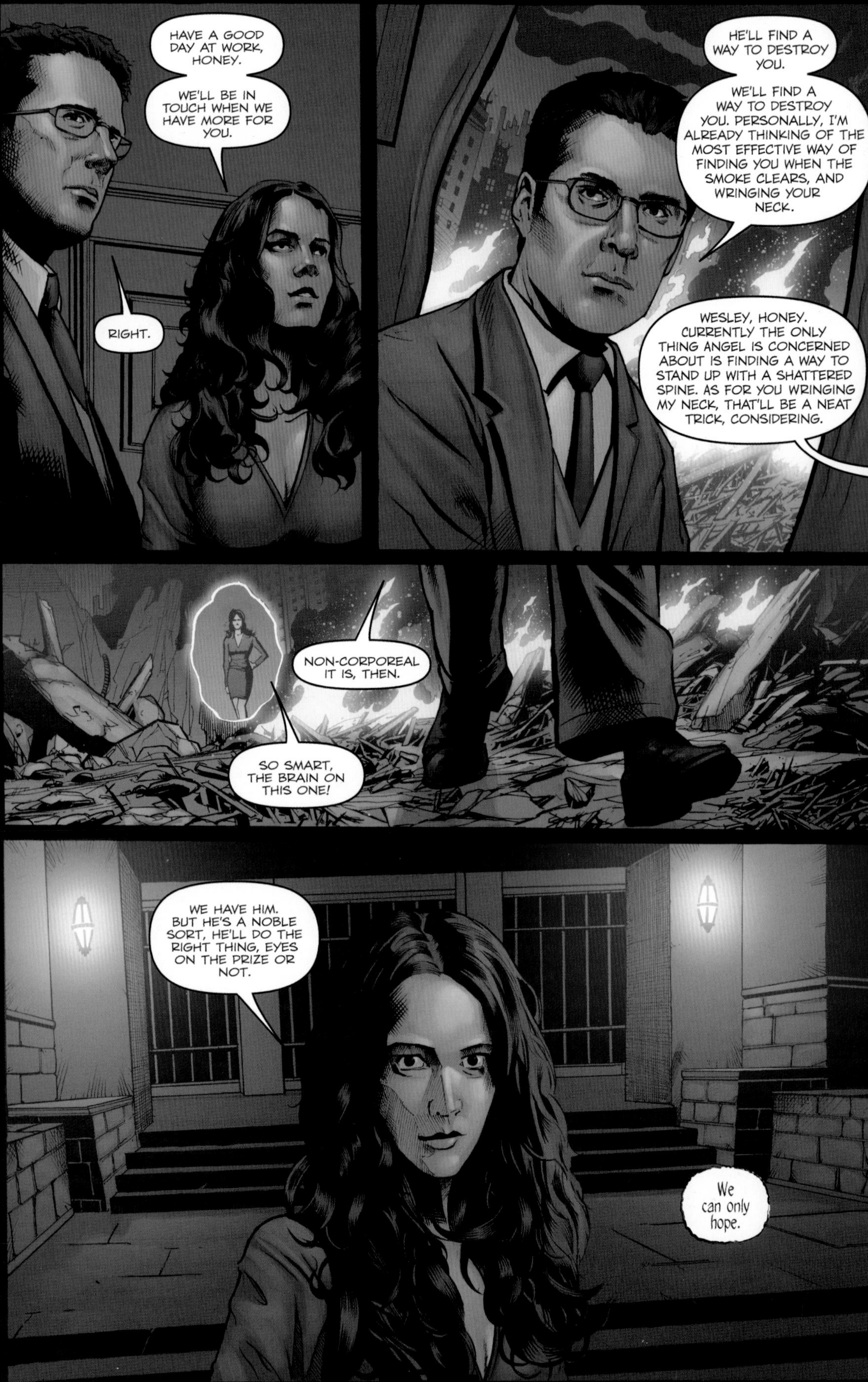
HAVE A GOOD DAY AT WORK, HONEY.
WE'LL BE IN TOUCH WHEN WE HAVE MORE FOR YOU.
RIGHT.
HE'LL FIND A WAY TO DESTROY YOU.
WE'LL FIND A WAY TO DESTROY YOU. PERSONALLY, I'M ALREADY THINKING OF THE MOST EFFECTIVE WAY OF FINDING YOU WHEN THE SMOKE CLEARS, AND WRINGING YOUR NECK.
WESLEY, HONEY. CURRENTLY THE ONLY THING ANGEL IS CONCERNED ABOUT IS FINDING A WAY TO STAND UP WITH A SHATTERED SPINE. AS FOR YOU WRINGING MY NECK, THAT'LL BE A NEAT TRICK, CONSIDERING.
NON-CORPOREAL IT IS, THEN.
SO SMART, THE BRAIN ON THIS ONE!
WE HAVE HIM. BUT HE'S A NOBLE SORT, HE'LL DO THE RIGHT THING, EYES ON THE PRIZE OR NOT.
We can only hope.

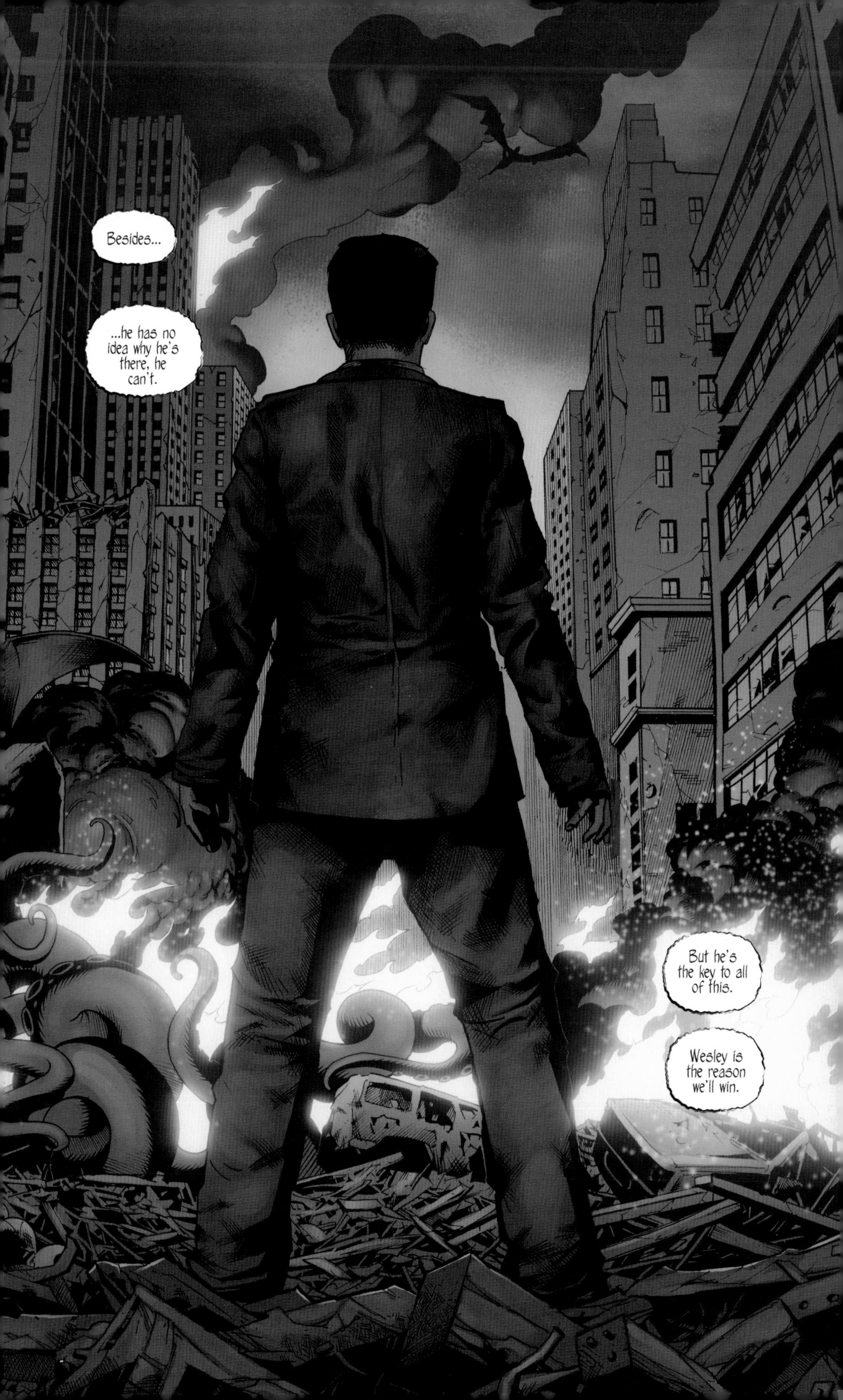
Besides...
...he has no idea why he's there, he can't.
But he's the key to all of this.
Wesley is the reason we'll win.

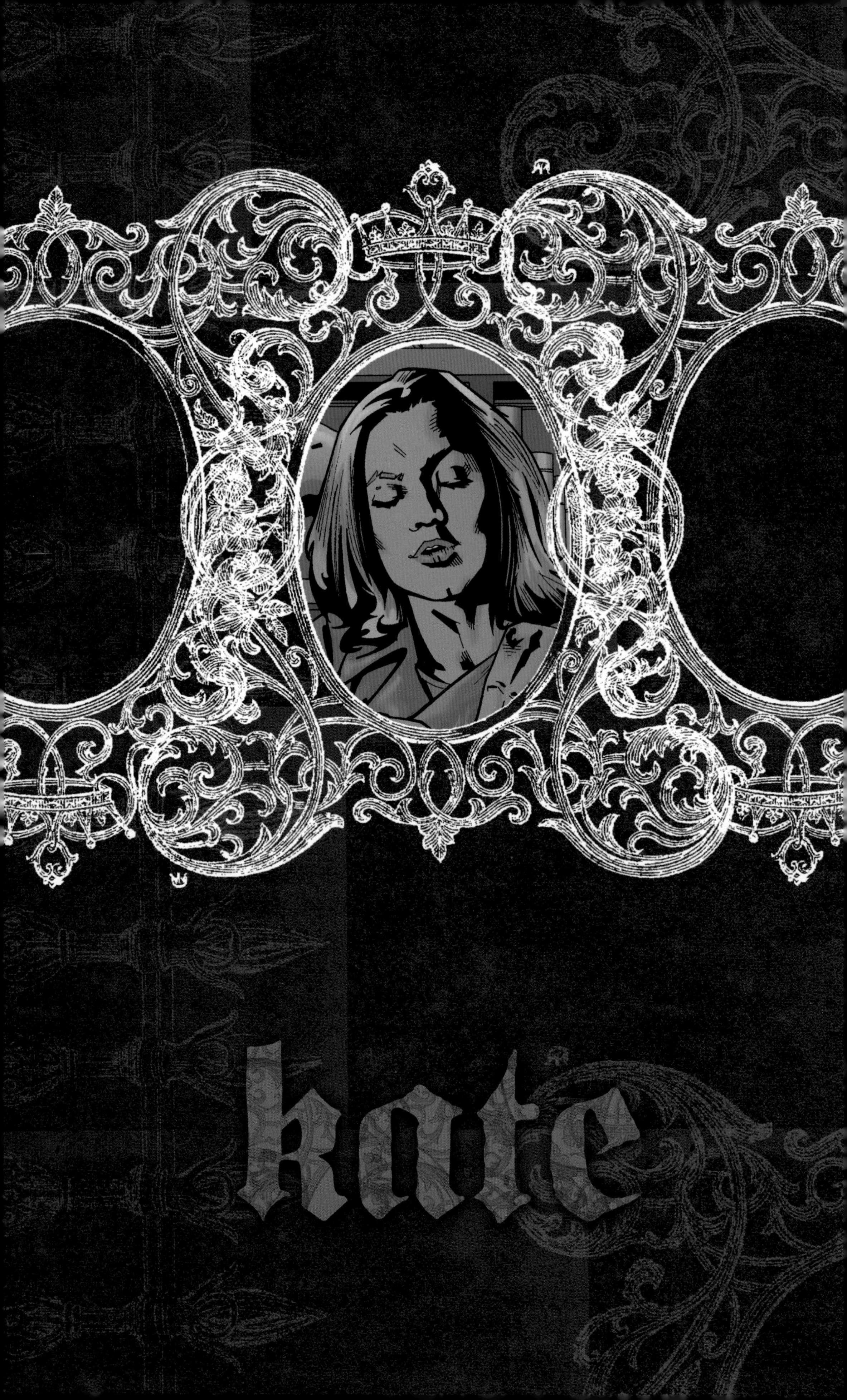

kate

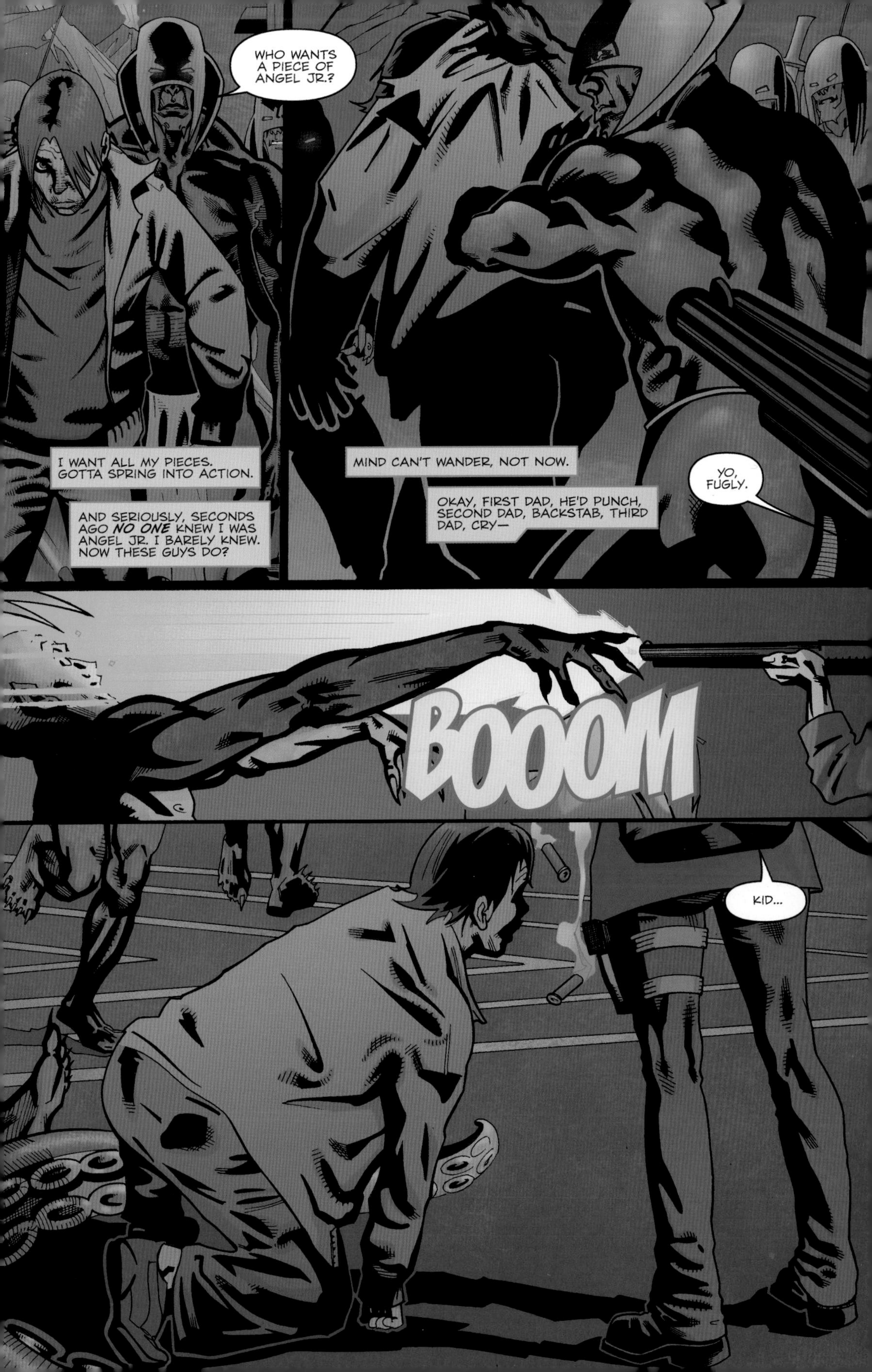
WHO WANTS A PIECE OF ANGEL JR.?
I WANT ALL MY PIECES. GOTTA SPRING INTO ACTION.
AND SERIOUSLY, SECONDS AGO NO ONE KNEW I WAS ANGEL JR. I BARELY KNEW. NOW THESE GUYS DO?
MIND CAN'T WANDER, NOT NOW.
OKAY, FIRST DAD, HE'D PUNCH, SECOND DAD, BACKSTAB, THIRD DAD, CRY—
YO, FUGLY.
BOOOM
KID...

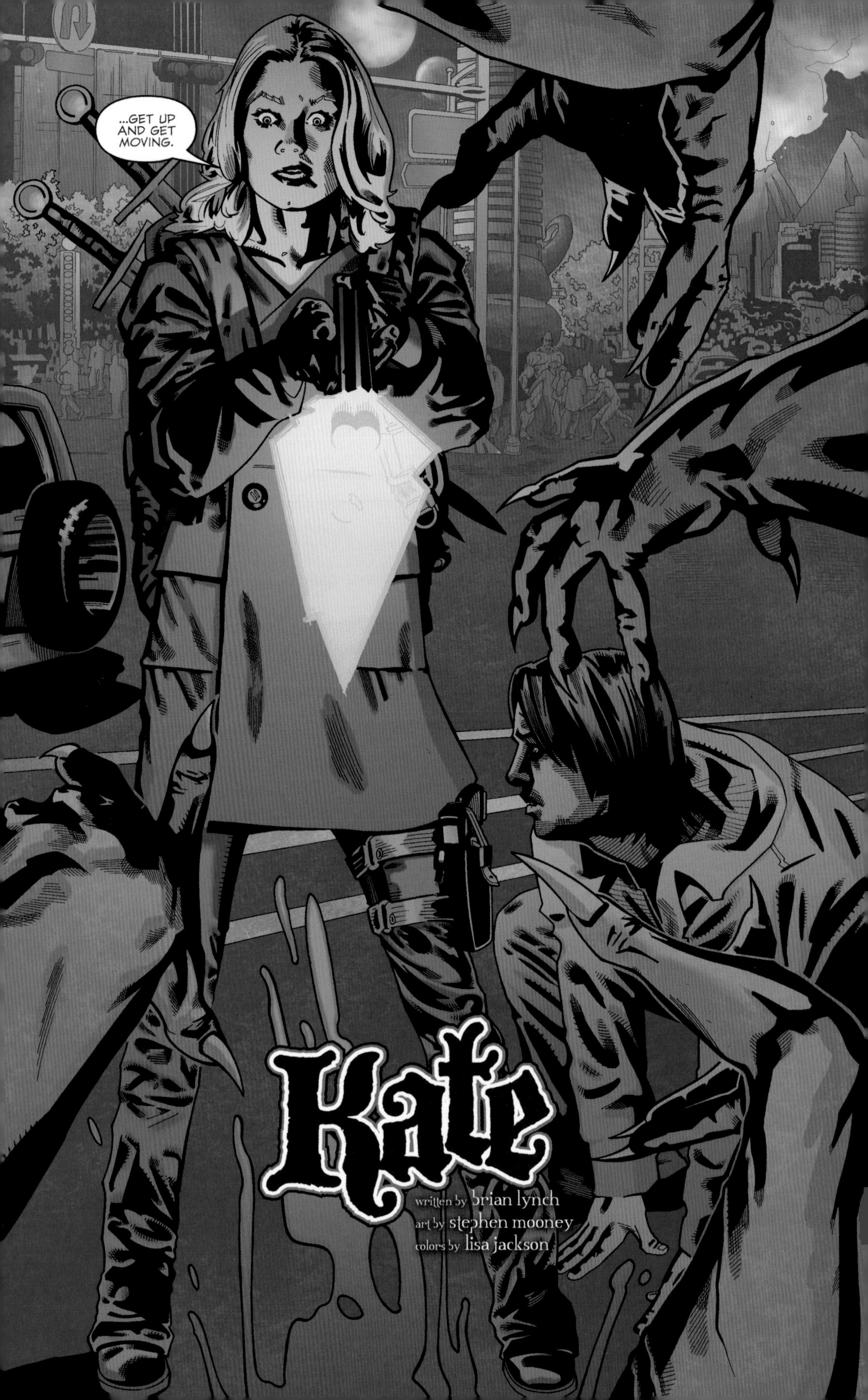
...GET UP AND GET MOVING.
Kate
written by brian lynch
art by stephen mooney
colors by lisa jackson

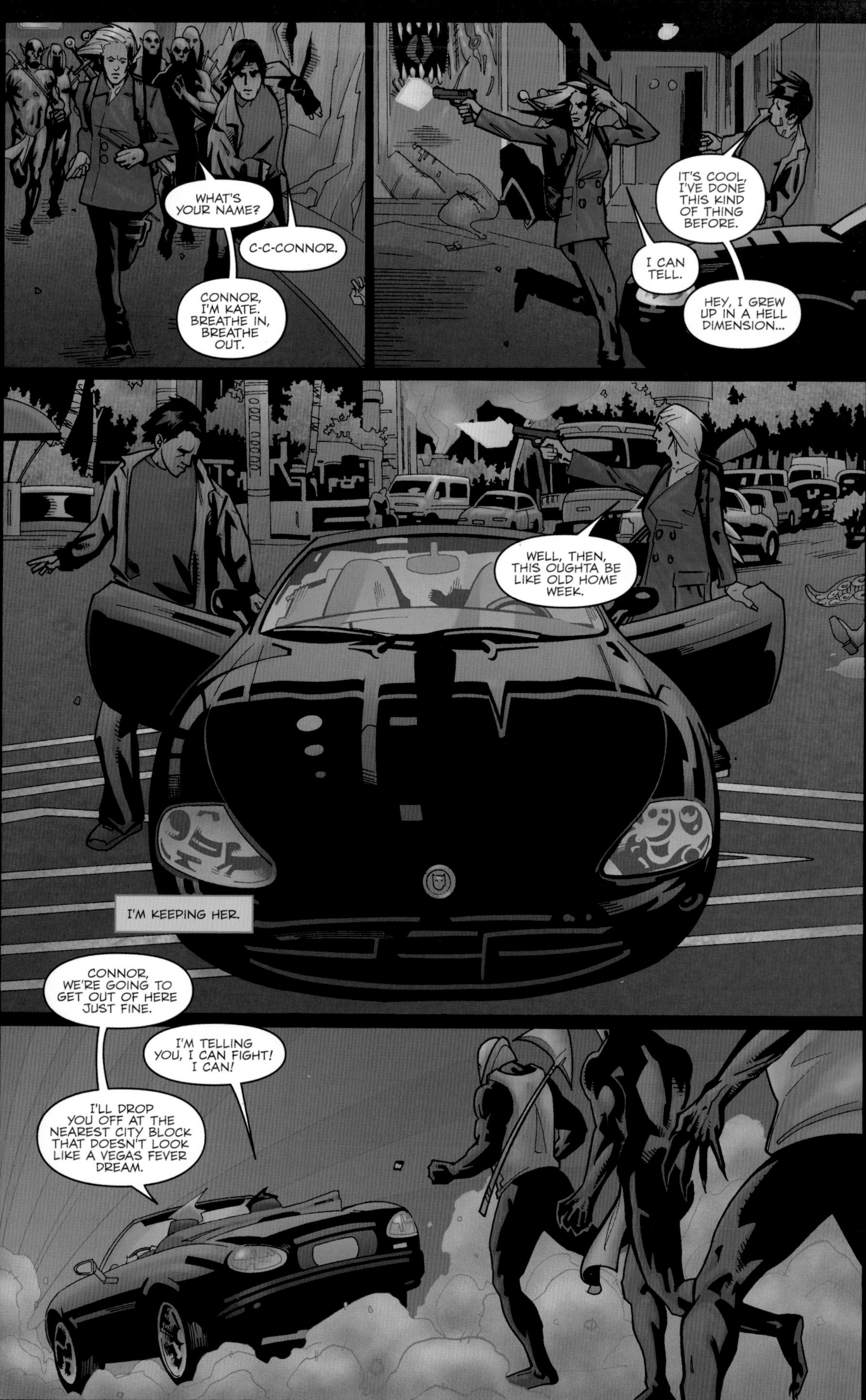
WHAT'S YOUR NAME?
C-C-CONNOR.
CONNOR, I'M KATE. BREATHE IN, BREATHE OUT.
IT'S COOL, I'VE DONE THIS KIND OF THING BEFORE.
I CAN TELL.
HEY, I GREW UP IN A HELL DIMENSION...
WELL, THEN, THIS OUGHTA BE LIKE OLD HOME WEEK.
I'M KEEPING HER.
CONNOR, WE'RE GOING TO GET OUT OF HERE JUST FINE.
I'M TELLING YOU, I CAN FIGHT! I CAN!
I'LL DROP YOU OFF AT THE NEAREST CITY BLOCK THAT DOESN'T LOOK LIKE A VEGAS FEVER DREAM.

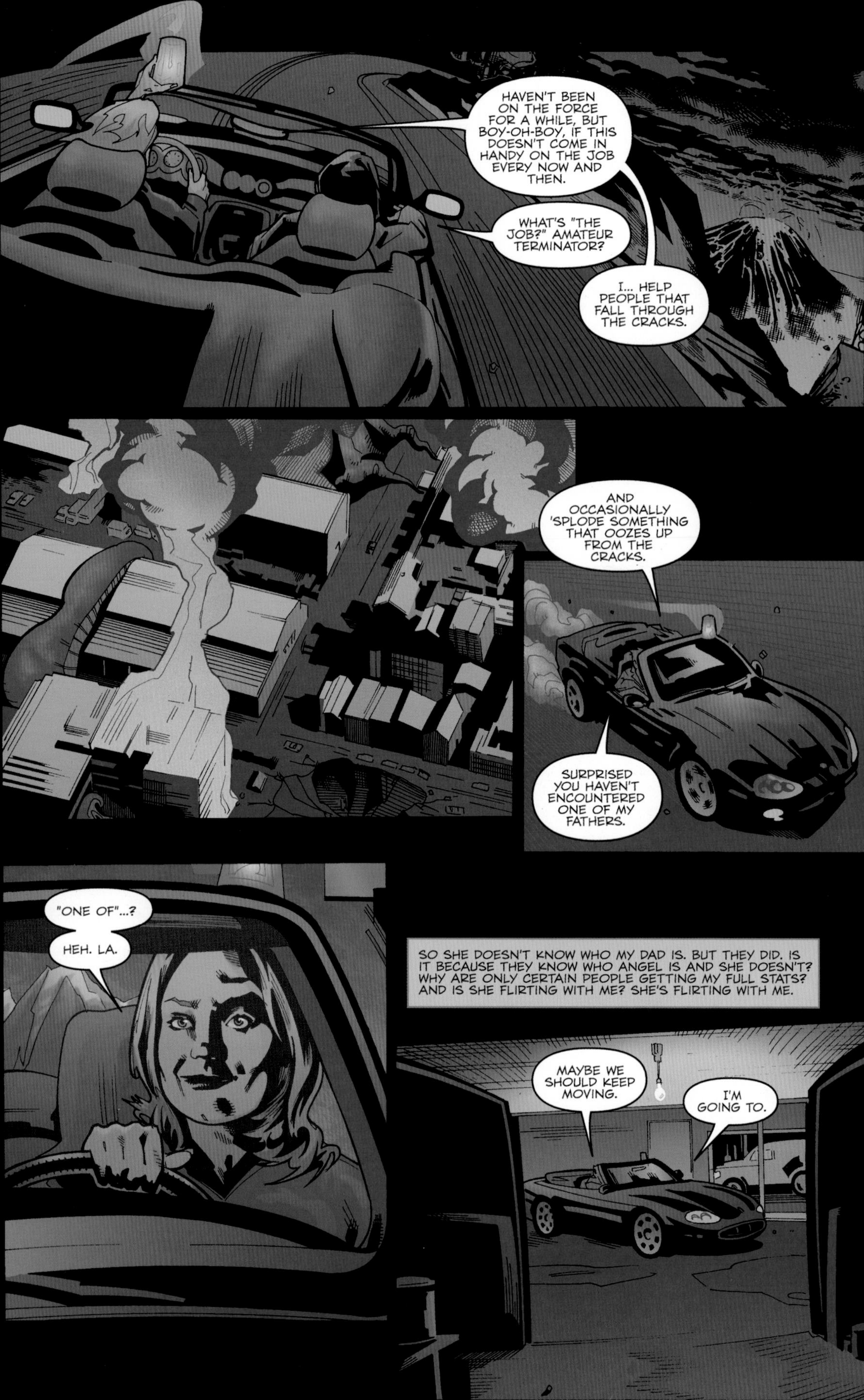
HAVEN'T BEEN ON THE FORCE FOR A WHILE, BUT BOY-OH-BOY, IF THIS DOESN'T COME IN HANDY ON THE JOB EVERY NOW AND THEN.
WHAT'S "THE JOB?" AMATEUR TERMINATOR?
I... HELP PEOPLE THAT FALL THROUGH THE CRACKS.
AND OCCASIONALLY 'SPLODE SOMETHING THAT OOZES UP FROM THE CRACKS.
SURPRISED YOU HAVEN'T ENCOUNTERED ONE OF MY FATHERS.
"ONE OF"...?
HEH. LA.
SO SHE DOESN'T KNOW WHO MY DAD IS. BUT THEY DID. IS IT BECAUSE THEY KNOW WHO ANGEL IS AND SHE DOESN'T? WHY ARE ONLY CERTAIN PEOPLE GETTING MY FULL STATS? AND IS SHE FLIRTING WITH ME? SHE'S FLIRTING WITH ME.
MAYBE WE SHOULD KEEP MOVING.
I'M GOING TO.

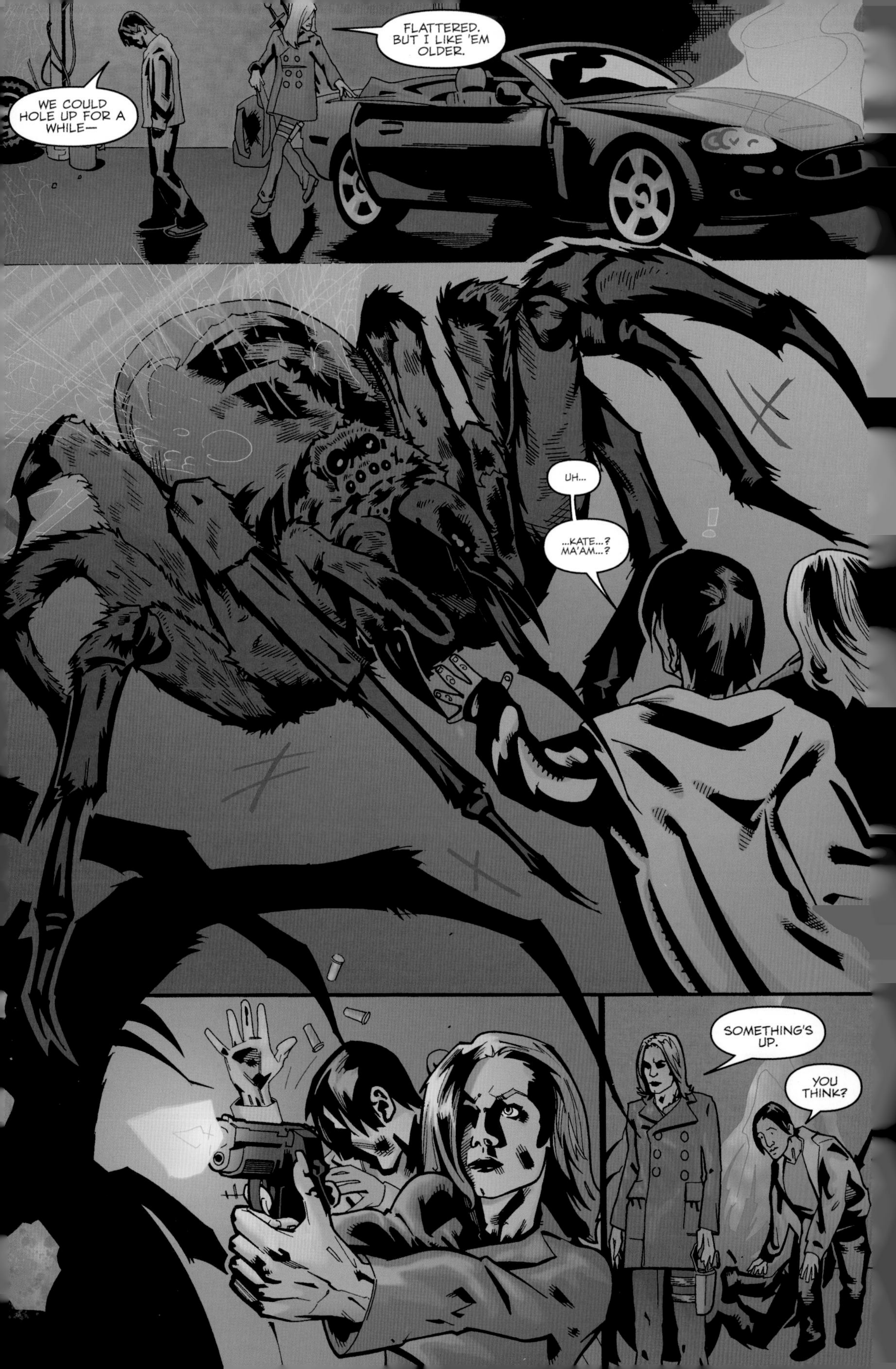
FLATTERED. BUT I LIKE 'EM OLDER.
WE COULD HOLE UP FOR A WHILE—
UH...
...KATE...? MA'AM...?
SOMETHING'S UP.
YOU THINK?

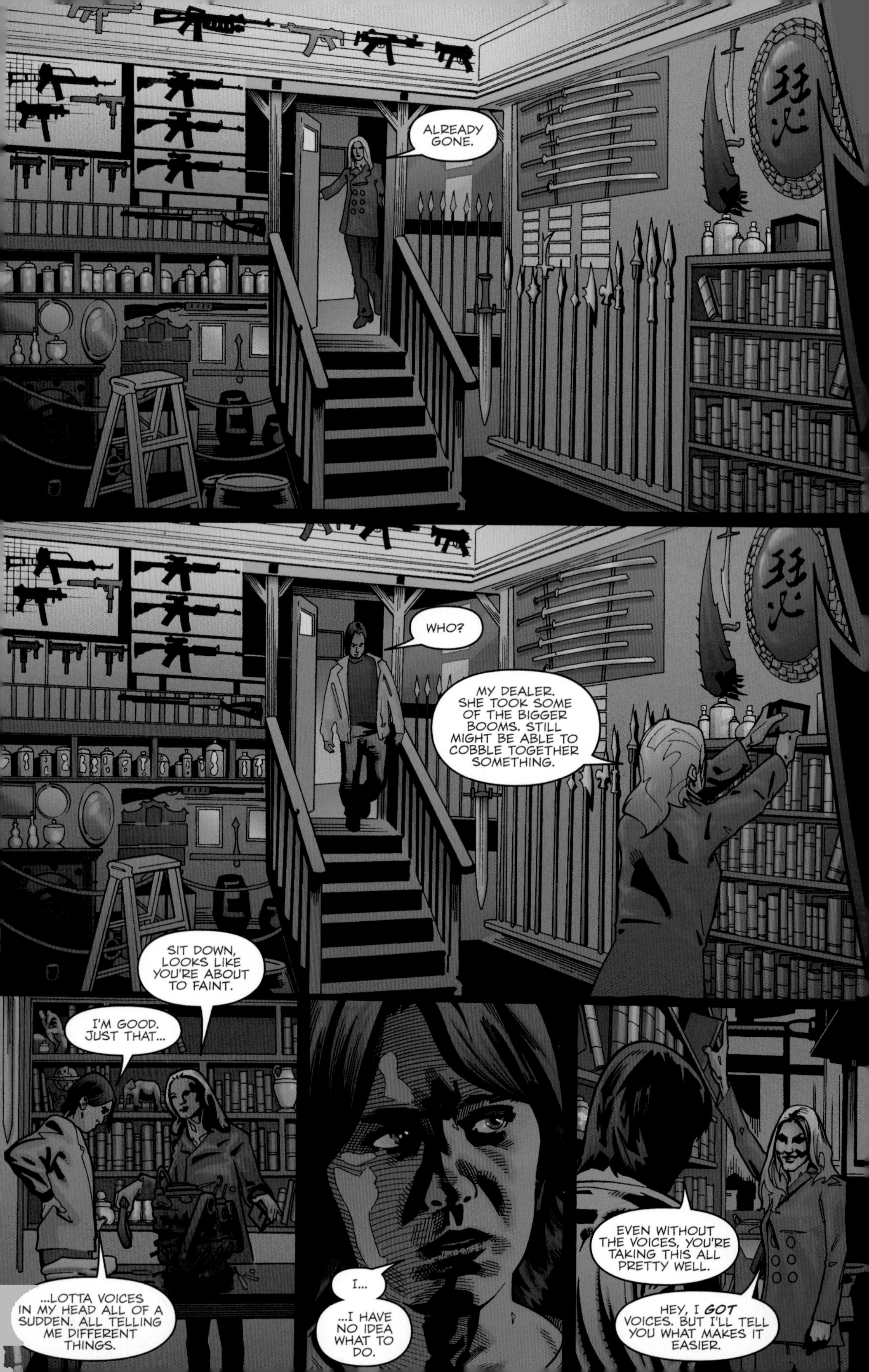
ALREADY GONE.
WHO?
MY DEALER. SHE TOOK SOME OF THE BIGGER BOOMS. STILL MIGHT BE ABLE TO COBBLE TOGETHER SOMETHING.
SIT DOWN, LOOKS LIKE YOU'RE ABOUT TO FAINT.
I'M GOOD. JUST THAT...
...LOTTA VOICES IN MY HEAD ALL OF A SUDDEN. ALL TELLING ME DIFFERENT THINGS.
I...
...I HAVE NO IDEA WHAT TO DO.
EVEN WITHOUT THE VOICES, YOU'RE TAKING THIS ALL PRETTY WELL.
HEY, I GOT VOICES. BUT I'LL TELL YOU WHAT MAKES IT EASIER.

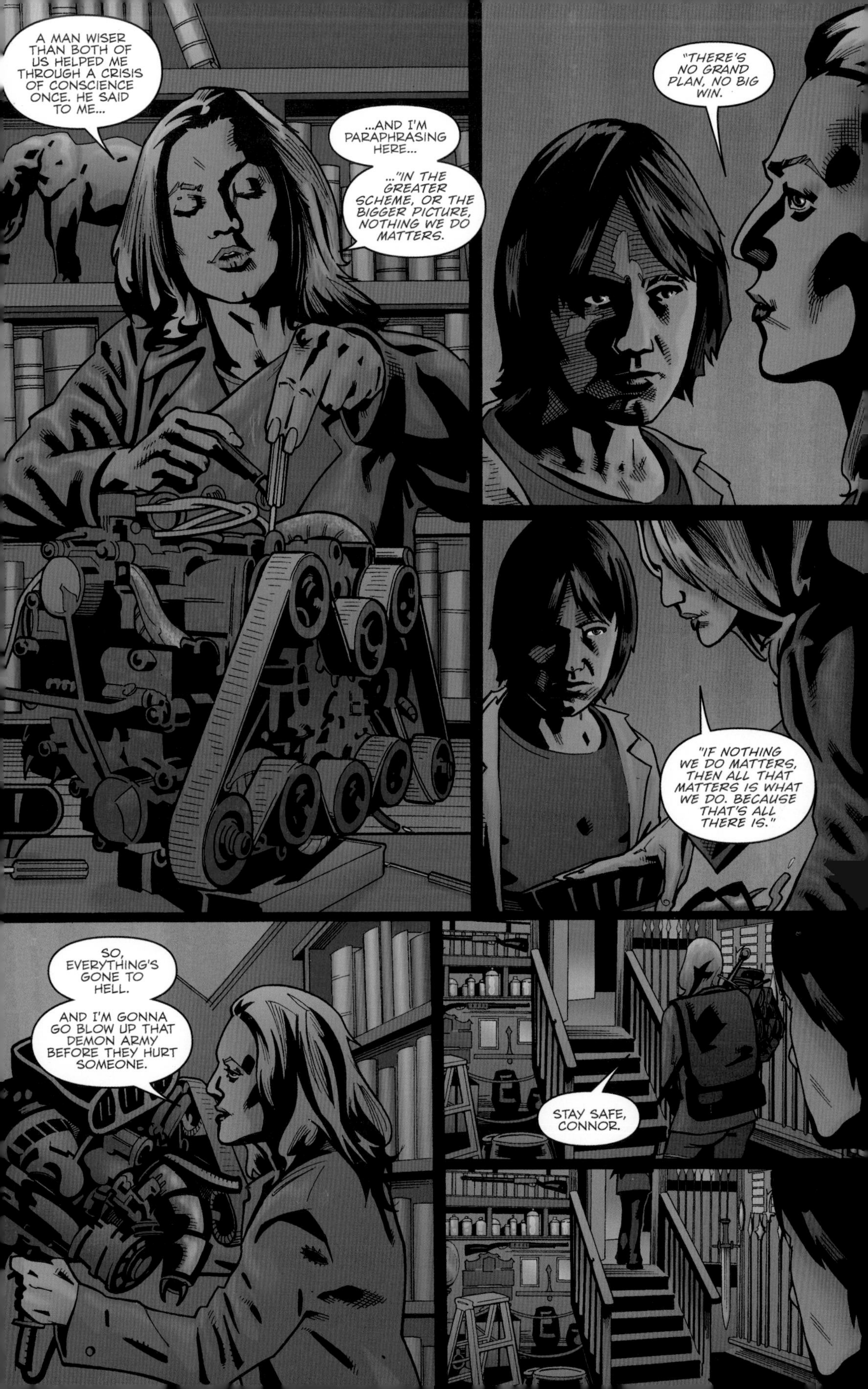
A MAN WISER THAN BOTH OF US HELPED ME THROUGH A CRISIS OF CONSCIENCE ONCE. HE SAID TO ME...
...AND I'M PARAPHRASING HERE...
..."IN THE GREATER SCHEME, OR THE BIGGER PICTURE, NOTHING WE DO MATTERS.
"THERE'S NO GRAND PLAN, NO BIG WIN.
"IF NOTHING WE DO MATTERS, THEN ALL THAT MATTERS IS WHAT WE DO. BECAUSE THAT'S ALL THERE IS."
SO, EVERYTHING'S GONE TO HELL.
AND I'M GONNA GO BLOW UP THAT DEMON ARMY BEFORE THEY HURT SOMEONE.
STAY SAFE, CONNOR.

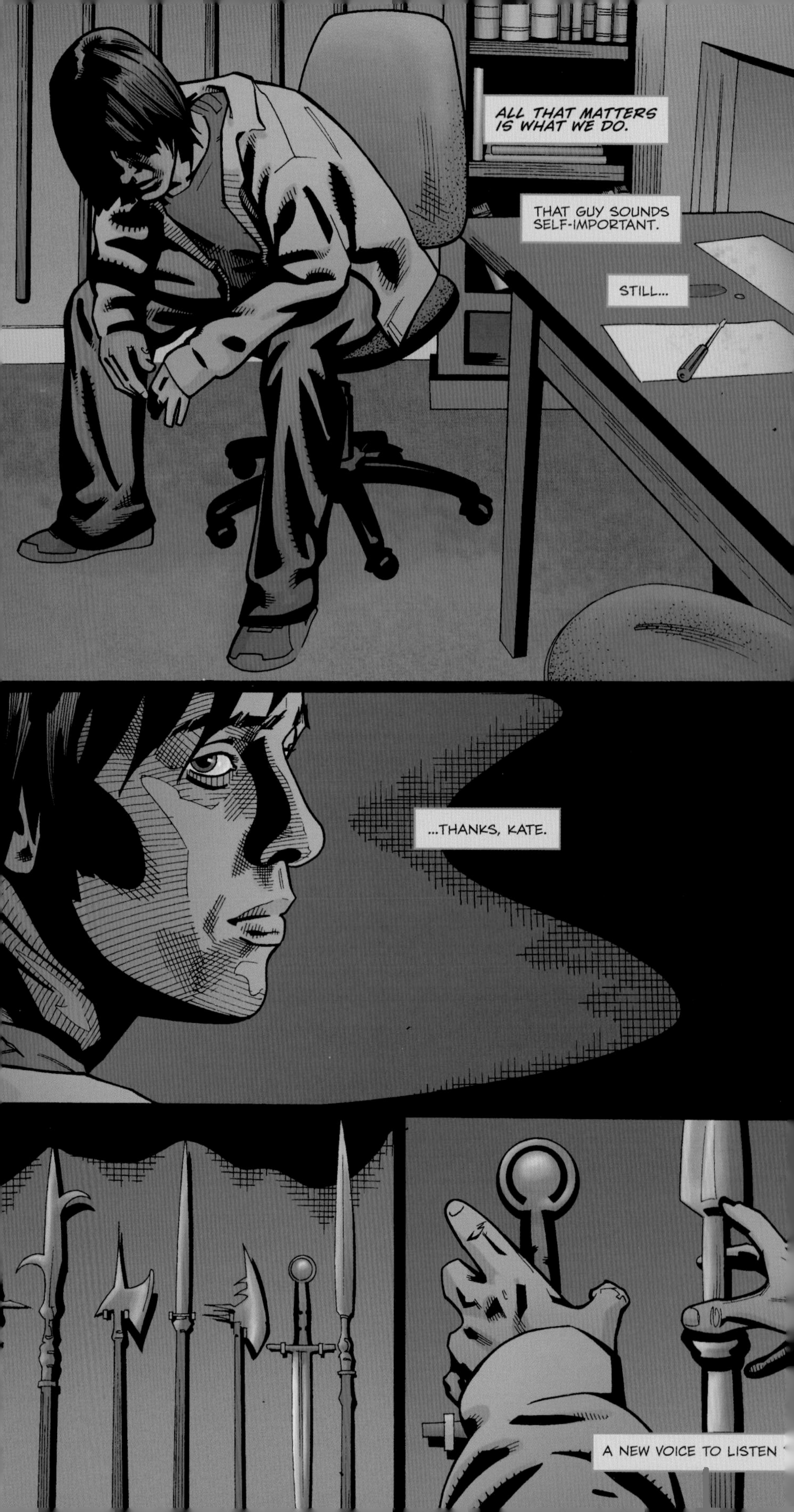
ALL THAT MATTERS IS WHAT WE DO.
THAT GUY SOUNDS SELF-IMPORTANT.
STILL...
...THANKS, KATE.
A NEW VOICE TO LISTEN

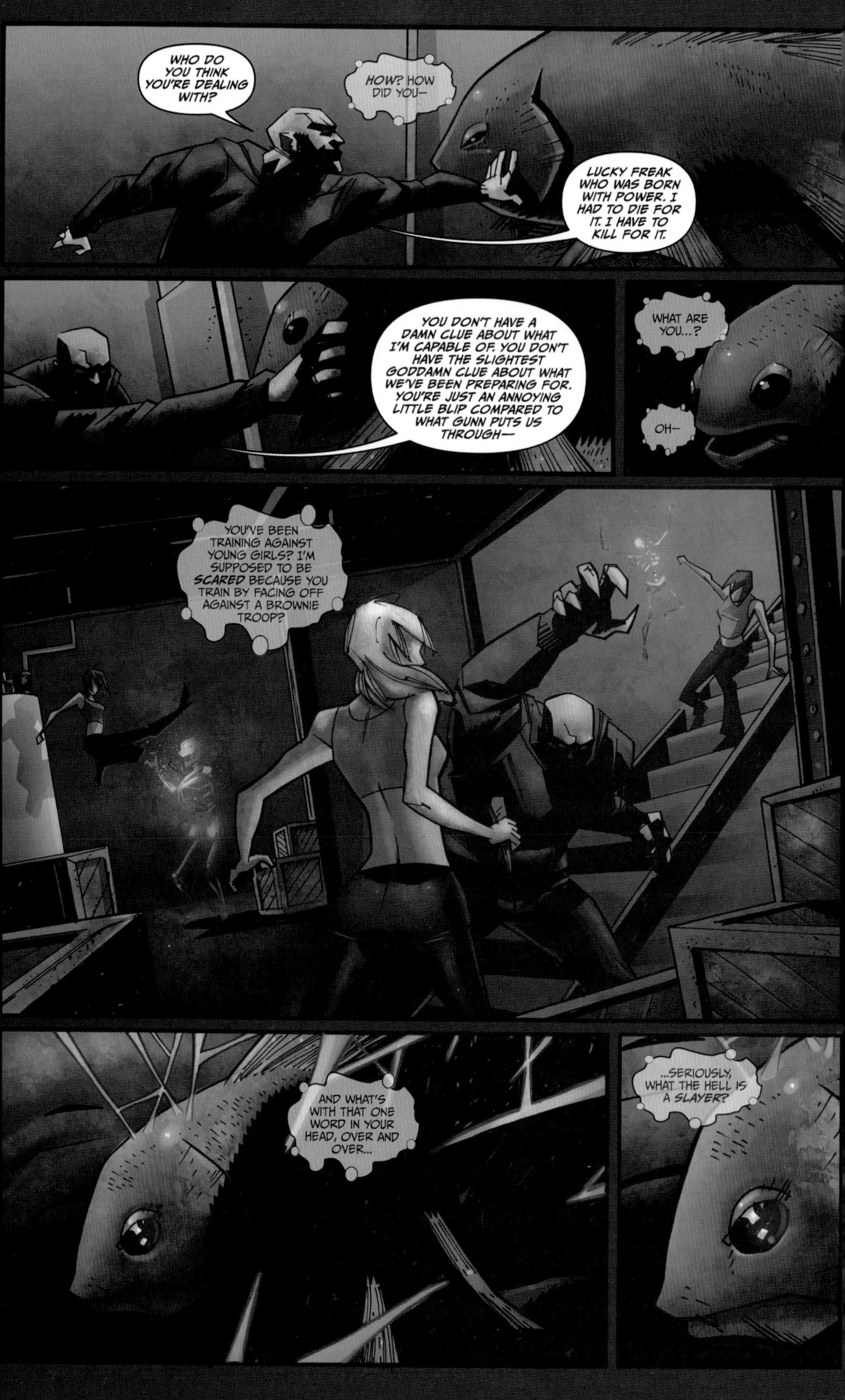
WHO DO YOU THINK YOU'RE DEALING WITH?
HOW? HOW DID YOU—
LUCKY FREAK WHO WAS BORN WITH POWER. I HAD TO DIE FOR IT. I HAVE TO KILL FOR IT.
YOU DON'T HAVE A DAMN CLUE ABOUT WHAT I'M CAPABLE OF. YOU DON'T HAVE THE SLIGHTEST GODDAMN CLUE ABOUT WHAT WE'VE BEEN PREPARING FOR. YOU'RE JUST AN ANNOYING LITTLE BLIP COMPARED TO WHAT GUNN PUTS US THROUGH—
WHAT ARE YOU...?
OH—
YOU'VE BEEN TRAINING AGAINST YOUNG GIRLS? I'M SUPPOSED TO BE SCARED BECAUSE YOU TRAIN BY FACING OFF AGAINST A BROWNIE TROOP?
AND WHAT'S WITH THAT ONE WORD IN YOUR HEAD, OVER AND OVER...
...SERIOUSLY, WHAT THE HELL IS A SLAYER?

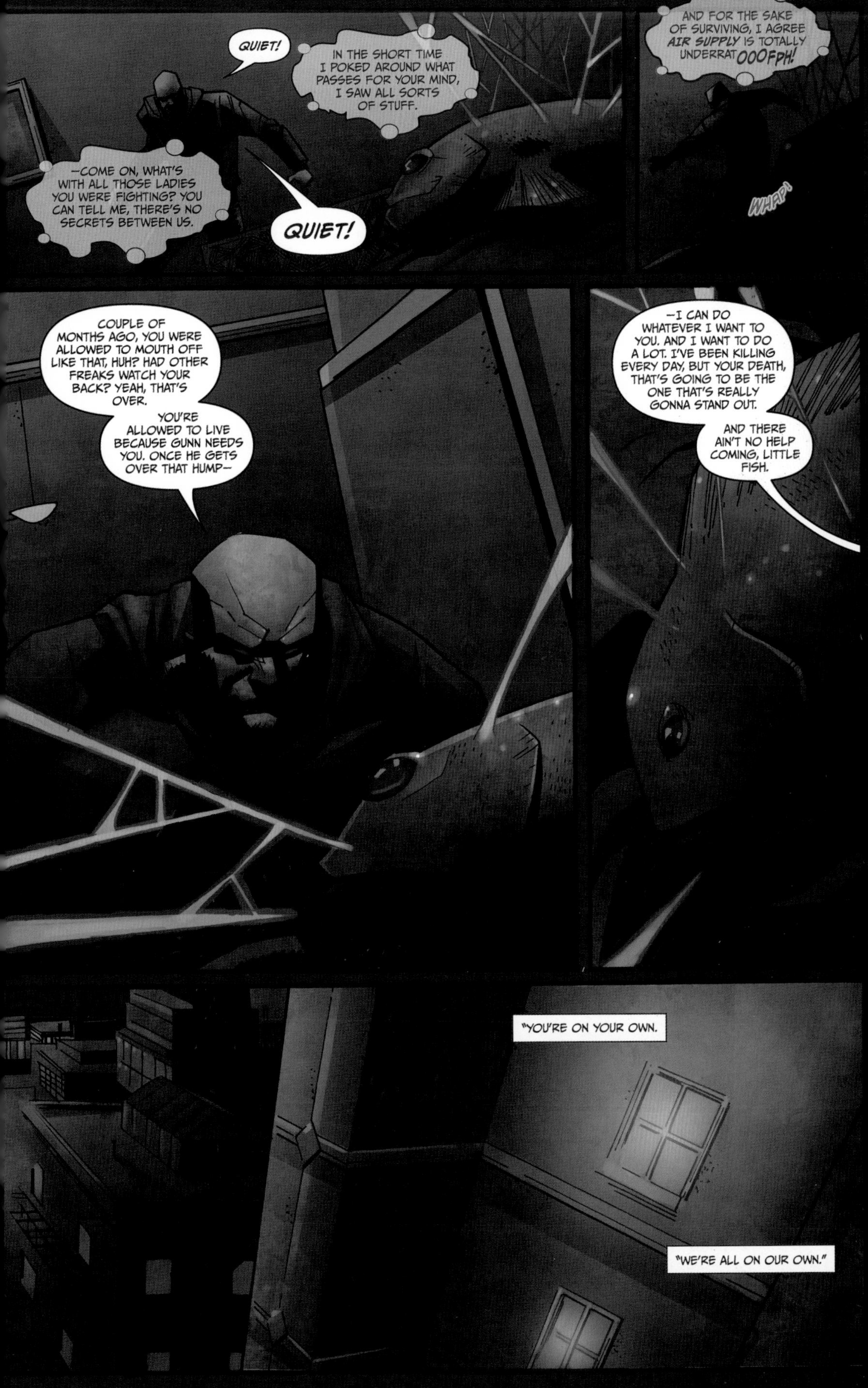
QUIET!
IN THE SHORT TIME I POKED AROUND WHAT PASSES FOR YOUR MIND, I SAW ALL SORTS OF STUFF.
—COME ON, WHAT'S WITH ALL THOSE LADIES YOU WERE FIGHTING? YOU CAN TELL ME, THERE'S NO SECRETS BETWEEN US.
QUIET!
AND FOR THE SAKE OF SURVIVING, I AGREE AIR SUPPLY IS TOTALLY UNDERRATOOOFPH!
WHAP!
COUPLE OF MONTHS AGO, YOU WERE ALLOWED TO MOUTH OFF LIKE THAT, HUH? HAD OTHER FREAKS WATCH YOUR BACK? YEAH, THAT'S OVER.
YOU'RE ALLOWED TO LIVE BECAUSE GUNN NEEDS YOU. ONCE HE GETS OVER THAT HUMP—
—I CAN DO WHATEVER I WANT TO YOU. AND I WANT TO DO A LOT. I'VE BEEN KILLING EVERY DAY, BUT YOUR DEATH, THAT'S GOING TO BE THE ONE THAT'S REALLY GONNA STAND OUT.
AND THERE AIN'T NO HELP COMING, LITTLE FISH.
"YOU'RE ON YOUR OWN.
"WE'RE ALL ON OUR OWN."

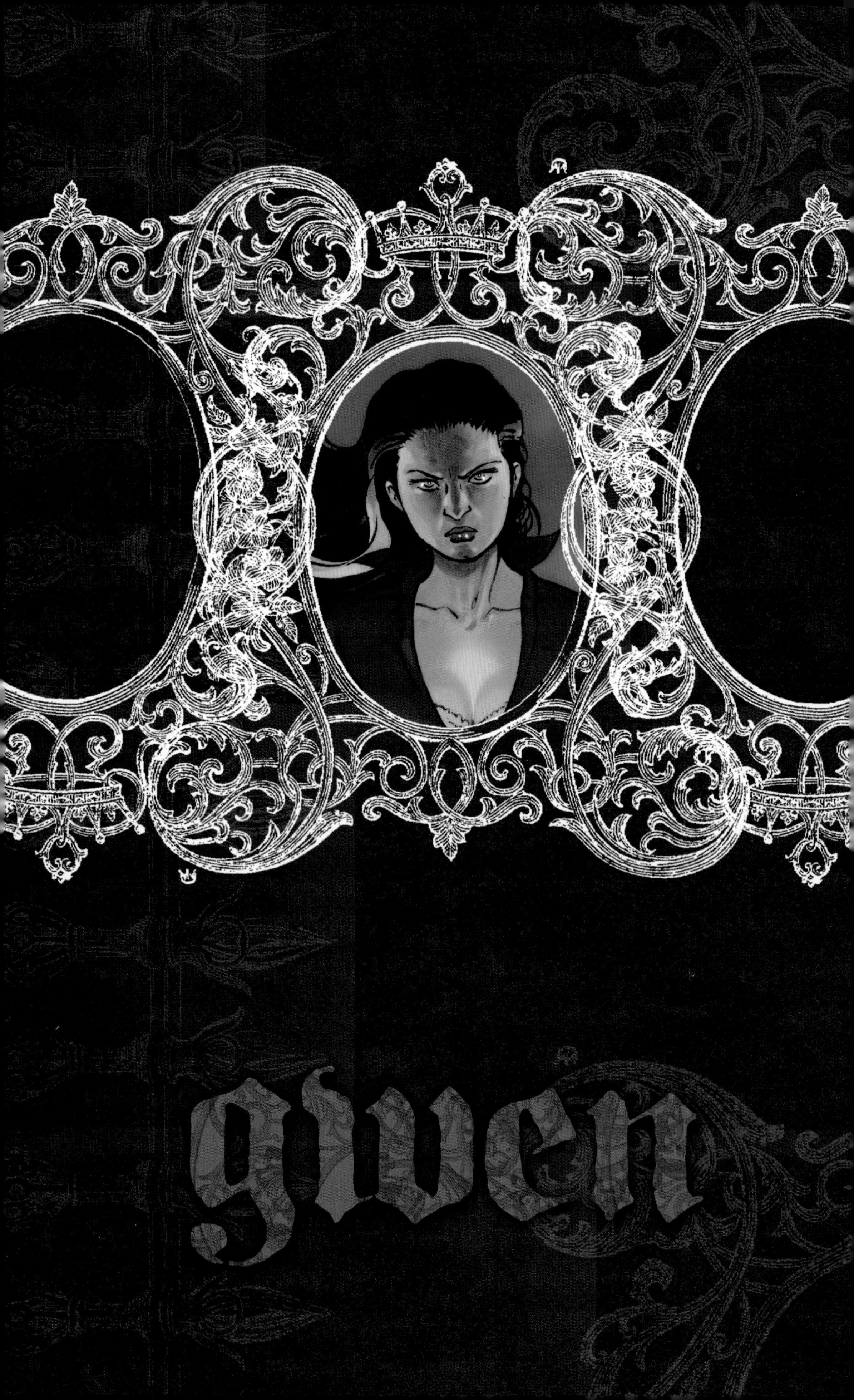
given

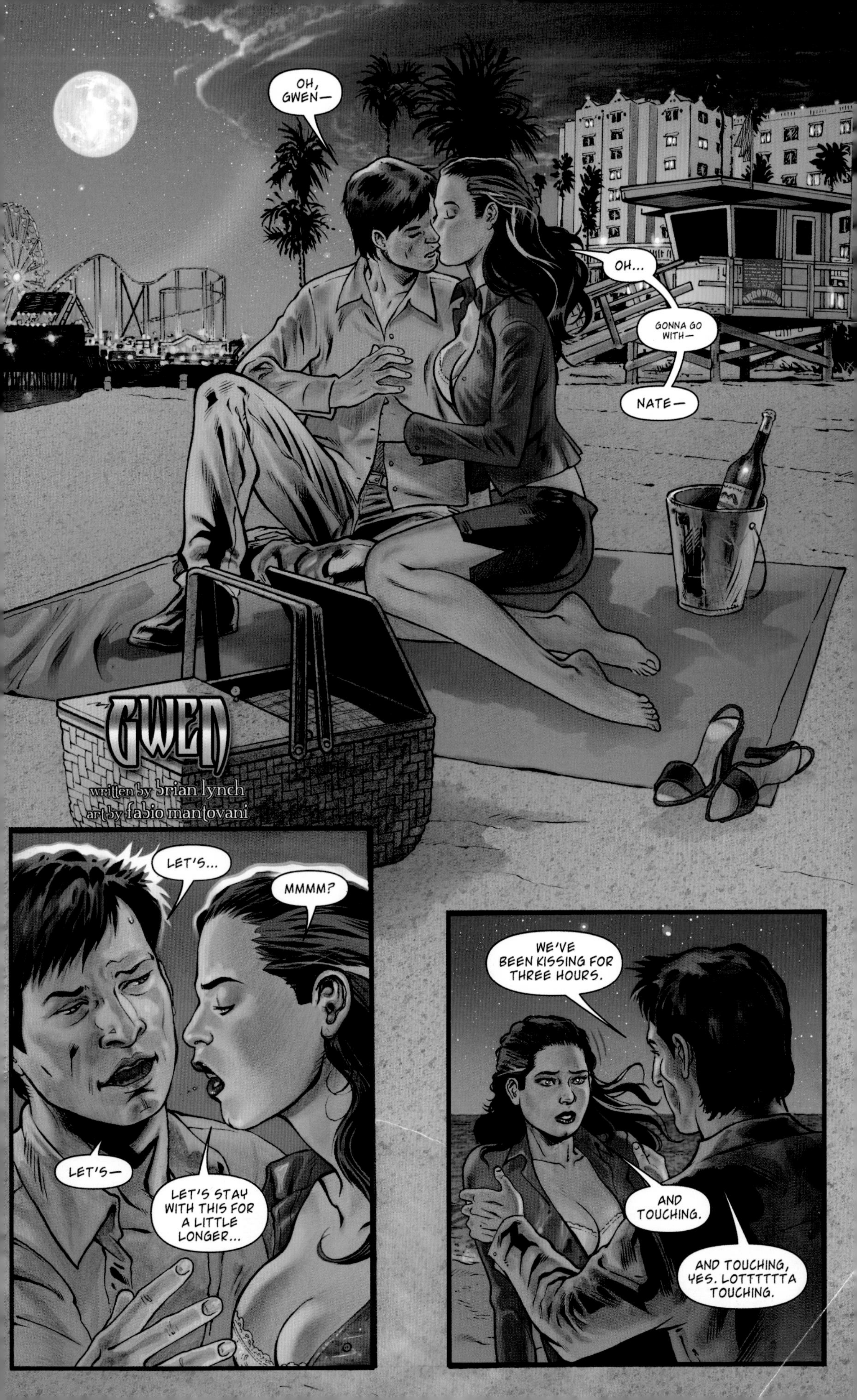
OH, GWEN—
OH...
GONNA GO WITH—
NATE—
GWEN
written by brian lynch
art by fabio mantovani
LET'S...
MMMM?
LET'S—
LET'S STAY WITH THIS FOR A LITTLE LONGER...
WE'VE BEEN KISSING FOR THREE HOURS.
AND TOUCHING.
AND TOUCHING, YES. LOTTTTTTA TOUCHING.

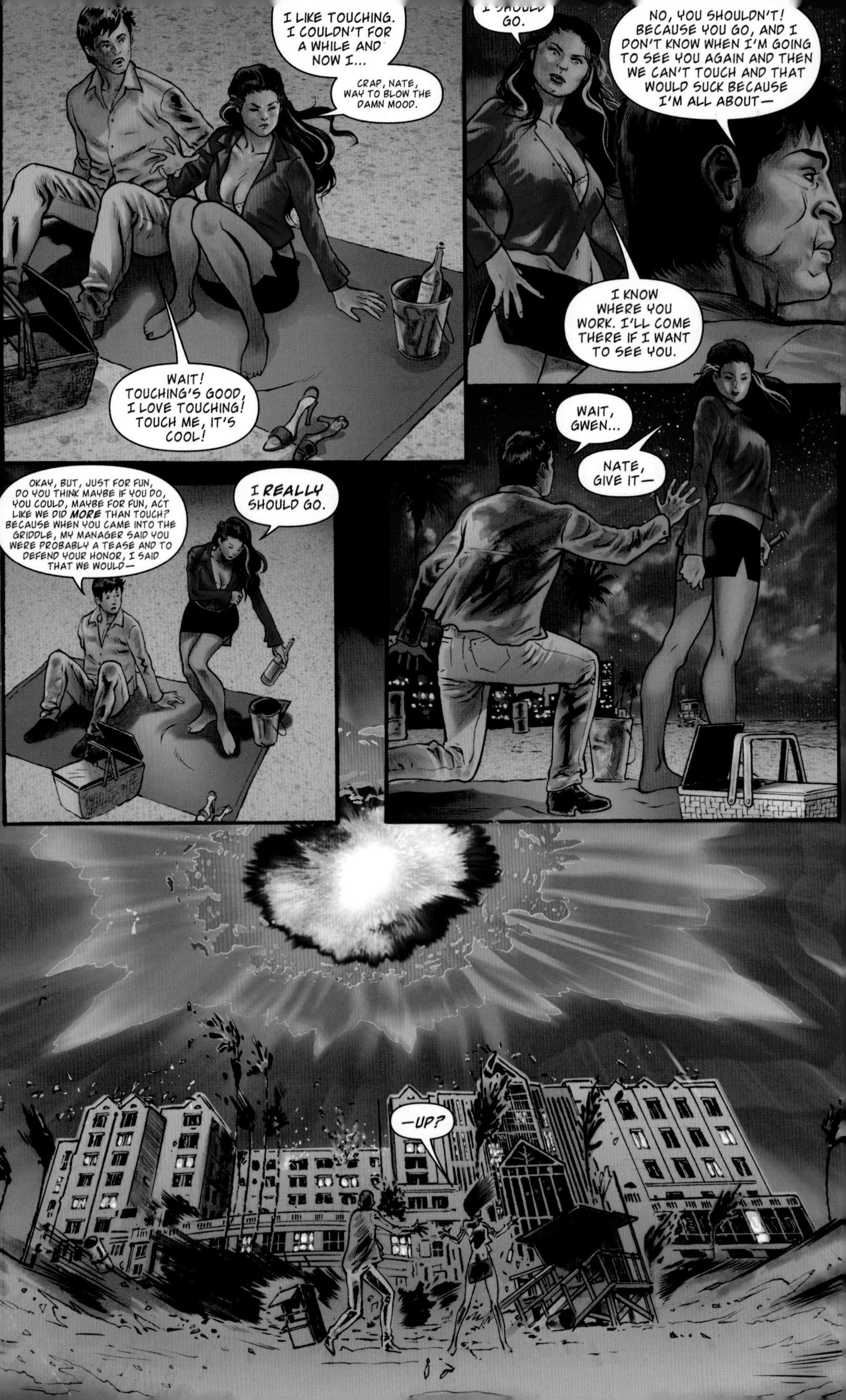
I LIKE TOUCHING. I COULDN'T FOR A WHILE AND NOW I...
CRAP, NATE, WAY TO BLOW THE DAMN MOOD.
WAIT! TOUCHING'S GOOD, I LOVE TOUCHING! TOUCH ME, IT'S COOL!
GO.
NO, YOU SHOULDN'T! BECAUSE YOU GO, AND I DON'T KNOW WHEN I'M GOING TO SEE YOU AGAIN AND THEN WE CAN'T TOUCH AND THAT WOULD SUCK BECAUSE I'M ALL ABOUT—
I KNOW WHERE YOU WORK. I'LL COME THERE IF I WANT TO SEE YOU.
OKAY, BUT, JUST FOR FUN, DO YOU THINK MAYBE IF YOU DO, YOU COULD, MAYBE FOR FUN, ACT LIKE WE DID MORE THAN TOUCH? BECAUSE WHEN YOU CAME INTO THE GRIDDLE, MY MANAGER SAID YOU WERE PROBABLY A TEASE AND TO DEFEND YOUR HONOR, I SAID THAT WE WOULD—
I REALLY SHOULD GO.
WAIT, GWEN...
NATE, GIVE IT—
—UP?

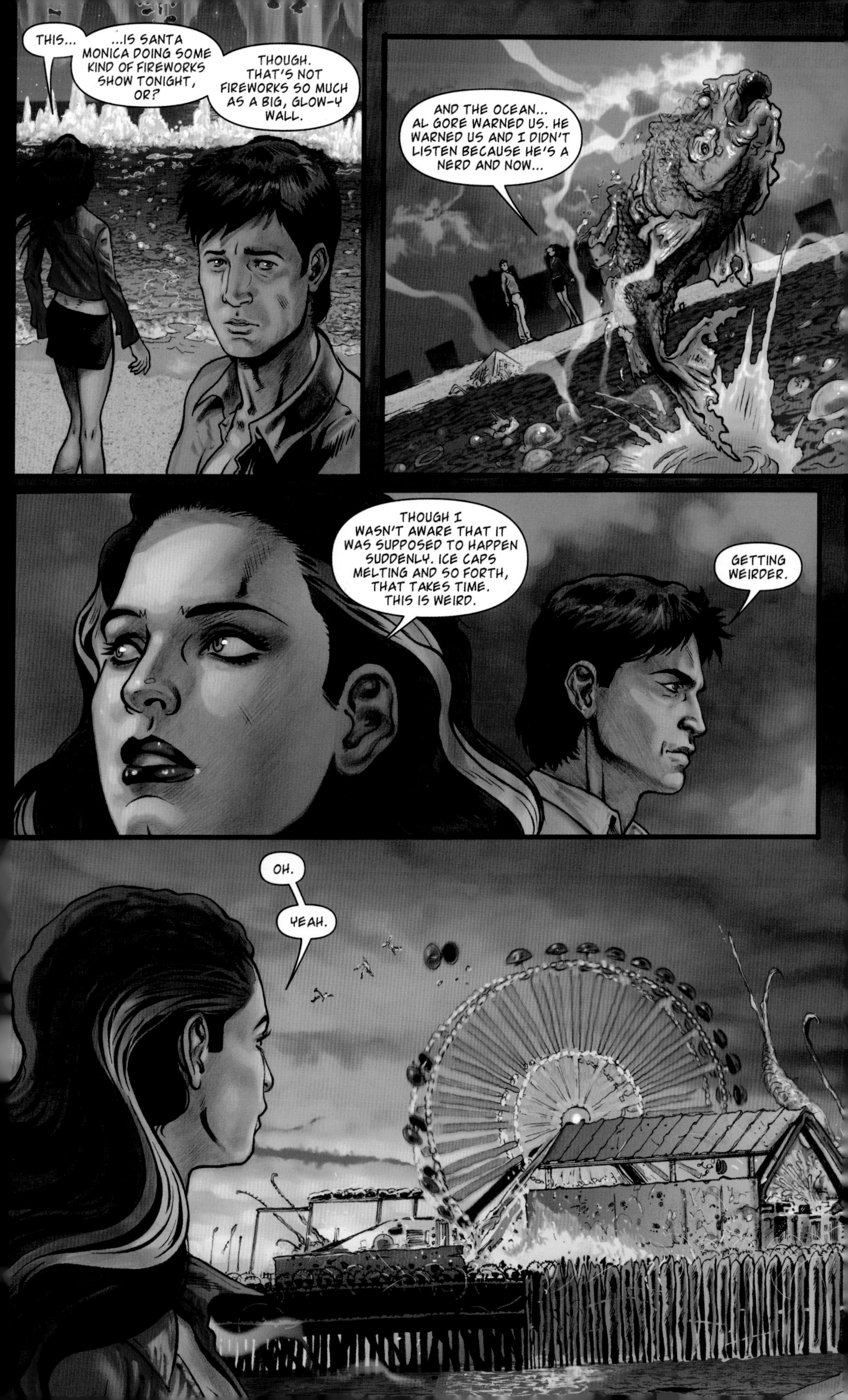
THIS...
...IS SANTA MONICA DOING SOME KIND OF FIREWORKS SHOW TONIGHT, OR?
THOUGH. THAT'S NOT FIREWORKS SO MUCH AS A BIG, GLOW-Y WALL.
AND THE OCEAN... AL GORE WARNED US. HE WARNED US AND I DIDN'T LISTEN BECAUSE HE'S A NERD AND NOW...
THOUGH I WASN'T AWARE THAT IT WAS SUPPOSED TO HAPPEN SUDDENLY. ICE CAPS MELTING AND SO FORTH, THAT TAKES TIME. THIS IS WEIRD.
GETTING WEIRDER.
OH.
YEAH.

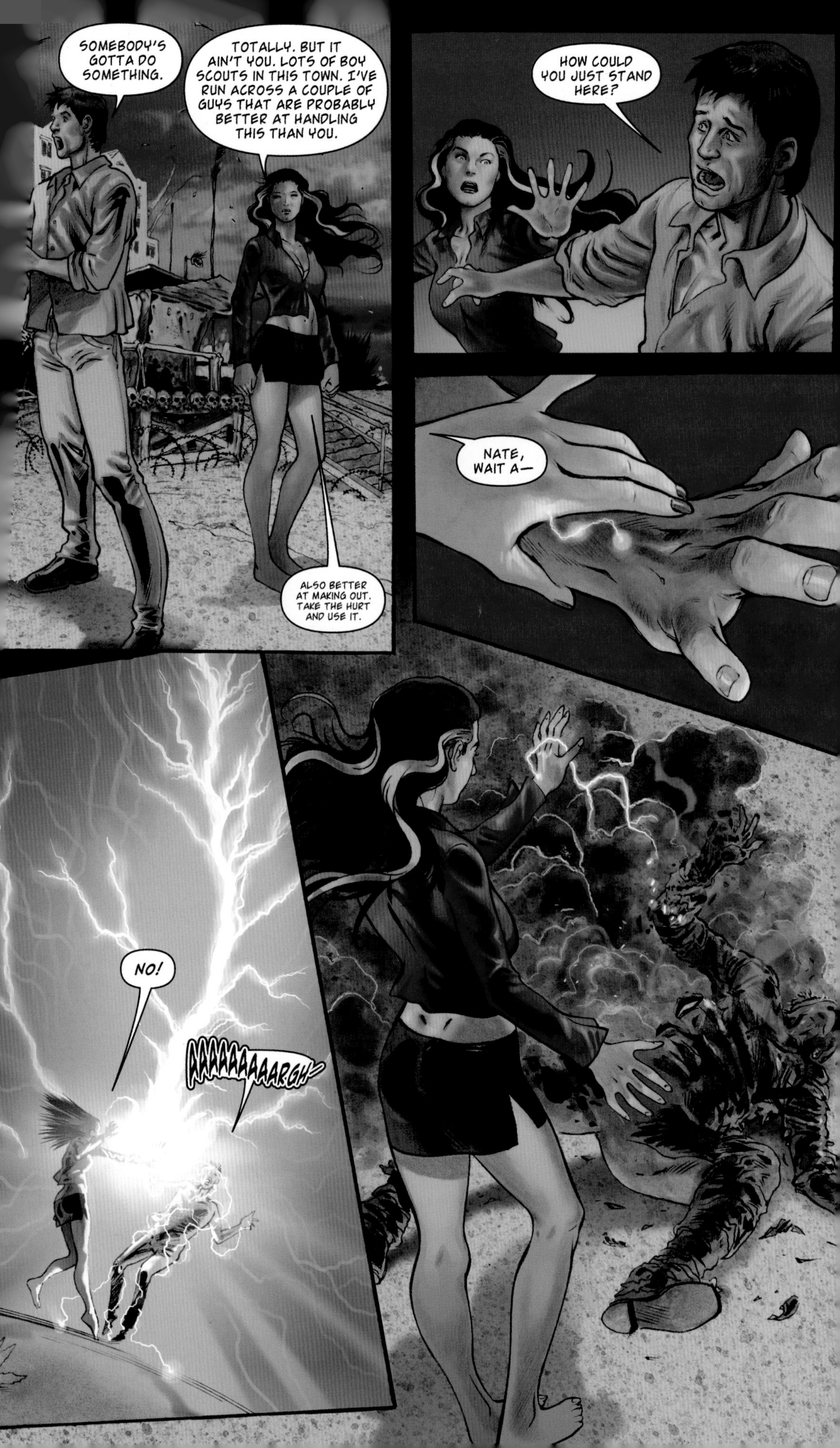
SOMEBODY'S GOTTA DO SOMETHING.
TOTALLY. BUT IT AIN'T YOU. LOTS OF BOY SCOUTS IN THIS TOWN. I'VE RUN ACROSS A COUPLE OF GUYS THAT ARE PROBABLY BETTER AT HANDLING THIS THAN YOU.
ALSO BETTER AT MAKING OUT. TAKE THE HURT AND USE IT.
HOW COULD YOU JUST STAND HERE?
NATE, WAIT A—
NO!
AAAAAAAAARGH—

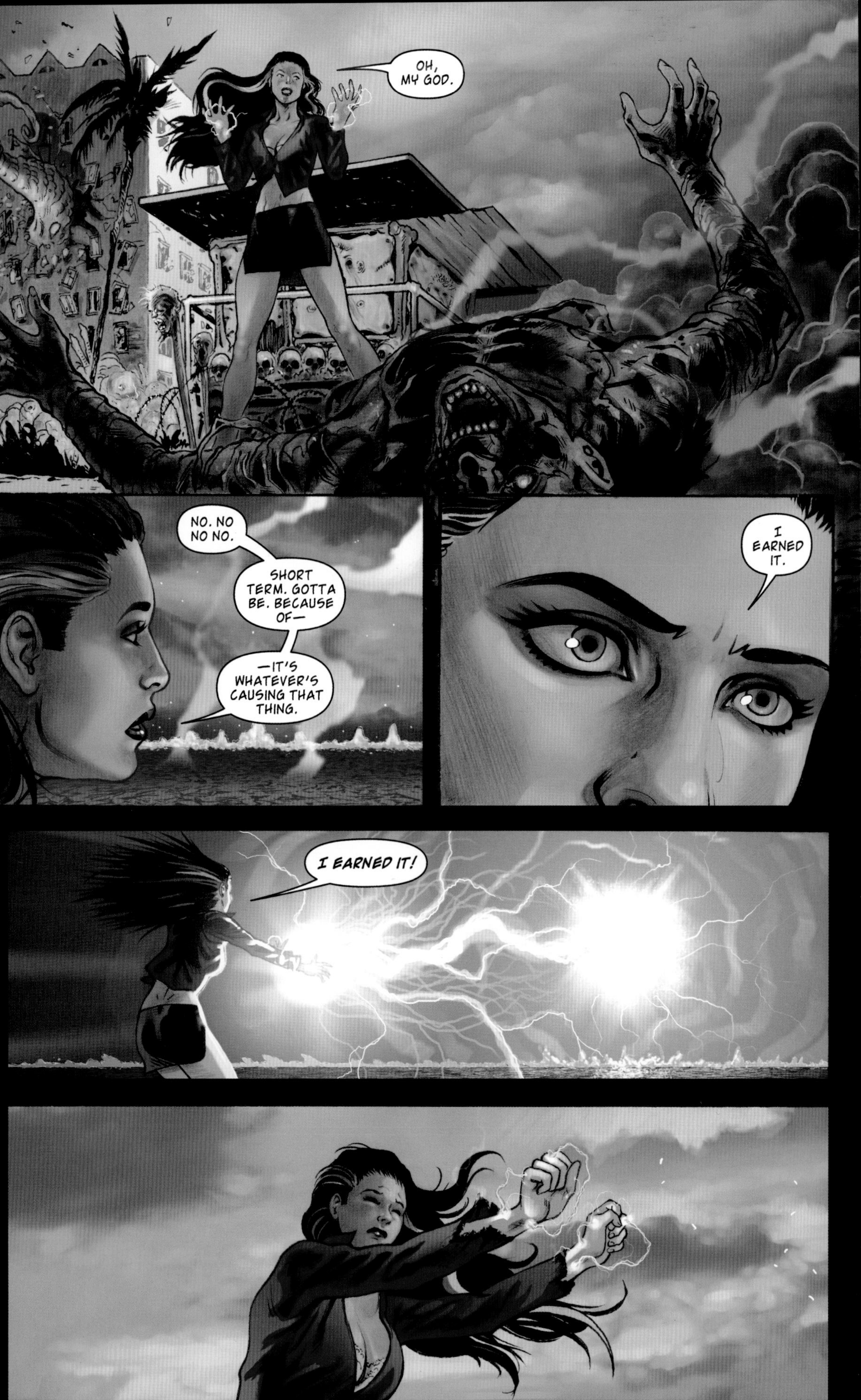
OH, MY GOD.
NO. NO NO NO.
SHORT TERM. GOTTA BE. BECAUSE OF—
—IT'S WHATEVER'S CAUSING THAT THING.
I EARNED IT.
I EARNED IT!

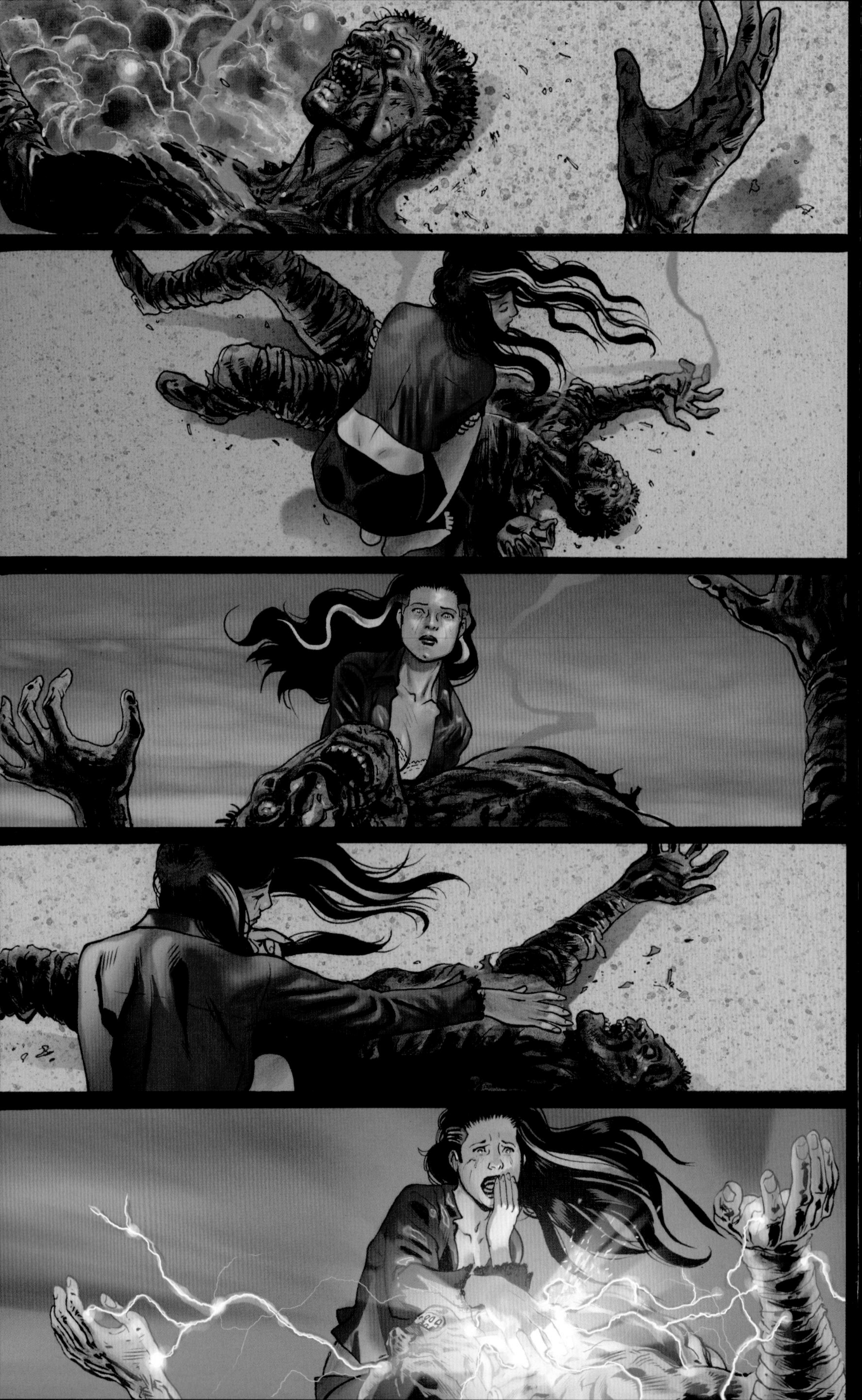

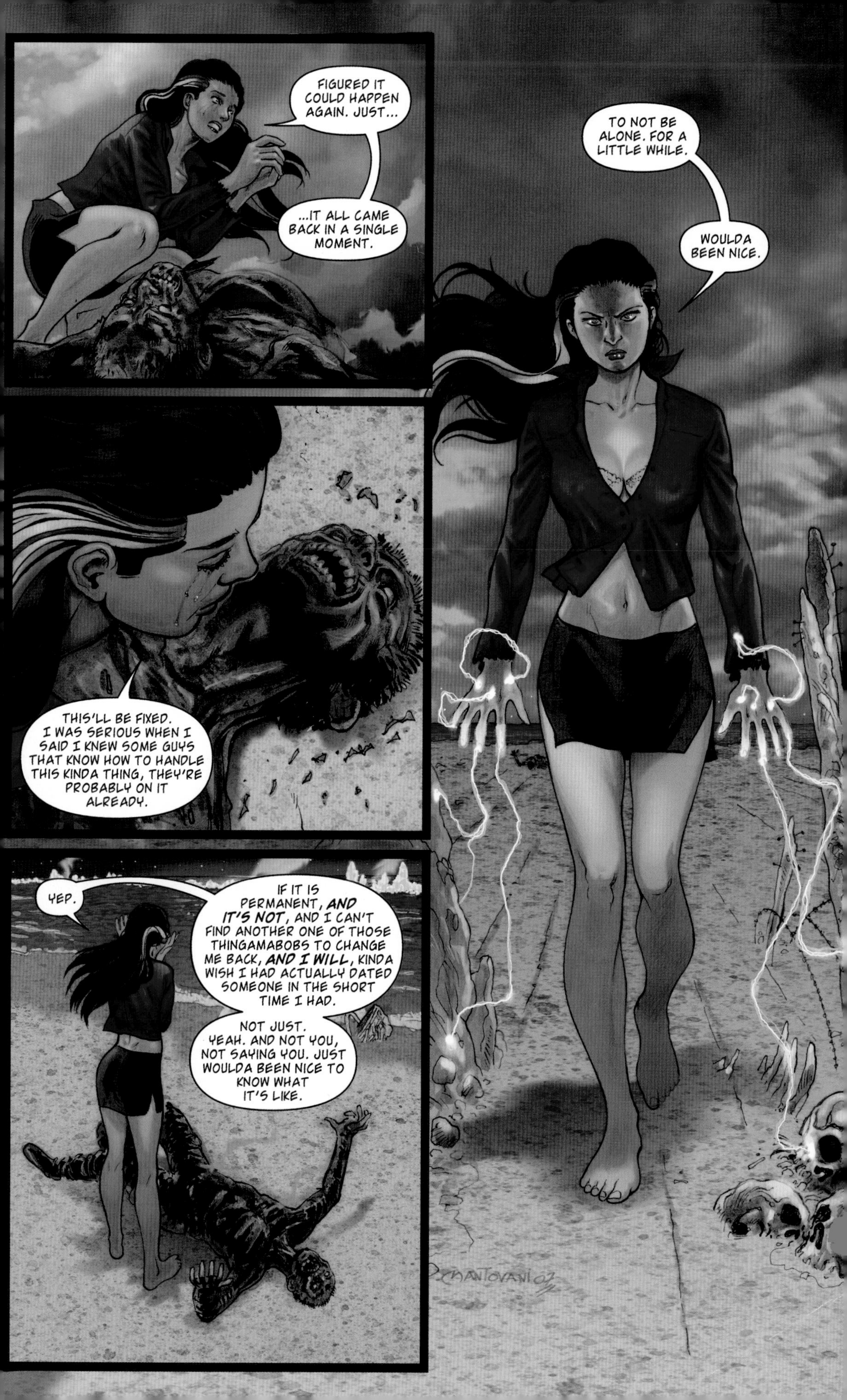

FIGURED IT COULD HAPPEN AGAIN. JUST...
...IT ALL CAME BACK IN A SINGLE MOMENT.
THIS'LL BE FIXED. I WAS SERIOUS WHEN I SAID I KNEW SOME GUYS THAT KNOW HOW TO HANDLE THIS KINDA THING, THEY'RE PROBABLY ON IT ALREADY.
YEP.
IF IT IS PERMANENT, **AND IT'S NOT**, AND I CAN'T FIND ANOTHER ONE OF THOSE THINGAMABOBS TO CHANGE ME BACK, **AND I WILL**, KINDA WISH I HAD ACTUALLY DATED SOMEONE IN THE SHORT TIME I HAD.
NOT JUST. YEAH. AND NOT YOU, NOT SAYING YOU. JUST WOULDA BEEN NICE TO KNOW WHAT IT'S LIKE.
TO NOT BE ALONE. FOR A LITTLE WHILE.
WOULDA BEEN NICE.
MANTOVANI 07

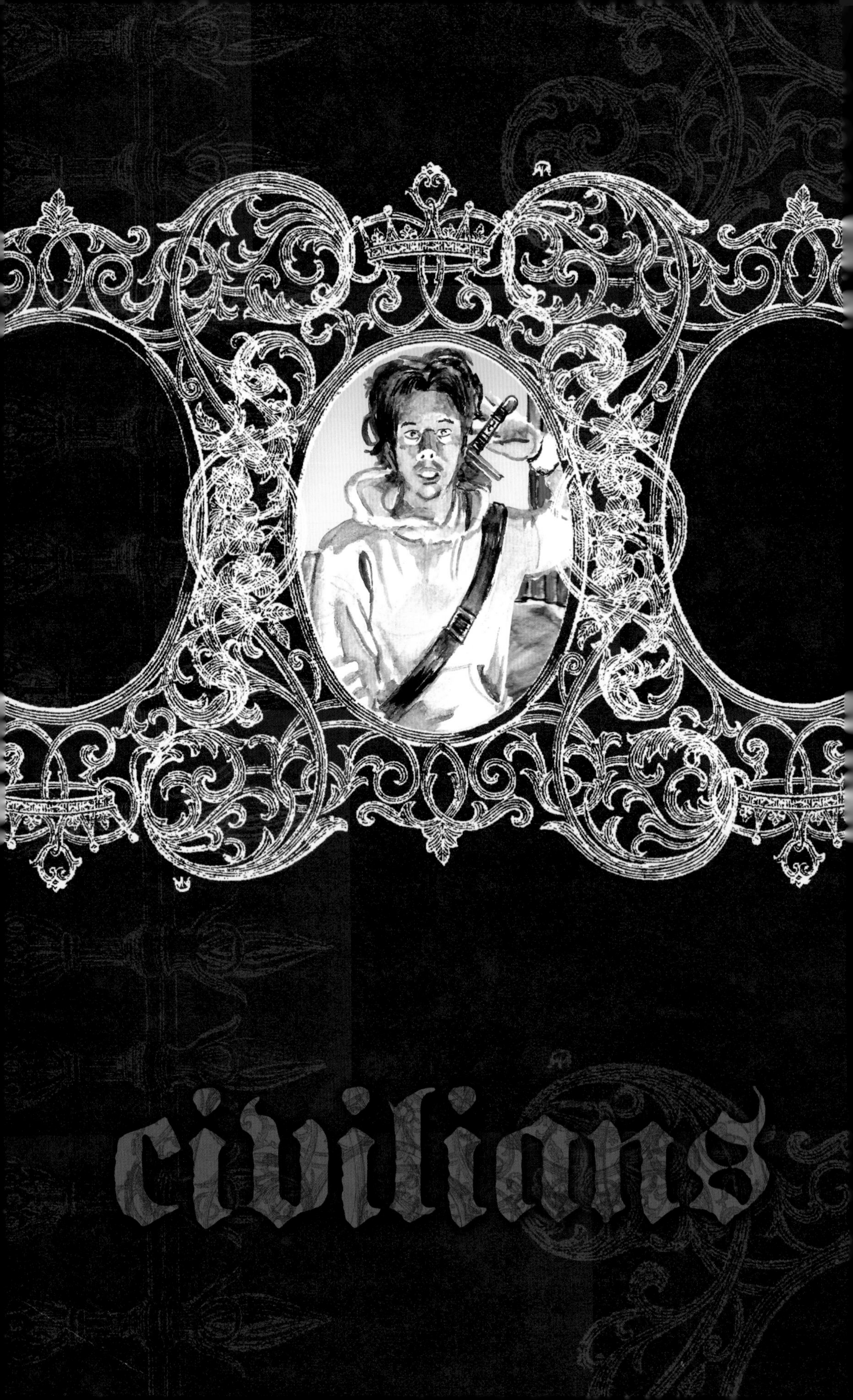
civilians

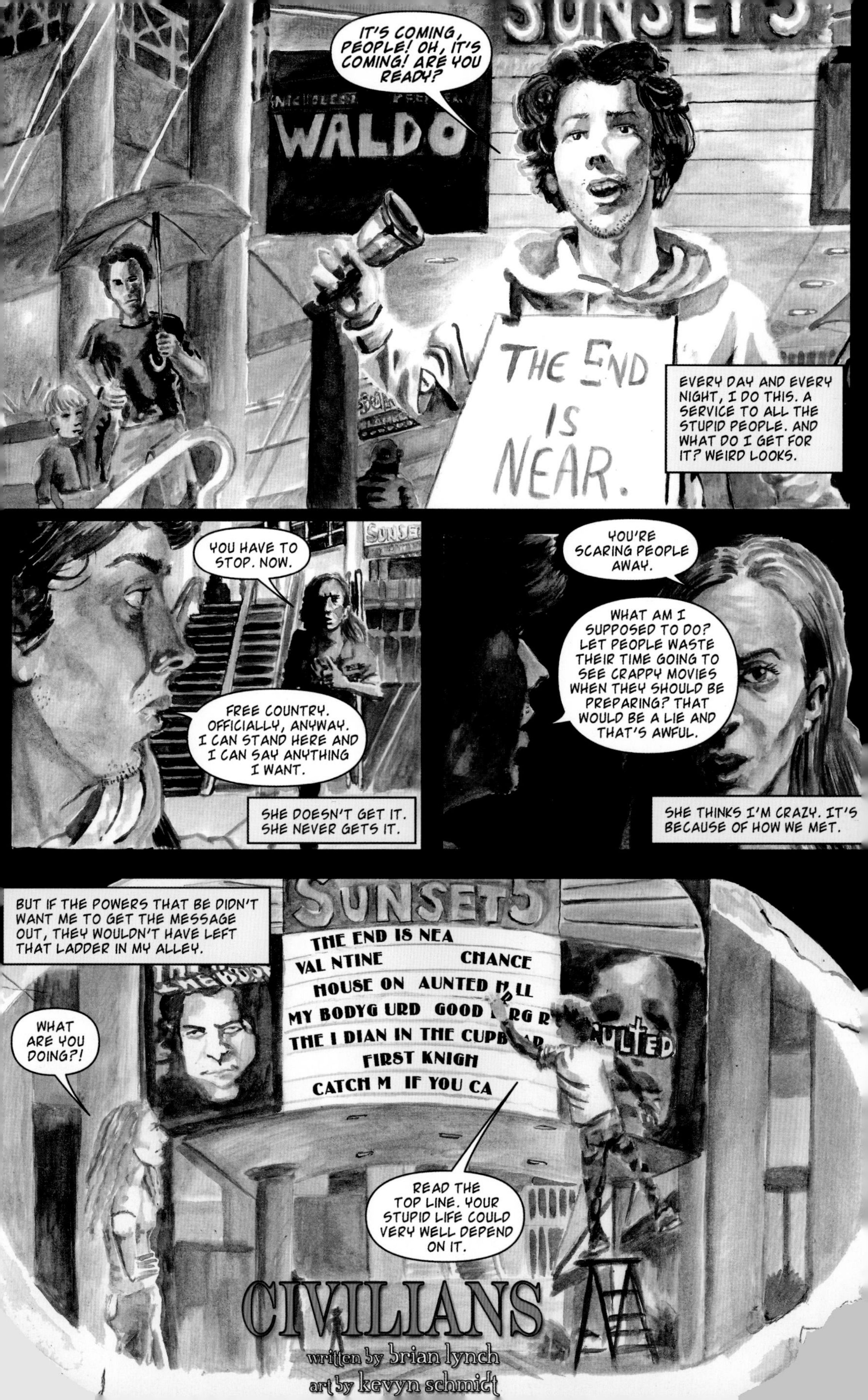
SUNSETS
WALDO
IT'S COMING, PEOPLE! OH, IT'S COMING! ARE YOU READY?
THE END IS NEAR.
EVERY DAY AND EVERY NIGHT, I DO THIS. A SERVICE TO ALL THE STUPID PEOPLE. AND WHAT DO I GET FOR IT? WEIRD LOOKS.
YOU HAVE TO STOP. NOW.
FREE COUNTRY. OFFICIALLY, ANYWAY. I CAN STAND HERE AND I CAN SAY ANYTHING I WANT.
SHE DOESN'T GET IT. SHE NEVER GETS IT.
YOU'RE SCARING PEOPLE AWAY.
WHAT AM I SUPPOSED TO DO? LET PEOPLE WASTE THEIR TIME GOING TO SEE CRAPPY MOVIES WHEN THEY SHOULD BE PREPARING? THAT WOULD BE A LIE AND THAT'S AWFUL.
SHE THINKS I'M CRAZY. IT'S BECAUSE OF HOW WE MET.
BUT IF THE POWERS THAT BE DIDN'T WANT ME TO GET THE MESSAGE OUT, THEY WOULDN'T HAVE LEFT THAT LADDER IN MY ALLEY.
SUNSETS
THE END IS NEA
VAL NTINE CHANCE
HOUSE ON AUNTED H LL
MY BODYG URD GOOD RG R
THE I DIAN IN THE CUPB AR
FIRST KNIGH
CATCH M IF YOU CA
WHAT ARE YOU DOING?!
READ THE TOP LINE. YOUR STUPID LIFE COULD VERY WELL DEPEND ON IT.
CIVILIANS
written by brian lynch
art by kevyn schmidt

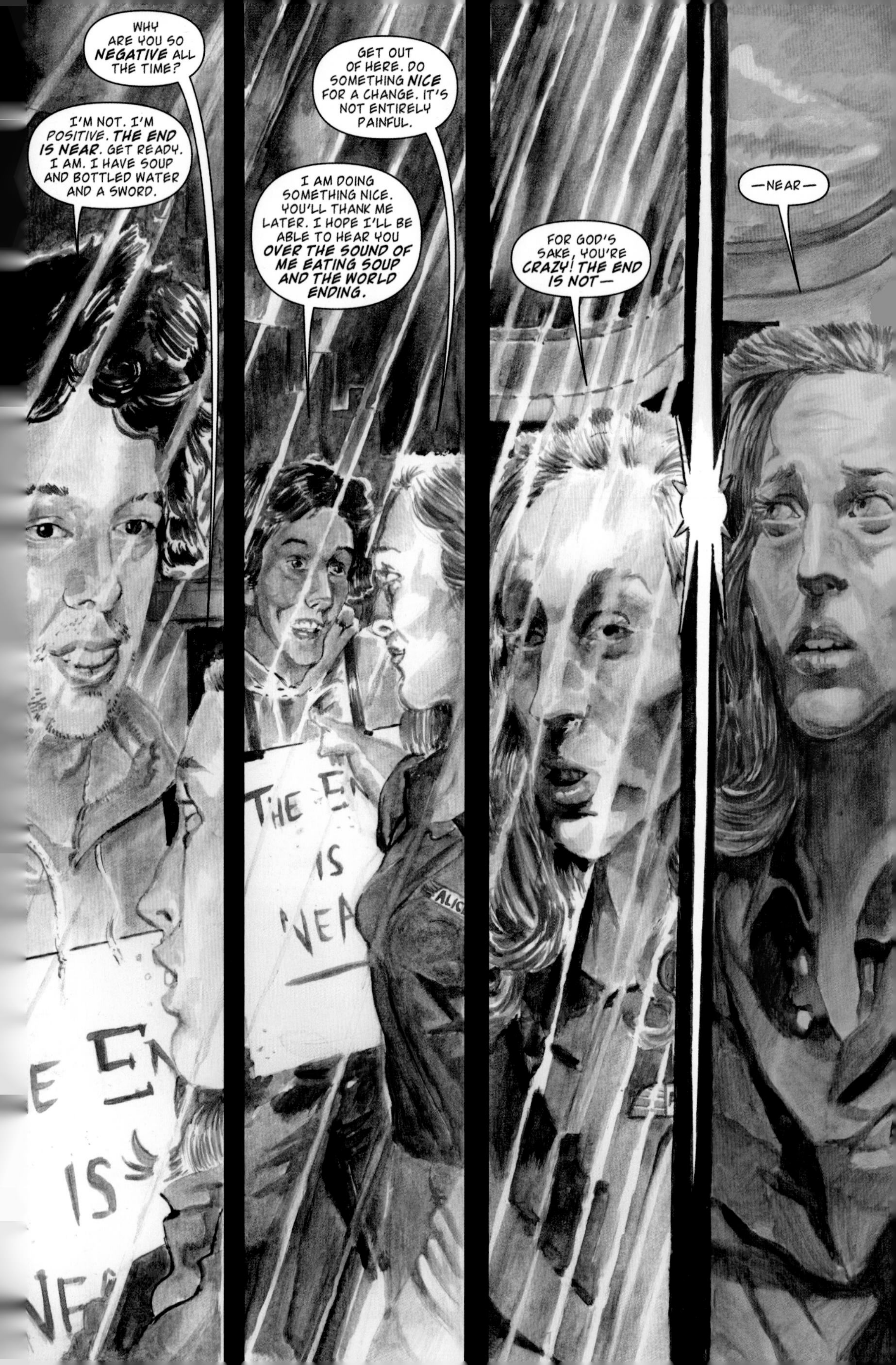
WHY ARE YOU SO NEGATIVE ALL THE TIME?
I'M NOT. I'M POSITIVE. THE END IS NEAR. GET READY. I AM. I HAVE SOUP AND BOTTLED WATER AND A SWORD.
THE END IS NEAR
GET OUT OF HERE. DO SOMETHING NICE FOR A CHANGE. IT'S NOT ENTIRELY PAINFUL.
I AM DOING SOMETHING NICE. YOU'LL THANK ME LATER. I HOPE I'LL BE ABLE TO HEAR YOU OVER THE SOUND OF ME EATING SOUP AND THE WORLD ENDING.
FOR GOD'S SAKE, YOU'RE CRAZY! THE END IS NOT—
—NEAR—

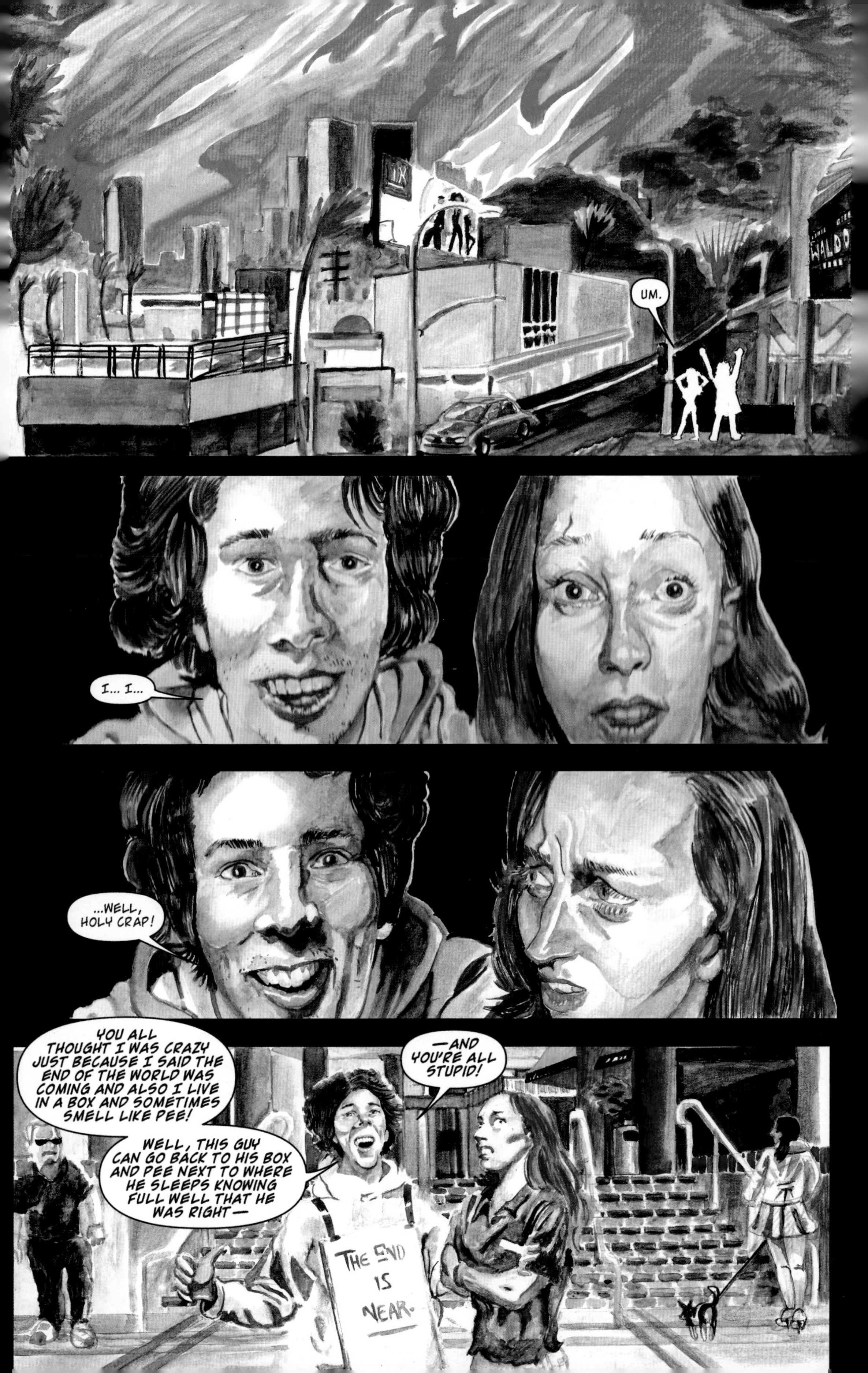
WALDO
UM.
I... I...
...WELL, HOLY CRAP!
YOU ALL THOUGHT I WAS CRAZY JUST BECAUSE I SAID THE END OF THE WORLD WAS COMING AND ALSO I LIVE IN A BOX AND SOMETIMES SMELL LIKE PEE!
WELL, THIS GUY CAN GO BACK TO HIS BOX AND PEE NEXT TO WHERE HE SLEEPS KNOWING FULL WELL THAT HE WAS RIGHT—
—AND YOU'RE ALL STUPID!
THE END IS NEAR.

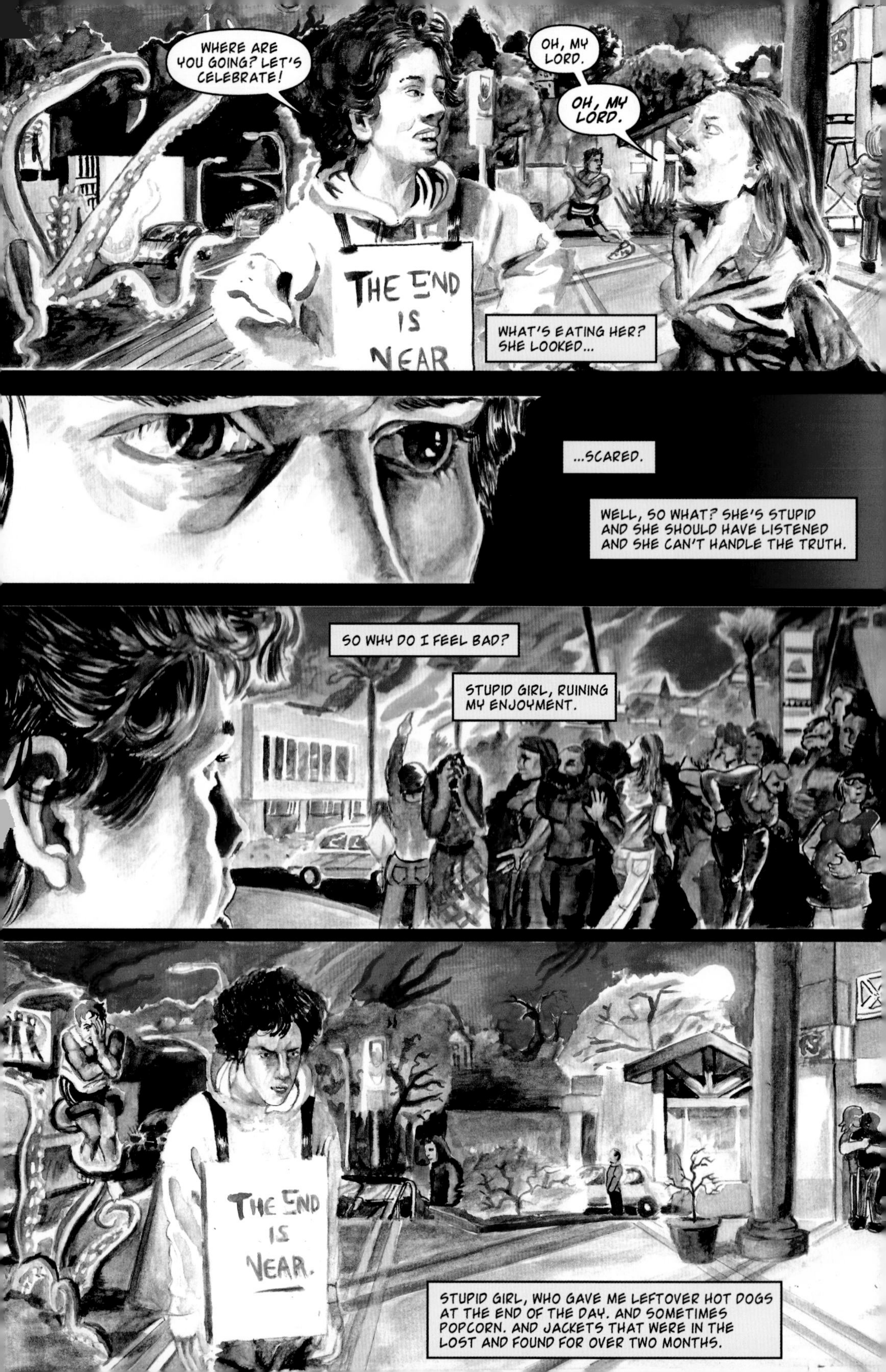

WHERE ARE YOU GOING? LET'S CELEBRATE!
OH, MY LORD.
OH, MY LORD.
THE END IS NEAR
WHAT'S EATING HER? SHE LOOKED...
...SCARED.
WELL, SO WHAT? SHE'S STUPID AND SHE SHOULD HAVE LISTENED AND SHE CAN'T HANDLE THE TRUTH.
SO WHY DO I FEEL BAD?
STUPID GIRL, RUINING MY ENJOYMENT.
THE END IS NEAR.
STUPID GIRL, WHO GAVE ME LEFTOVER HOT DOGS AT THE END OF THE DAY. AND SOMETIMES POPCORN. AND JACKETS THAT WERE IN THE LOST AND FOUND FOR OVER TWO MONTHS.

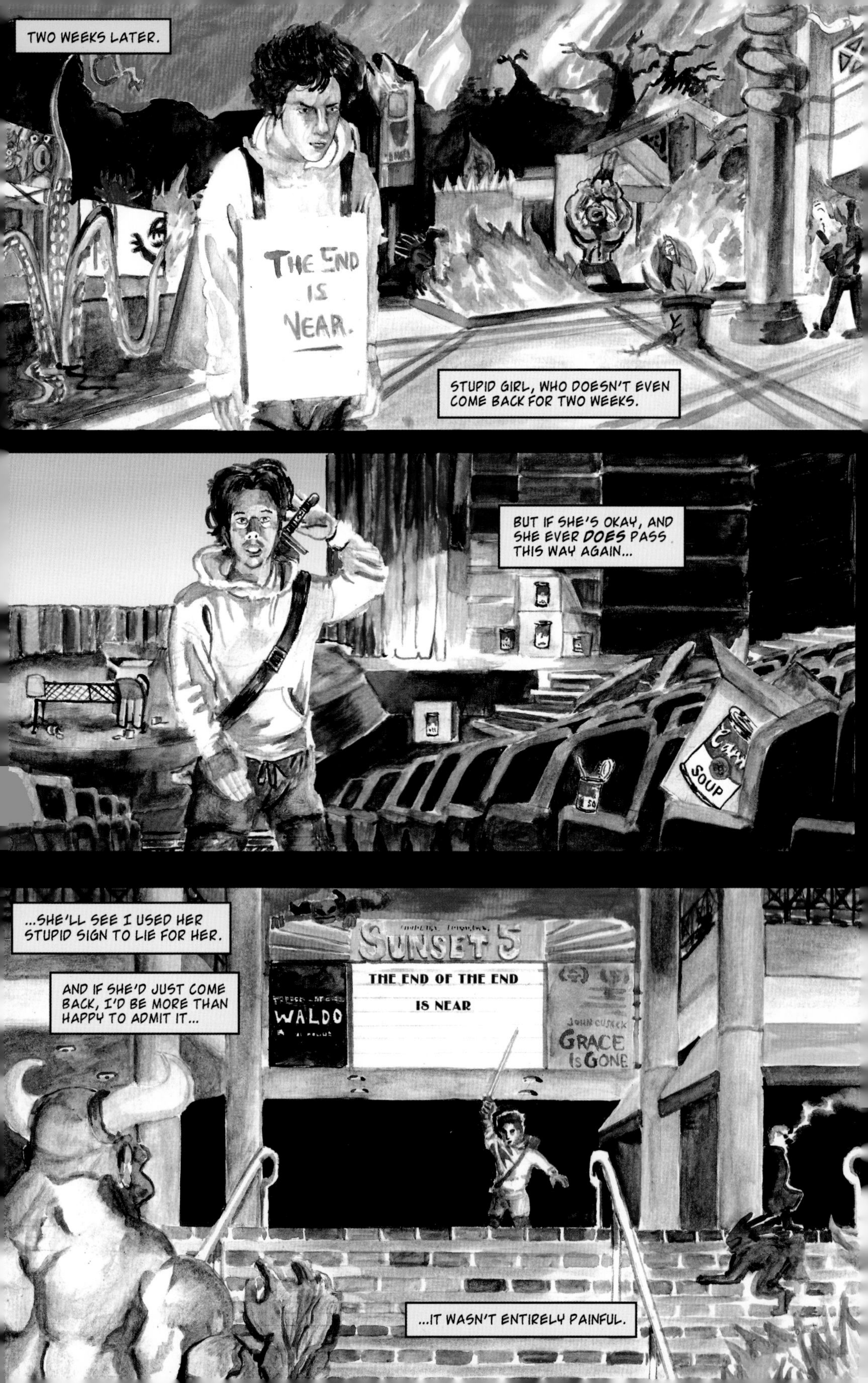
TWO WEEKS LATER.
THE END IS NEAR.
STUPID GIRL, WHO DOESN'T EVEN COME BACK FOR TWO WEEKS.
BUT IF SHE'S OKAY, AND SHE EVER **DOES** PASS THIS WAY AGAIN...
SOUP
...SHE'LL SEE I USED HER STUPID SIGN TO LIE FOR HER.
SUNSET 5
THE END OF THE END
IS NEAR
WALDO
GRACE IS GONE
AND IF SHE'D JUST COME BACK, I'D BE MORE THAN HAPPY TO ADMIT IT...
...IT WASN'T ENTIRELY PAINFUL.

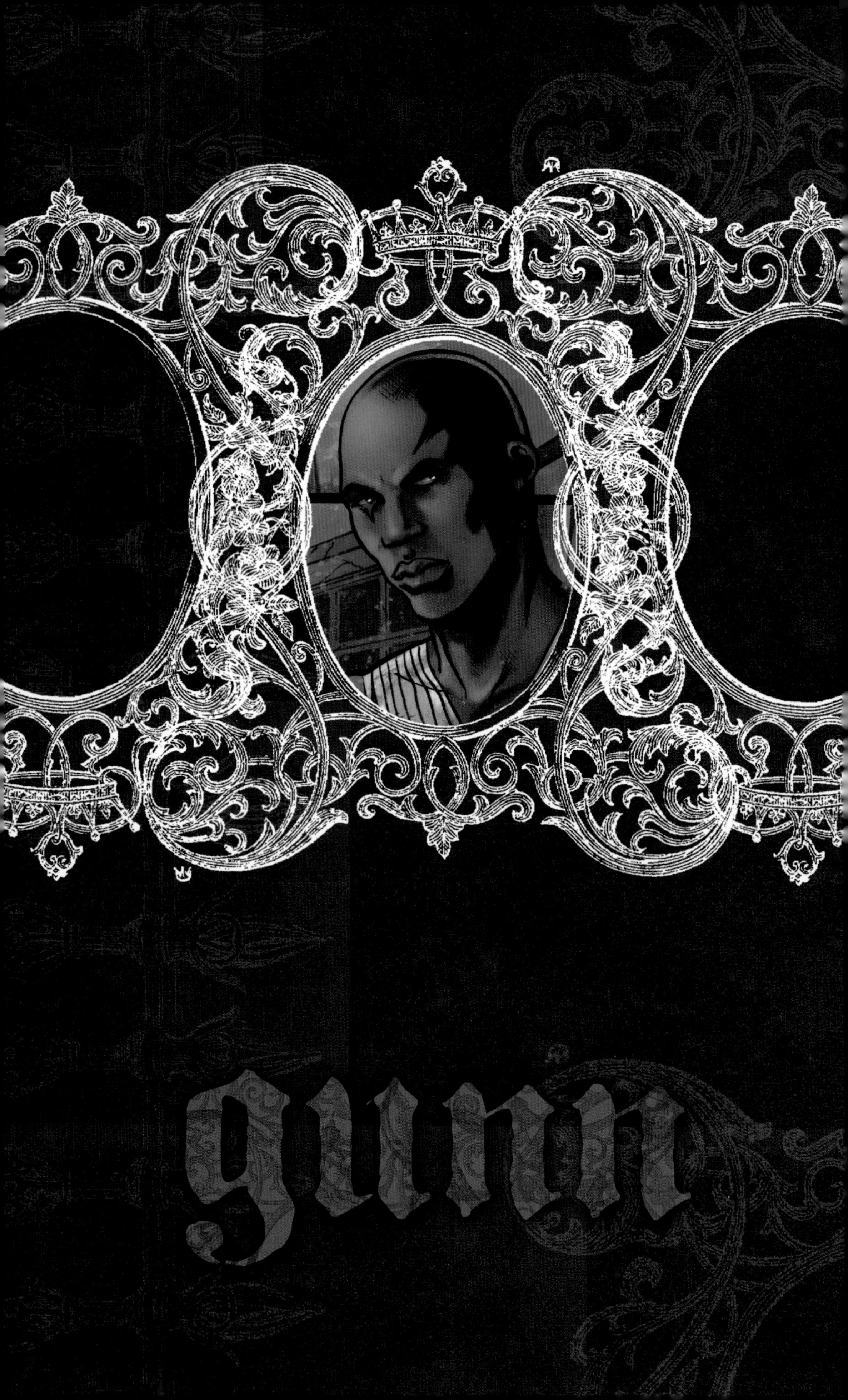
gunn

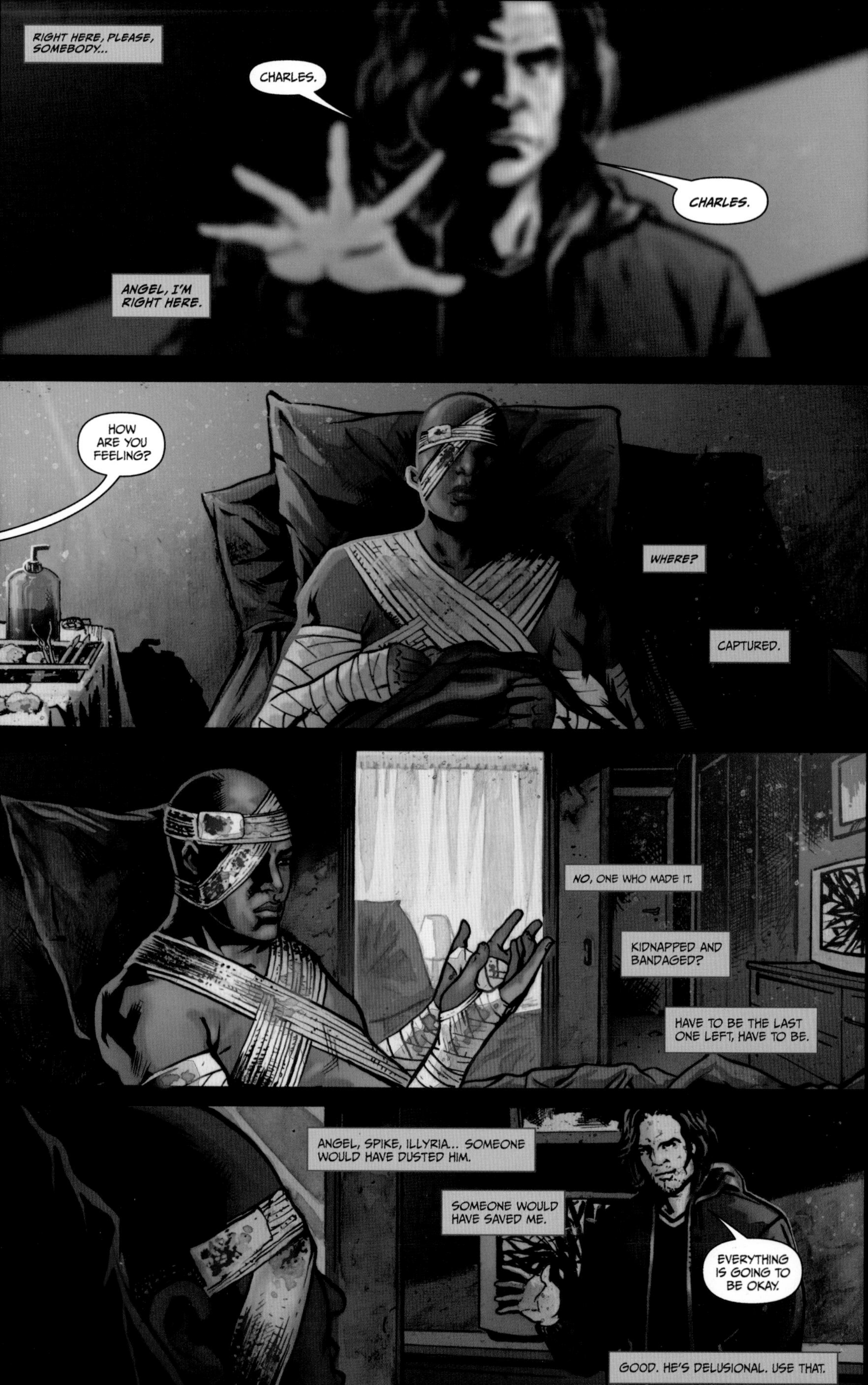
RIGHT HERE, PLEASE, SOMEBODY...
CHARLES.
CHARLES.
ANGEL, I'M RIGHT HERE.
HOW ARE YOU FEELING?
WHERE?
CAPTURED.
NO, ONE WHO MADE IT.
KIDNAPPED AND BANDAGED?
HAVE TO BE THE LAST ONE LEFT, HAVE TO BE.
ANGEL, SPIKE, ILLYRIA... SOMEONE WOULD HAVE DUSTED HIM.
SOMEONE WOULD HAVE SAVED ME.
EVERYTHING IS GOING TO BE OKAY.
GOOD. HE'S DELUSIONAL. USE THAT.

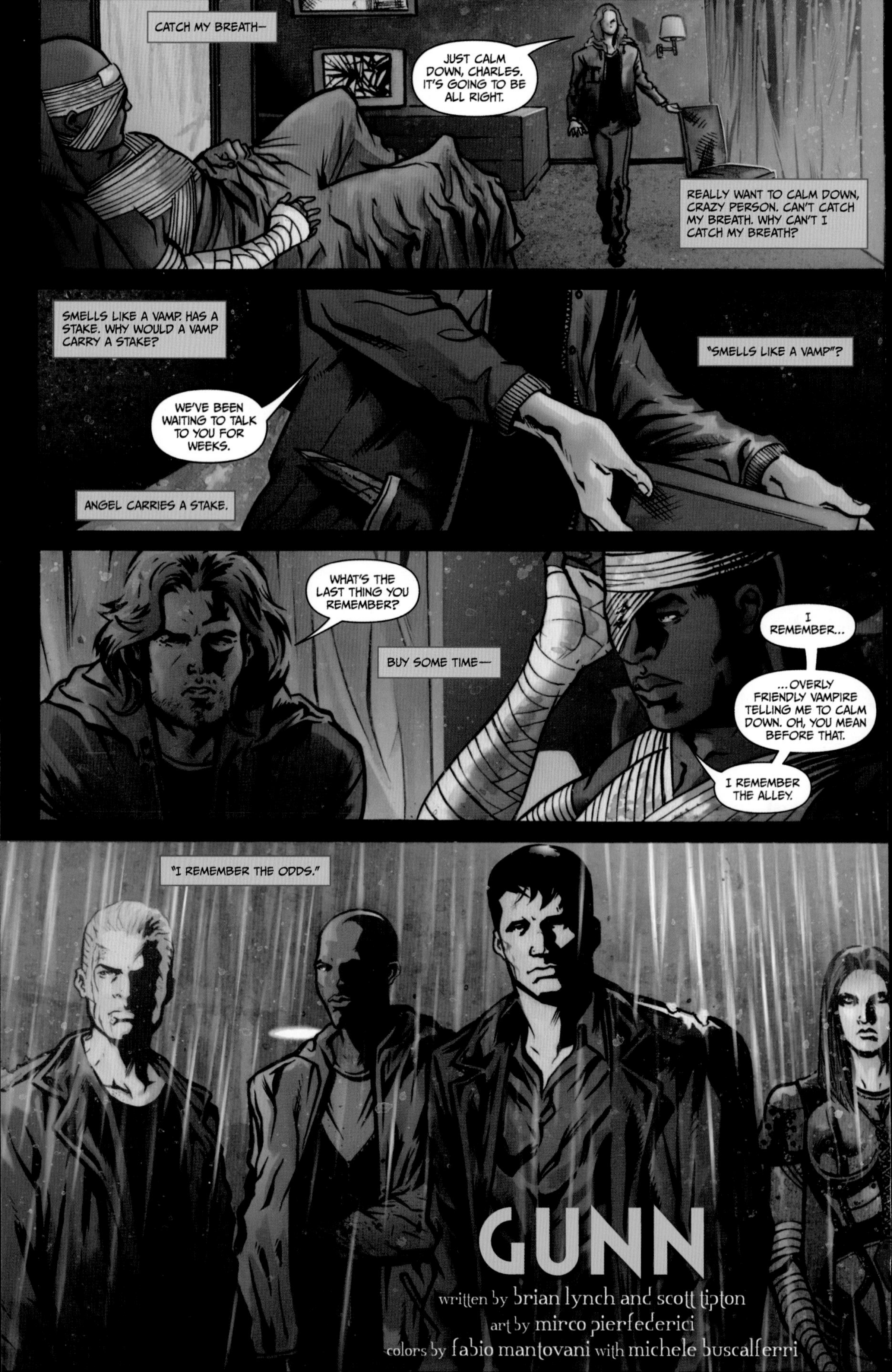
CATCH MY BREATH—
JUST CALM DOWN, CHARLES. IT'S GOING TO BE ALL RIGHT.
REALLY WANT TO CALM DOWN, CRAZY PERSON. CAN'T CATCH MY BREATH. WHY CAN'T I CATCH MY BREATH?
SMELLS LIKE A VAMP. HAS A STAKE. WHY WOULD A VAMP CARRY A STAKE?
"SMELLS LIKE A VAMP"?
WE'VE BEEN WAITING TO TALK TO YOU FOR WEEKS.
ANGEL CARRIES A STAKE.
WHAT'S THE LAST THING YOU REMEMBER?
BUY SOME TIME—
I REMEMBER...
...OVERLY FRIENDLY VAMPIRE TELLING ME TO CALM DOWN. OH, YOU MEAN BEFORE THAT.
I REMEMBER THE ALLEY.
"I REMEMBER THE ODDS."
GUNN
written by brian lynch and scott tipton
art by mirco pierfederici
colors by fabio mantovani with michele buscalferri

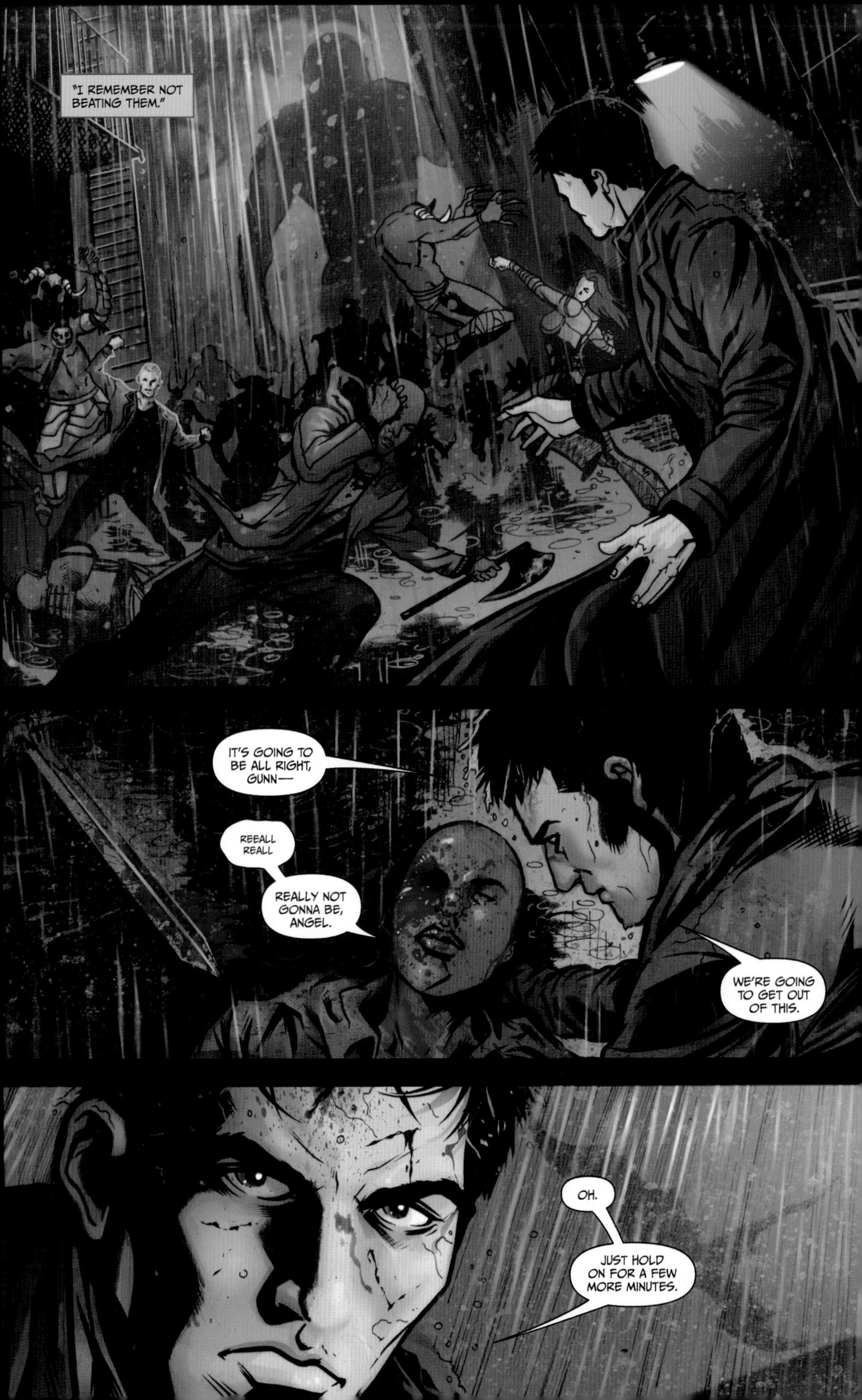
"I REMEMBER NOT BEATING THEM."
IT'S GOING TO BE ALL RIGHT, GUNN--
REEALL REALL
REALLY NOT GONNA BE, ANGEL.
WE'RE GOING TO GET OUT OF THIS.
OH.
JUST HOLD ON FOR A FEW MORE MINUTES.

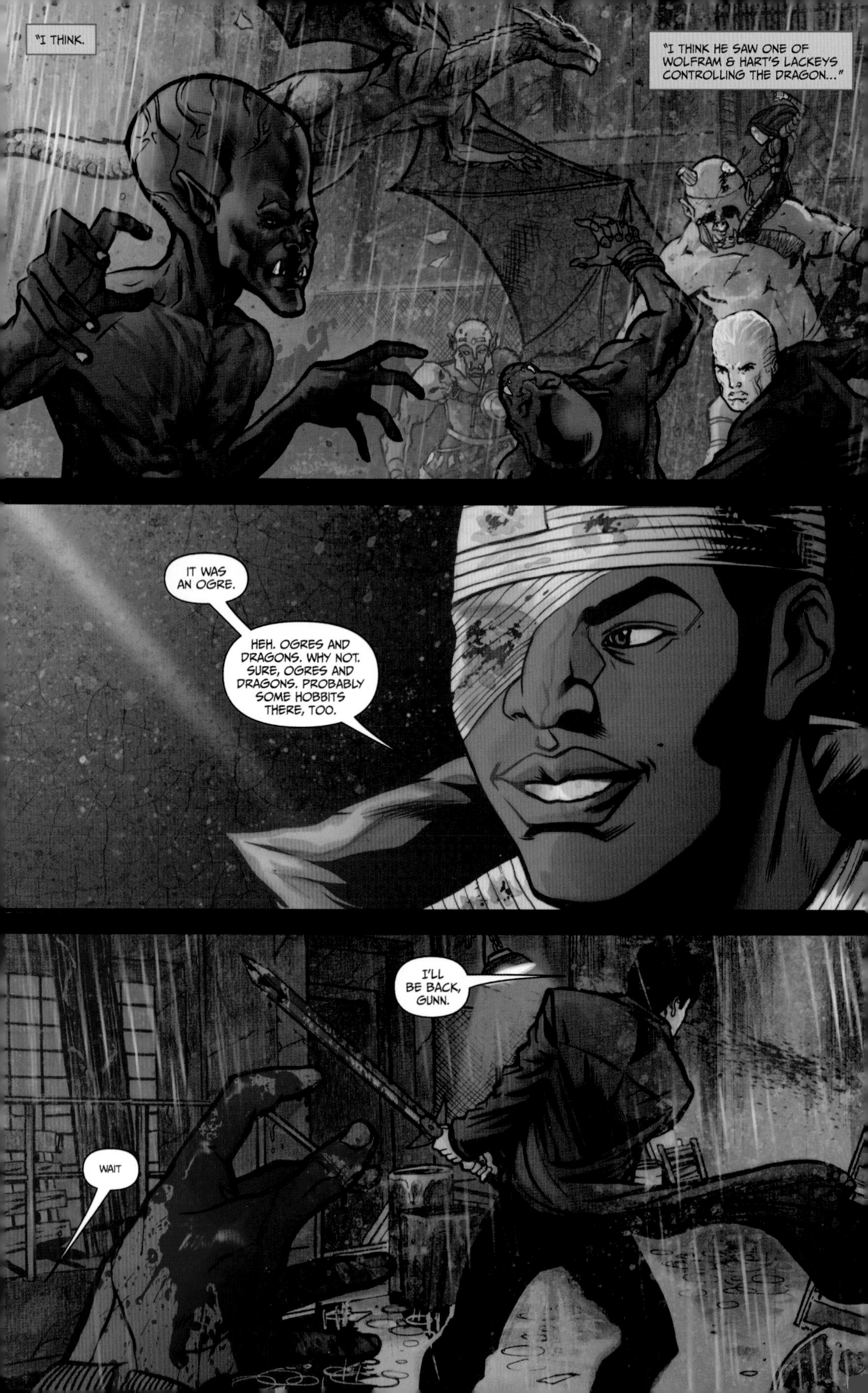
"I THINK.
"I THINK HE SAW ONE OF WOLFRAM & HART'S LACKEYS CONTROLLING THE DRAGON..."
IT WAS AN OGRE.
HEH. OGRES AND DRAGONS. WHY NOT. SURE, OGRES AND DRAGONS. PROBABLY SOME HOBBITS THERE, TOO.
I'LL BE BACK, GUNN.
WAIT

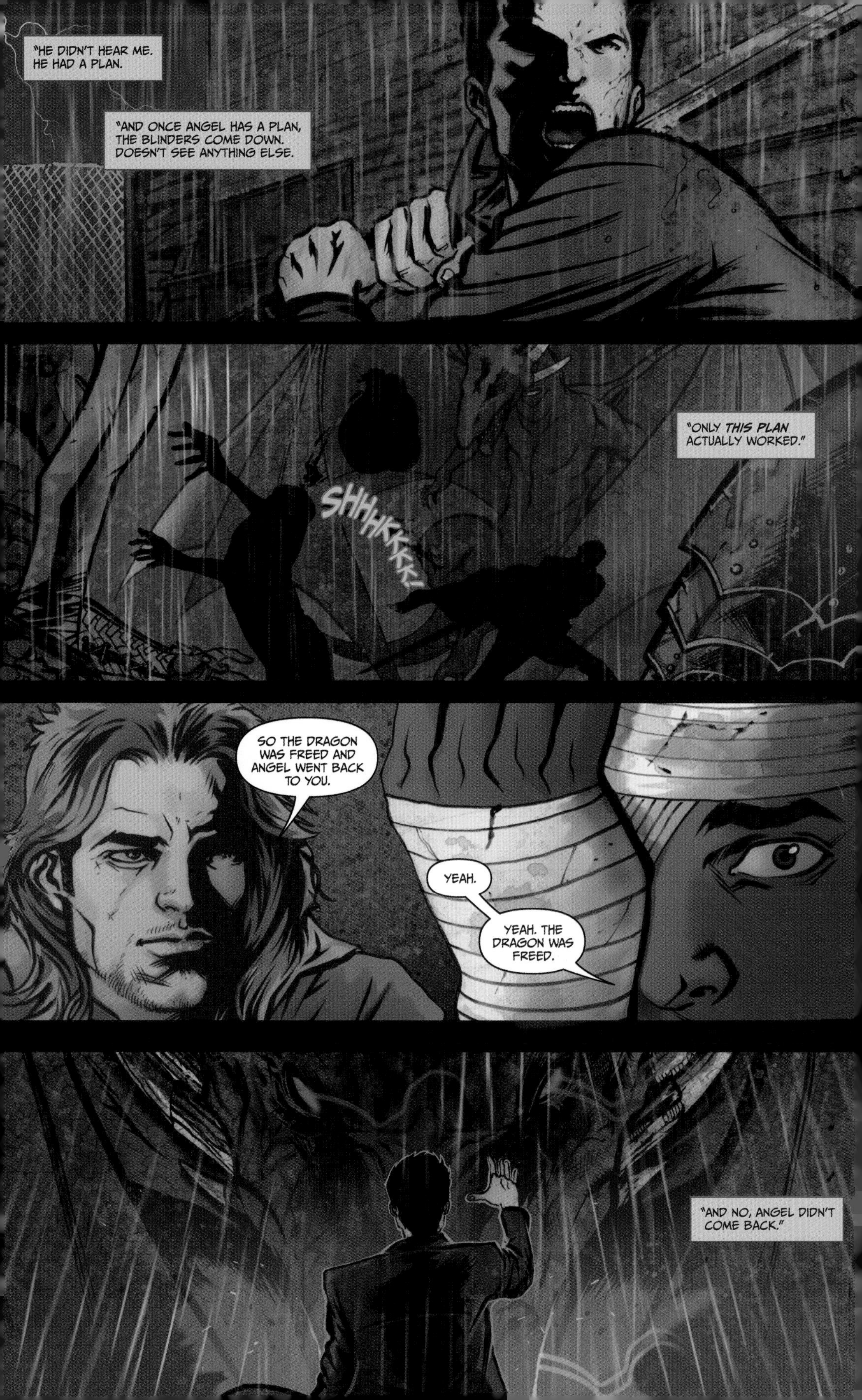
"HE DIDN'T HEAR ME. HE HAD A PLAN.
"AND ONCE ANGEL HAS A PLAN, THE BLINDERS COME DOWN. DOESN'T SEE ANYTHING ELSE.
"ONLY *THIS PLAN* ACTUALLY WORKED."
SHHHKKKK!
SO THE DRAGON WAS FREED AND ANGEL WENT BACK TO YOU.
YEAH.
YEAH. THE DRAGON WAS FREED.
"AND NO, ANGEL DIDN'T COME BACK."

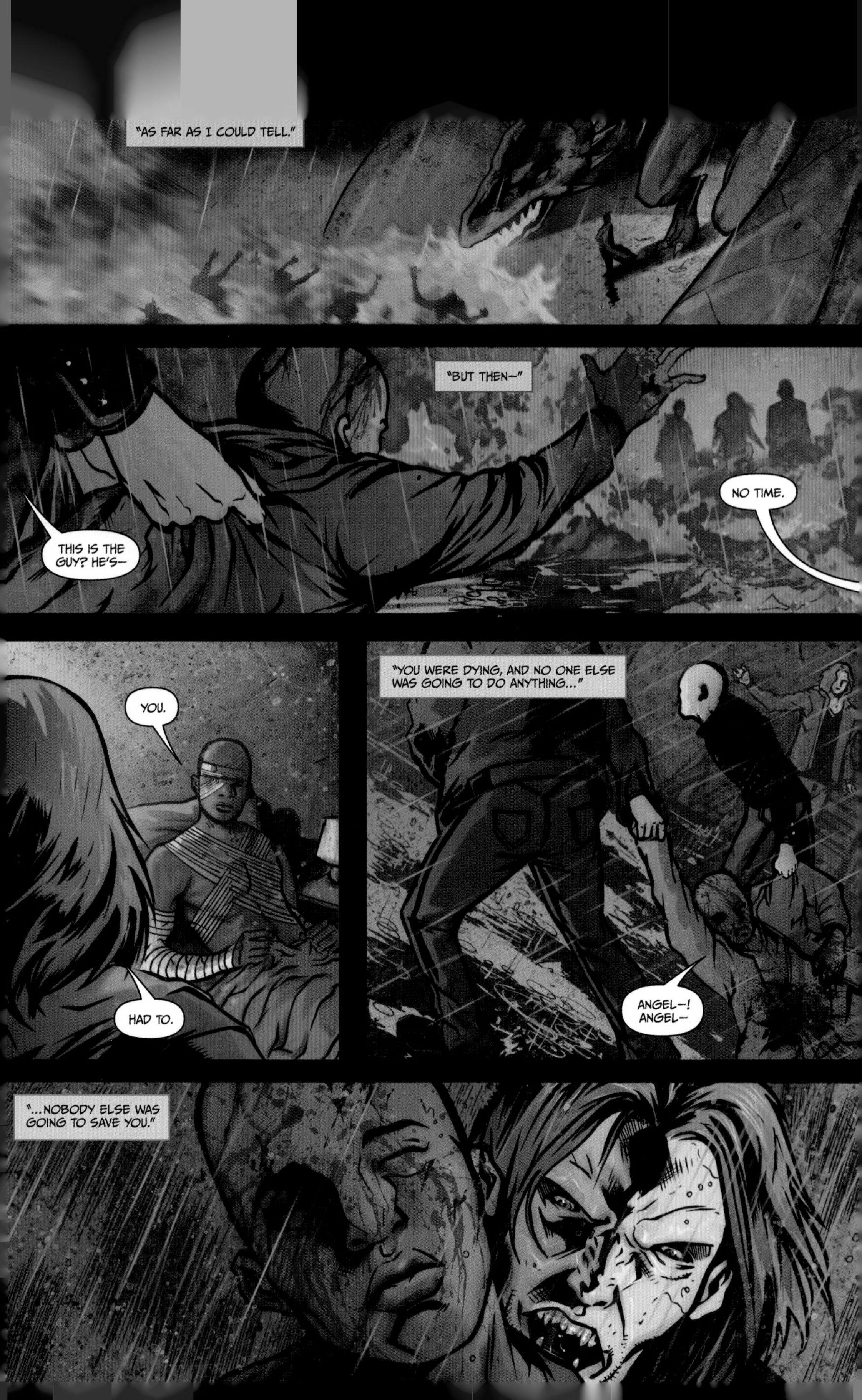
"AS FAR AS I COULD TELL."
"BUT THEN--"
THIS IS THE GUY? HE'S--
NO TIME.
YOU.
HAD TO.
"YOU WERE DYING, AND NO ONE ELSE WAS GOING TO DO ANYTHING..."
ANGEL--! ANGEL--
"...NOBODY ELSE WAS GOING TO SAVE YOU."

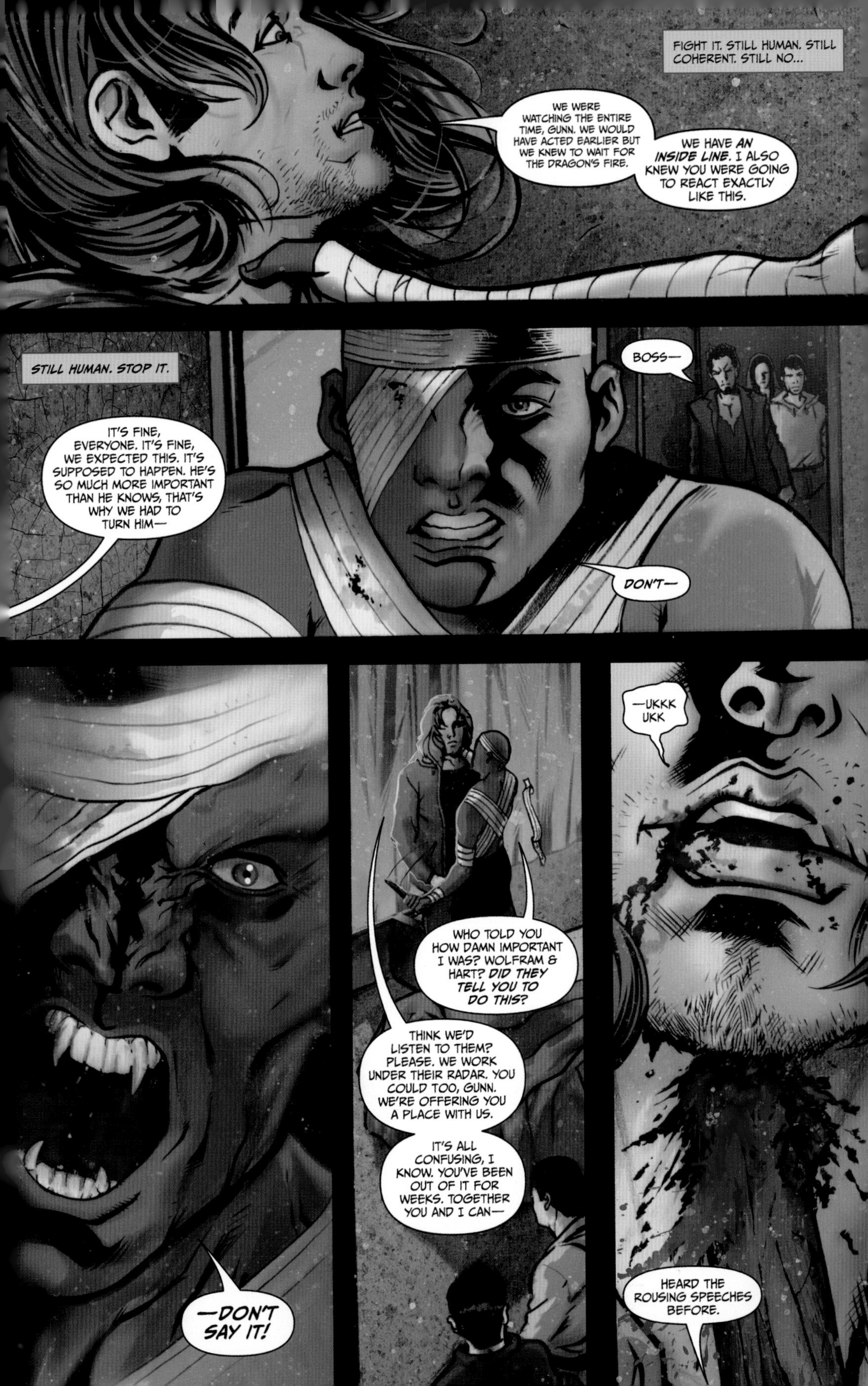
FIGHT IT. STILL HUMAN. STILL COHERENT. STILL NO...
WE WERE WATCHING THE ENTIRE TIME, GUNN. WE WOULD HAVE ACTED EARLIER BUT WE KNEW TO WAIT FOR THE DRAGON'S FIRE.
WE HAVE *AN INSIDE LINE*. I ALSO KNEW YOU WERE GOING TO REACT EXACTLY LIKE THIS.
STILL HUMAN. STOP IT.
BOSS—
IT'S FINE, EVERYONE. IT'S FINE, WE EXPECTED THIS. IT'S SUPPOSED TO HAPPEN. HE'S SO MUCH MORE IMPORTANT THAN HE KNOWS, THAT'S WHY WE HAD TO TURN HIM—
DON'T—
—DON'T SAY IT!
WHO TOLD YOU HOW DAMN IMPORTANT I WAS? WOLFRAM & HART? *DID THEY TELL YOU TO DO THIS?*
THINK WE'D LISTEN TO THEM? PLEASE. WE WORK UNDER THEIR RADAR. YOU COULD TOO, GUNN. WE'RE OFFERING YOU A PLACE WITH US.
IT'S ALL CONFUSING, I KNOW. YOU'VE BEEN OUT OF IT FOR WEEKS. TOGETHER YOU AND I CAN—
—UKKK UKK
HEARD THE ROUSING SPEECHES BEFORE.

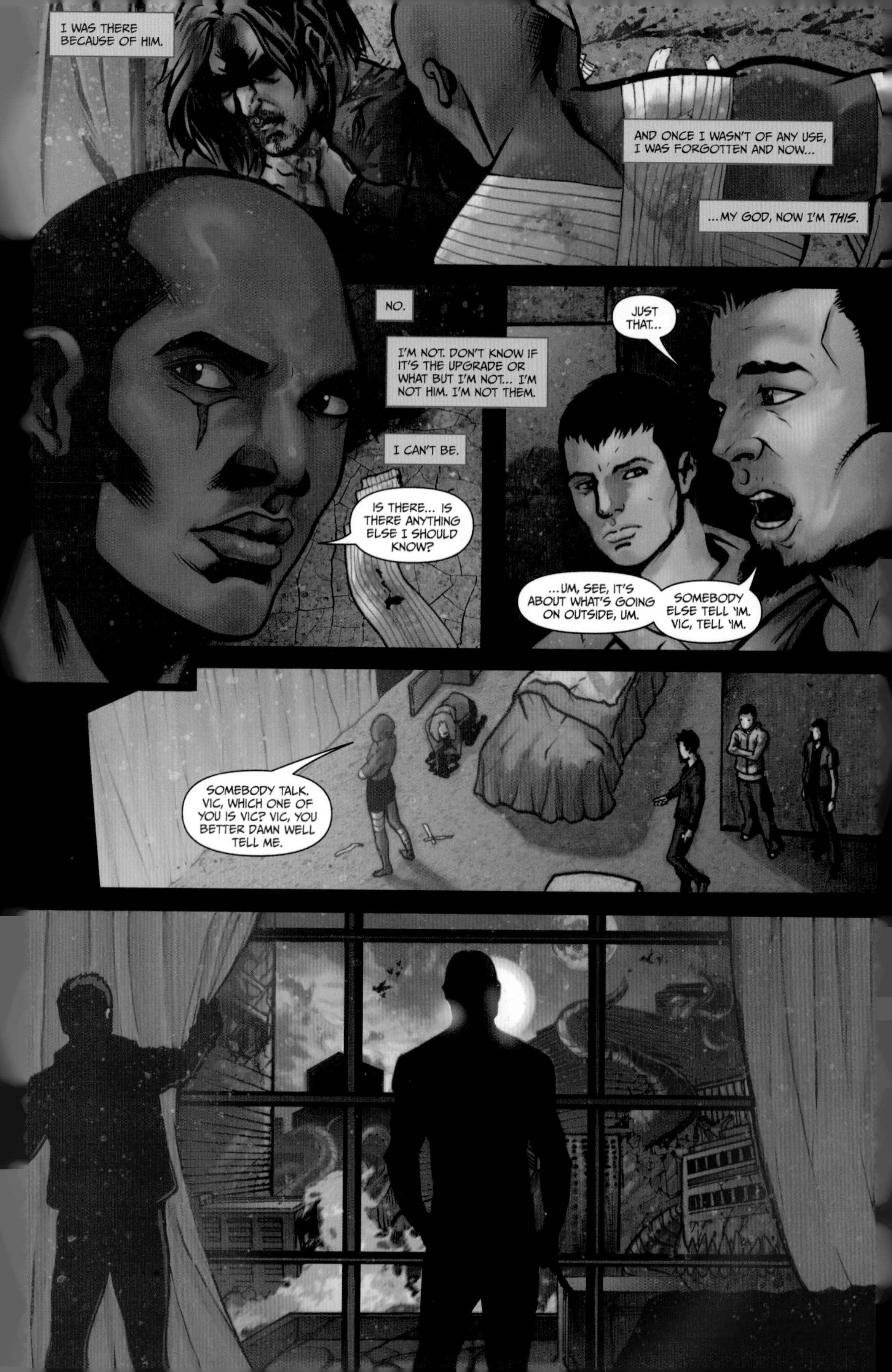
I WAS THERE BECAUSE OF HIM.
AND ONCE I WASN'T OF ANY USE, I WAS FORGOTTEN AND NOW...
...MY GOD, NOW I'M *THIS*.
NO.
I'M NOT. DON'T KNOW IF IT'S THE UPGRADE OR WHAT BUT I'M NOT... I'M NOT HIM. I'M NOT THEM.
I CAN'T BE.
IS THERE... IS THERE ANYTHING ELSE I SHOULD KNOW?
JUST THAT...
...UM, SEE, IT'S ABOUT WHAT'S GOING ON OUTSIDE, UM.
SOMEBODY ELSE TELL 'IM. VIC, TELL 'IM.
SOMEBODY TALK. VIC, WHICH ONE OF YOU IS VIC? VIC, YOU BETTER DAMN WELL TELL ME.

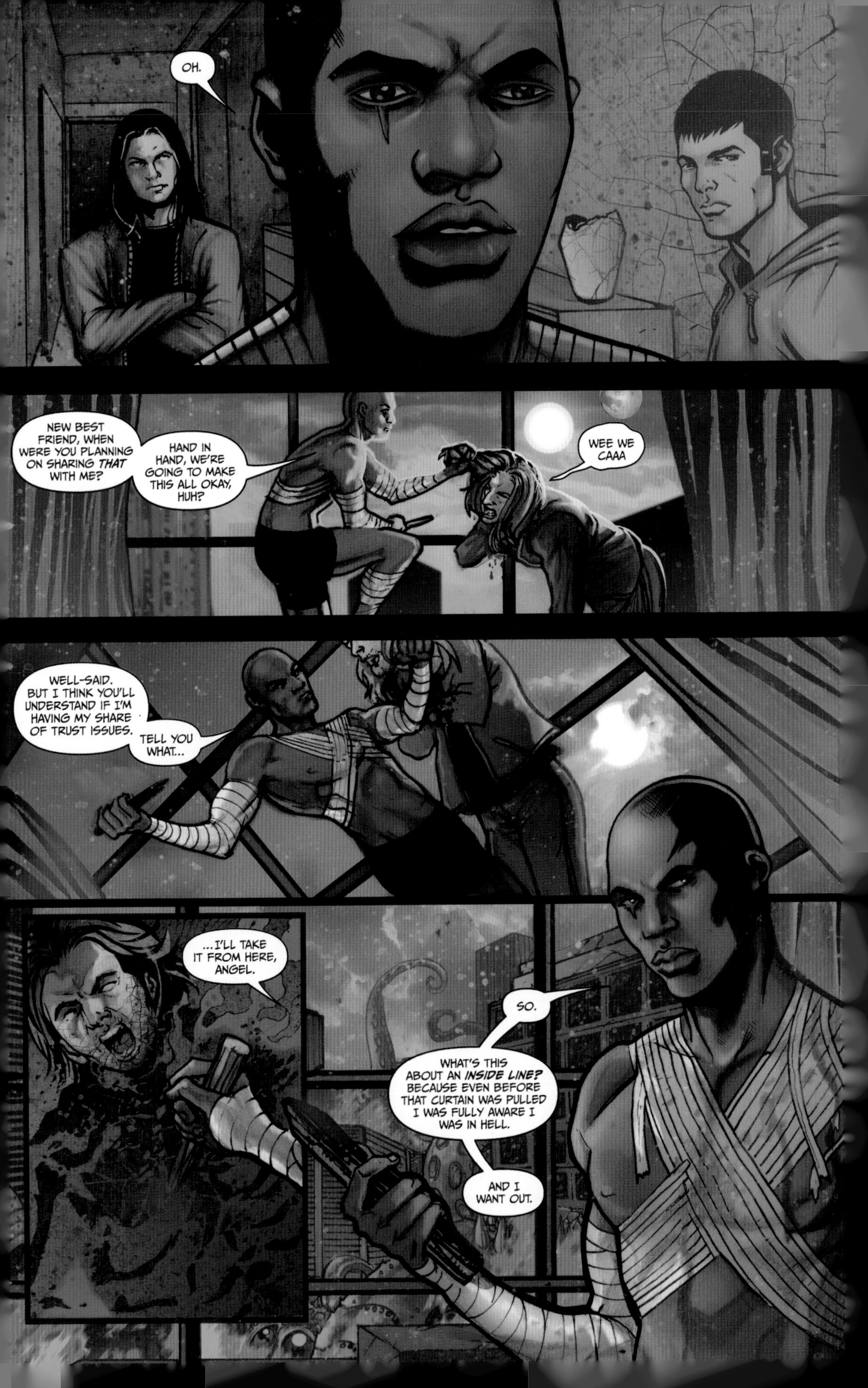
OH.
NEW BEST FRIEND, WHEN WERE YOU PLANNING ON SHARING *THAT* WITH ME?
HAND IN HAND, WE'RE GOING TO MAKE THIS ALL OKAY, HUH?
WEE WE CAAA
WELL-SAID. BUT I THINK YOU'LL UNDERSTAND IF I'M HAVING MY SHARE OF TRUST ISSUES.
TELL YOU WHAT...
...I'LL TAKE IT FROM HERE, ANGEL.
SO.
WHAT'S THIS ABOUT AN *INSIDE LINE?* BECAUSE EVEN BEFORE THAT CURTAIN WAS PULLED I WAS FULLY AWARE I WAS IN HELL.
AND I WANT OUT.

art gallery

Opposite Page: Art by David Messina

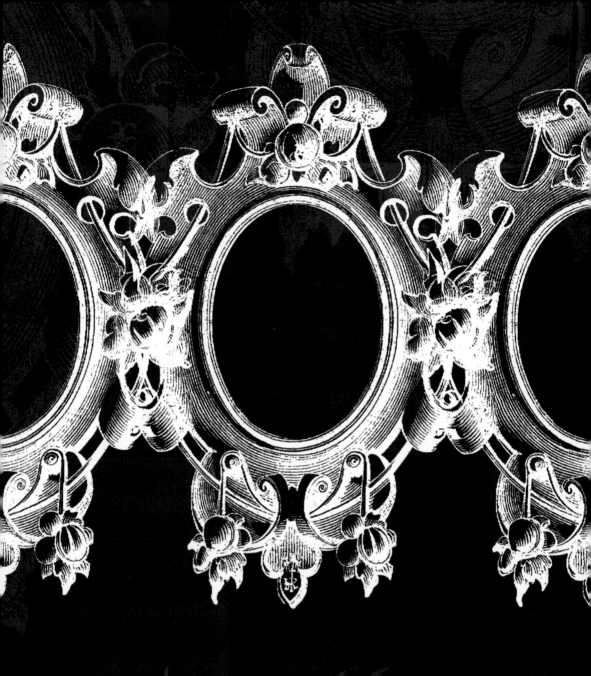

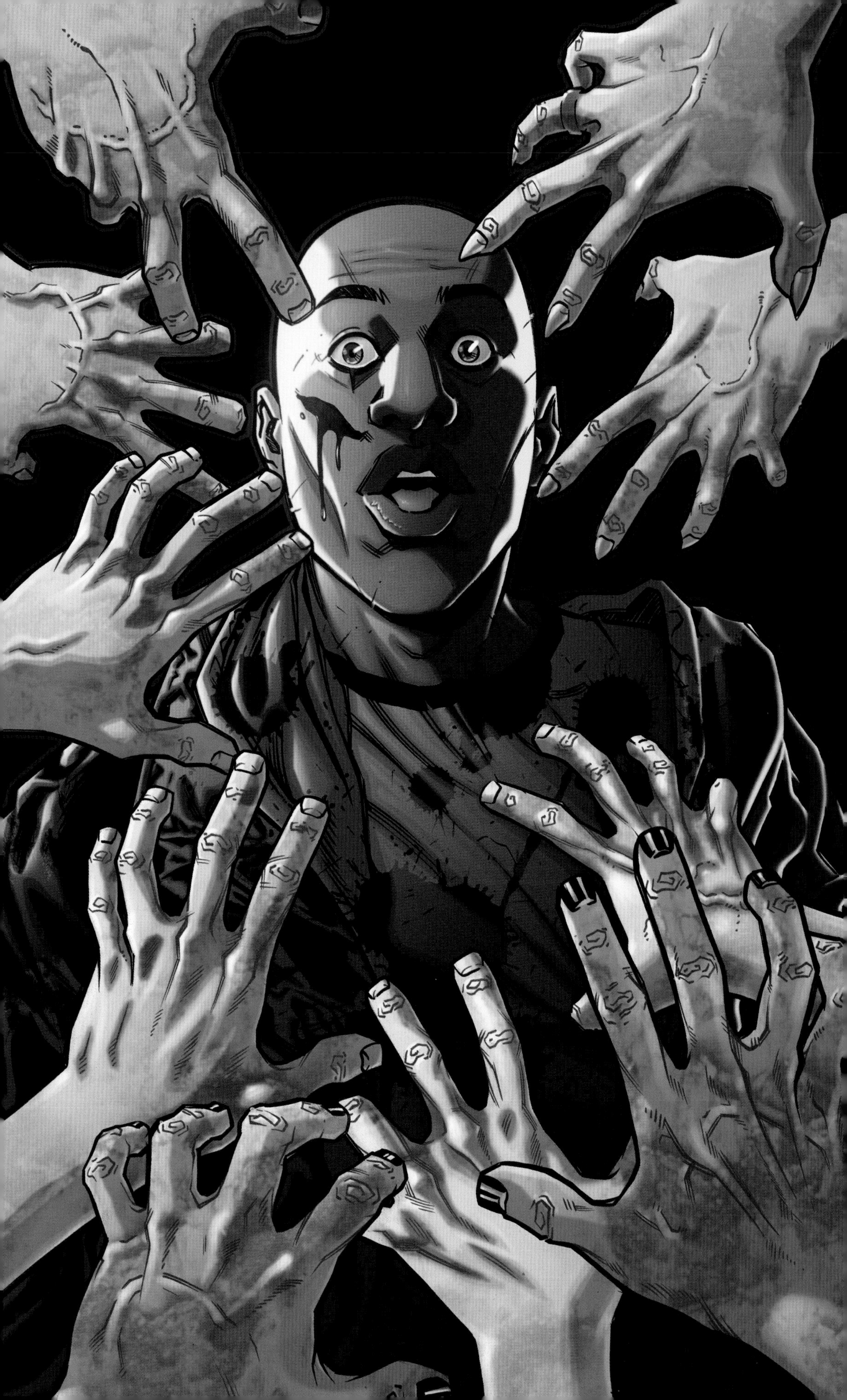

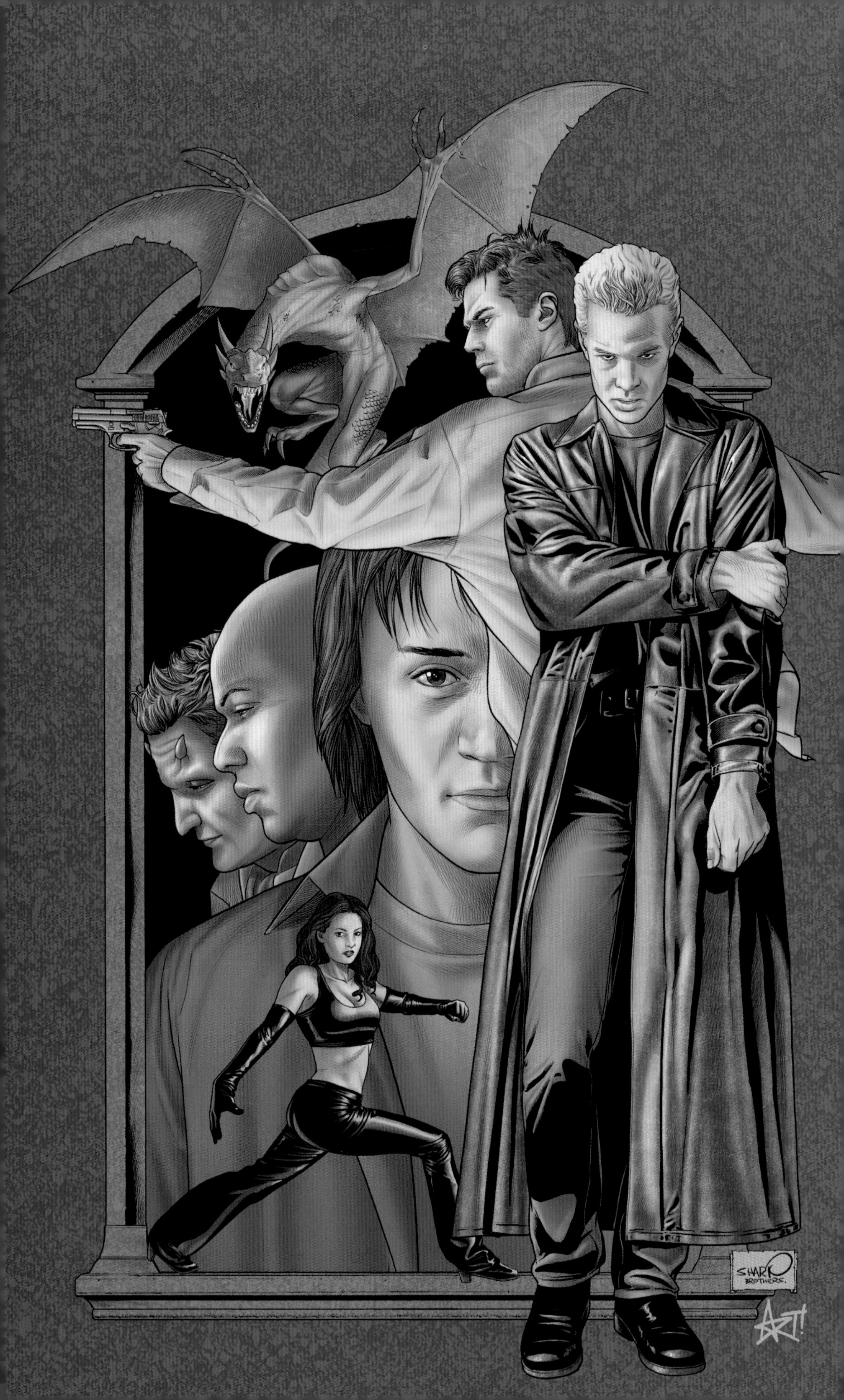
SHARP BROTHERS.

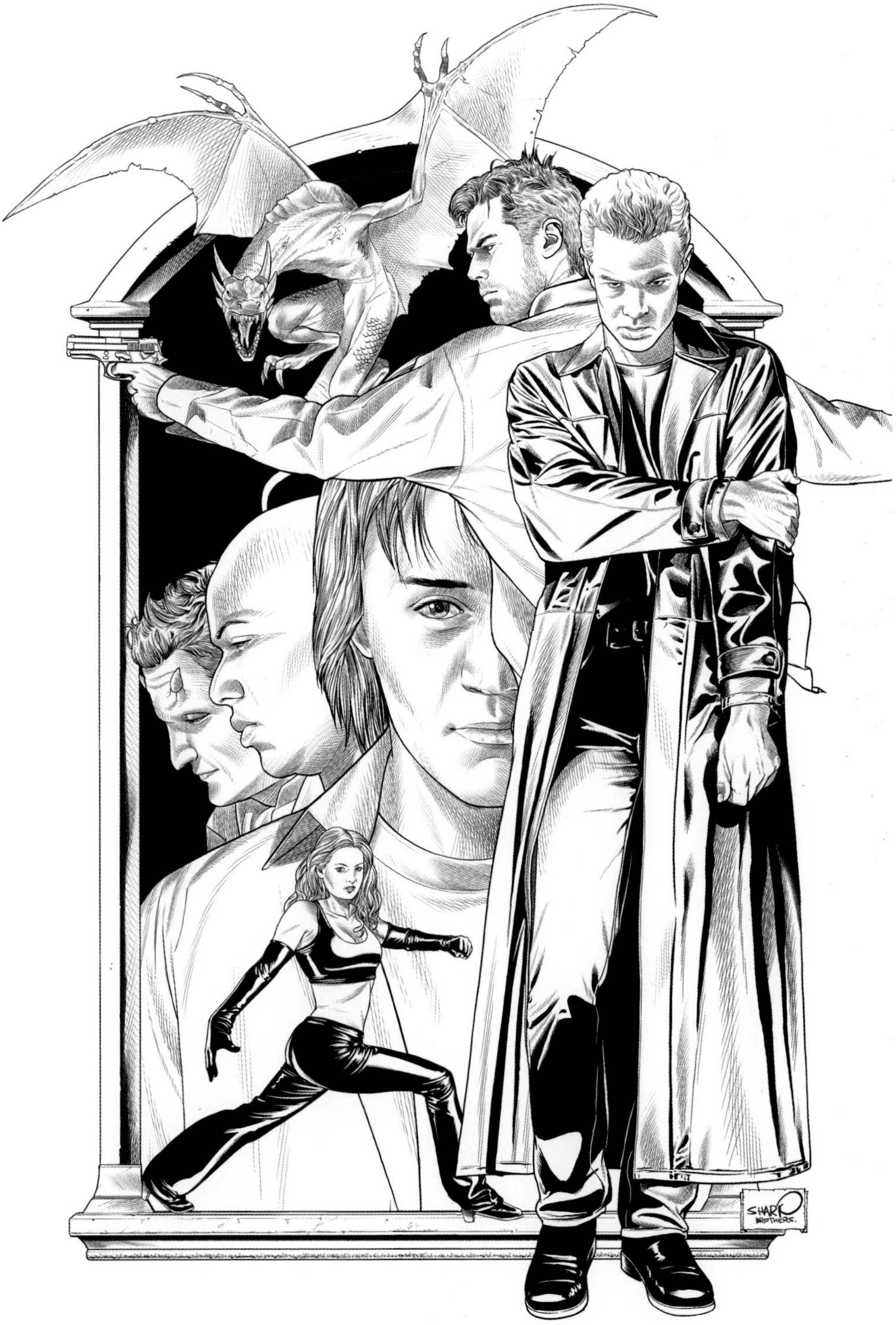

Opposite Page: Art by Joe & Rob Sharp
Colors by Art Lyon

This Page: Art by Joe & Rob Sharp

Next Page: Rebecca A. Wrigley

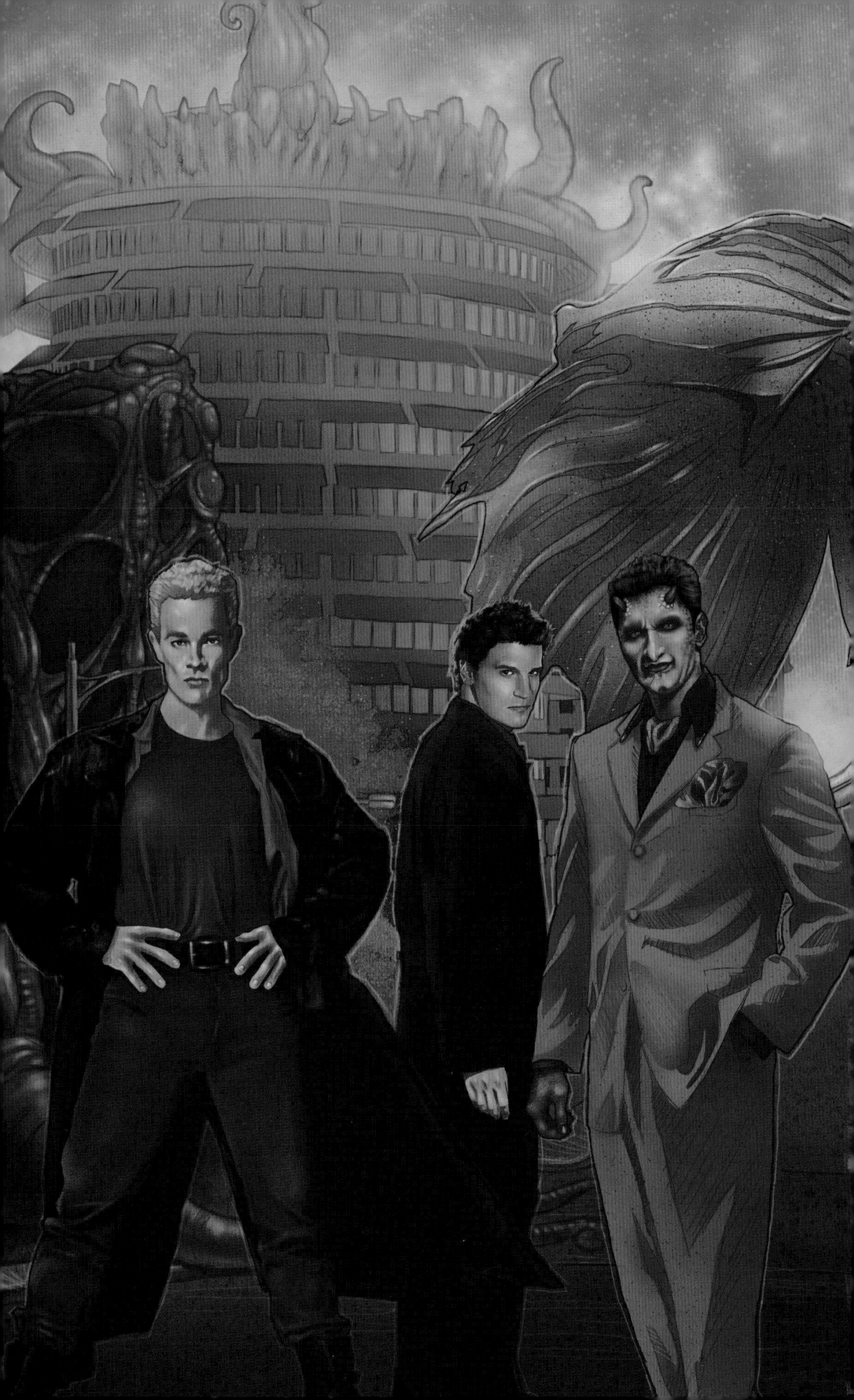

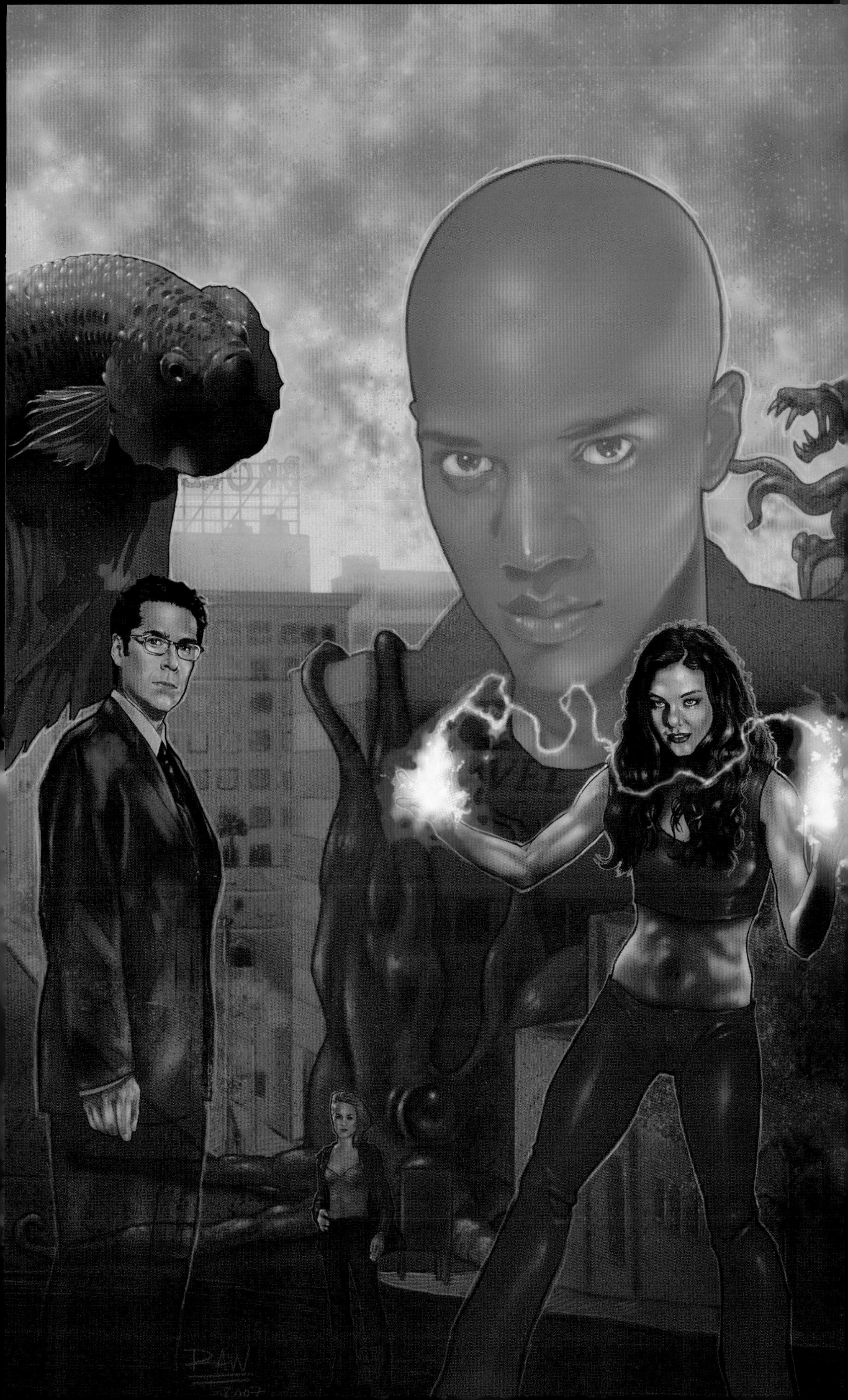

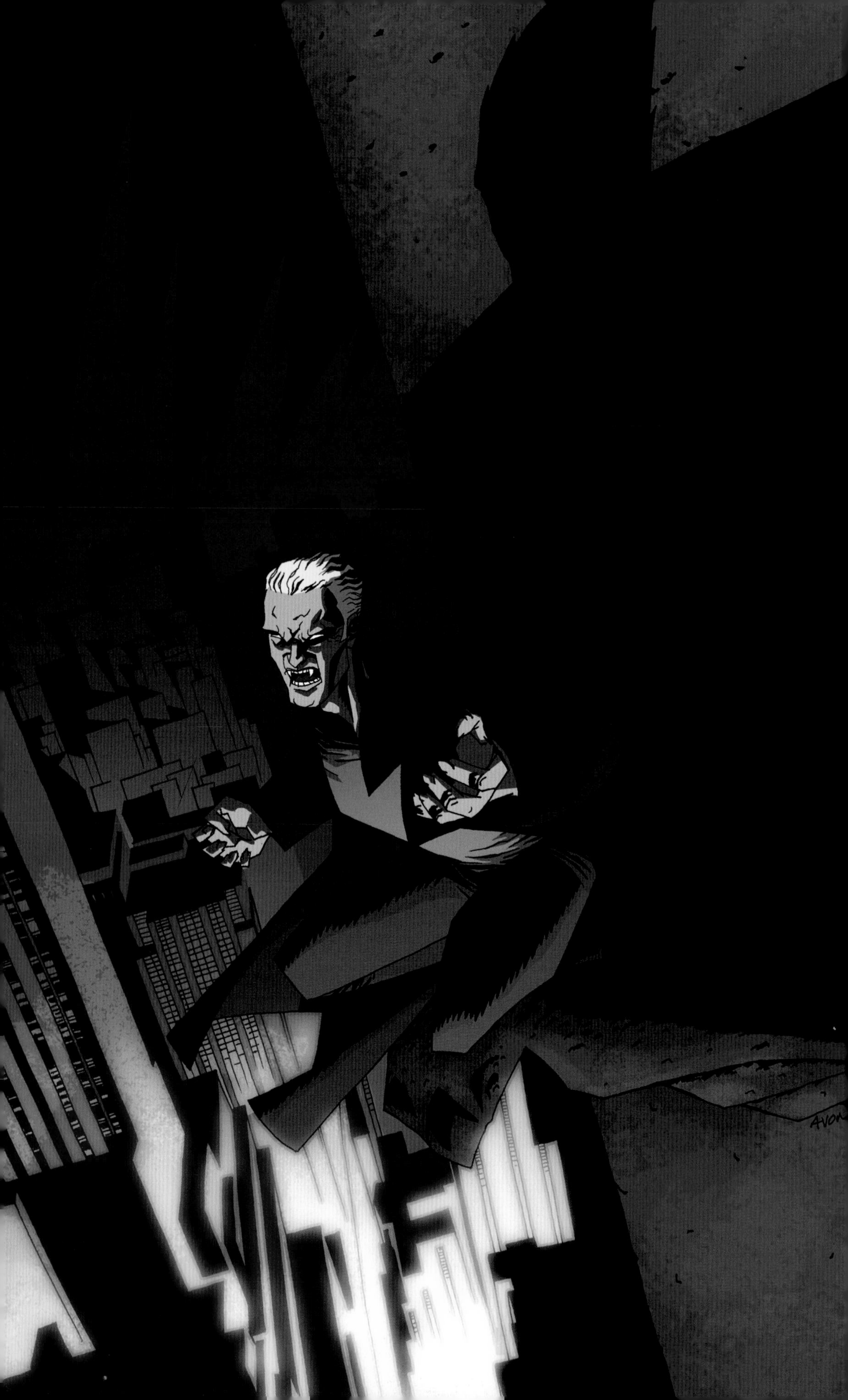
AVON

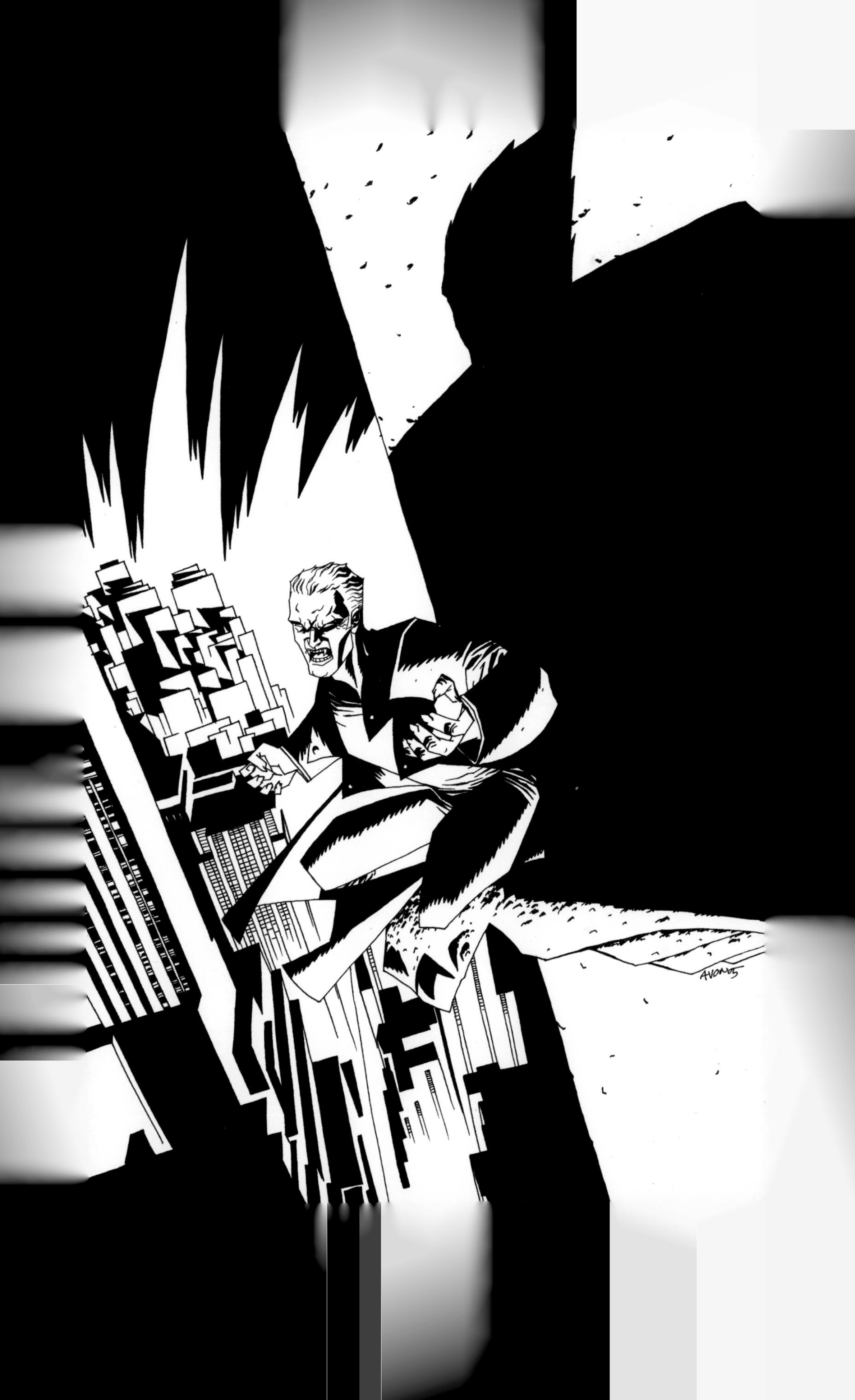

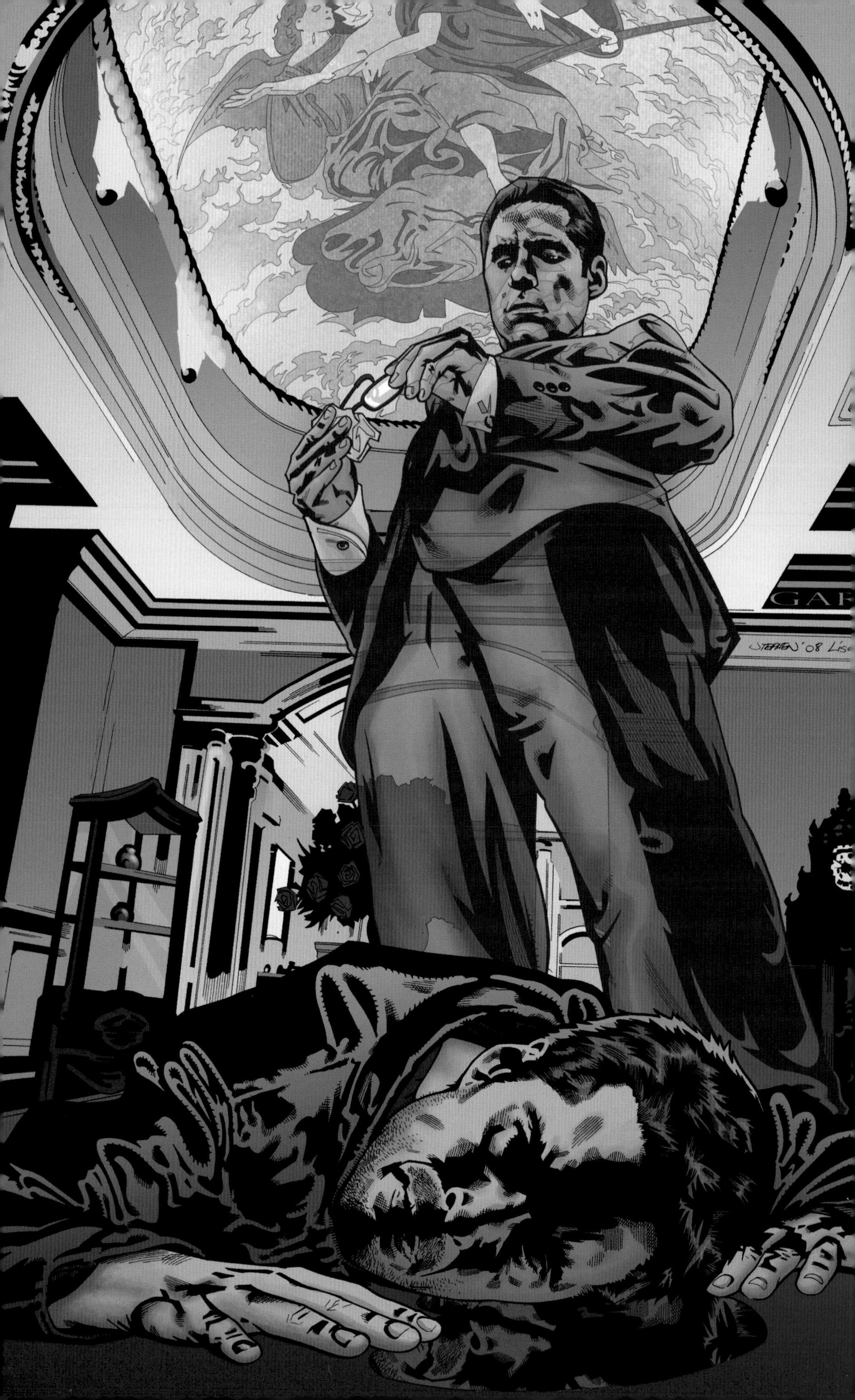

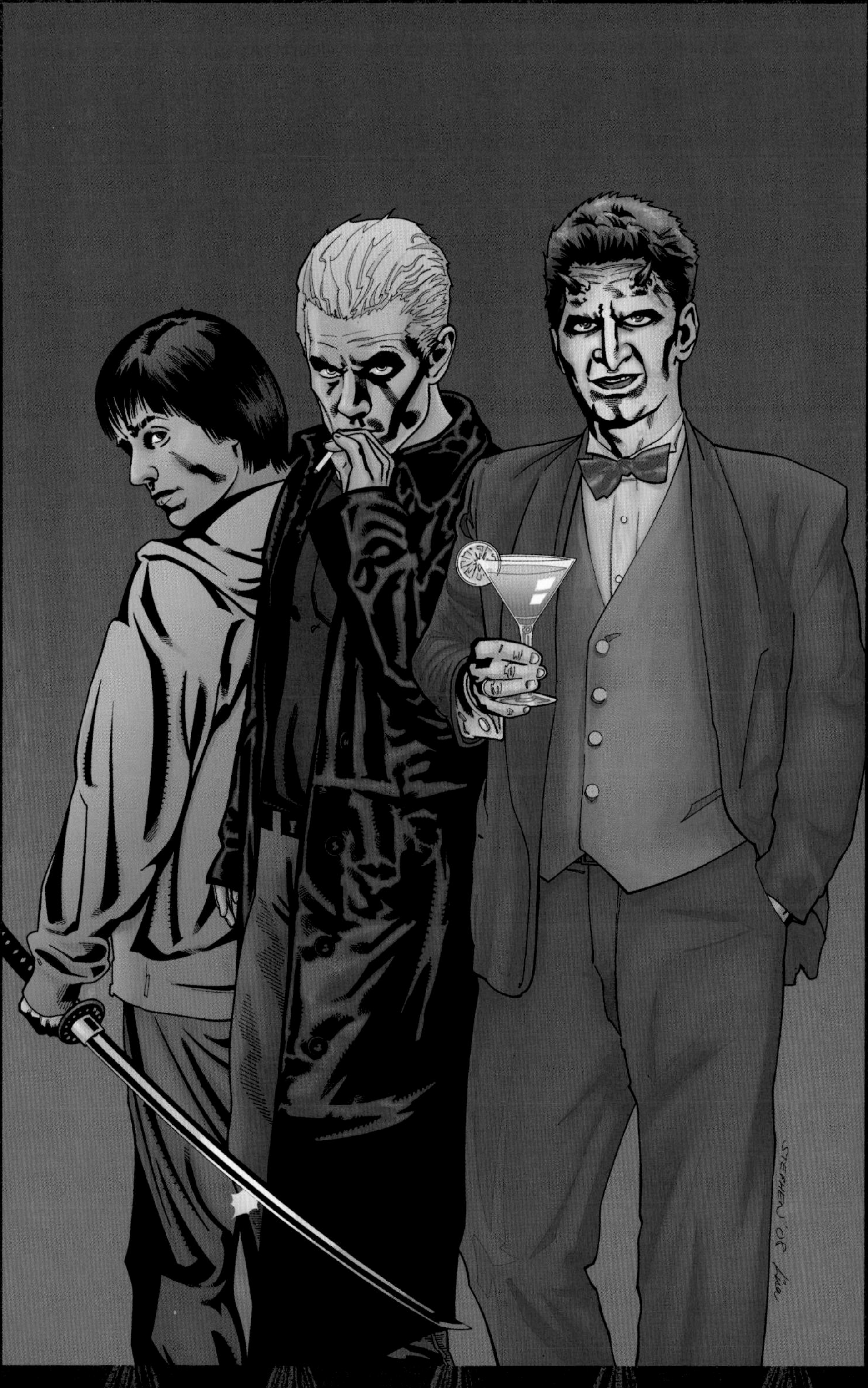

Opposite Page: Art by Stephen Mooney
Colors by Lisa Jackson

This Page: Art by Stephen Mooney
Colors by Lisa Jackson

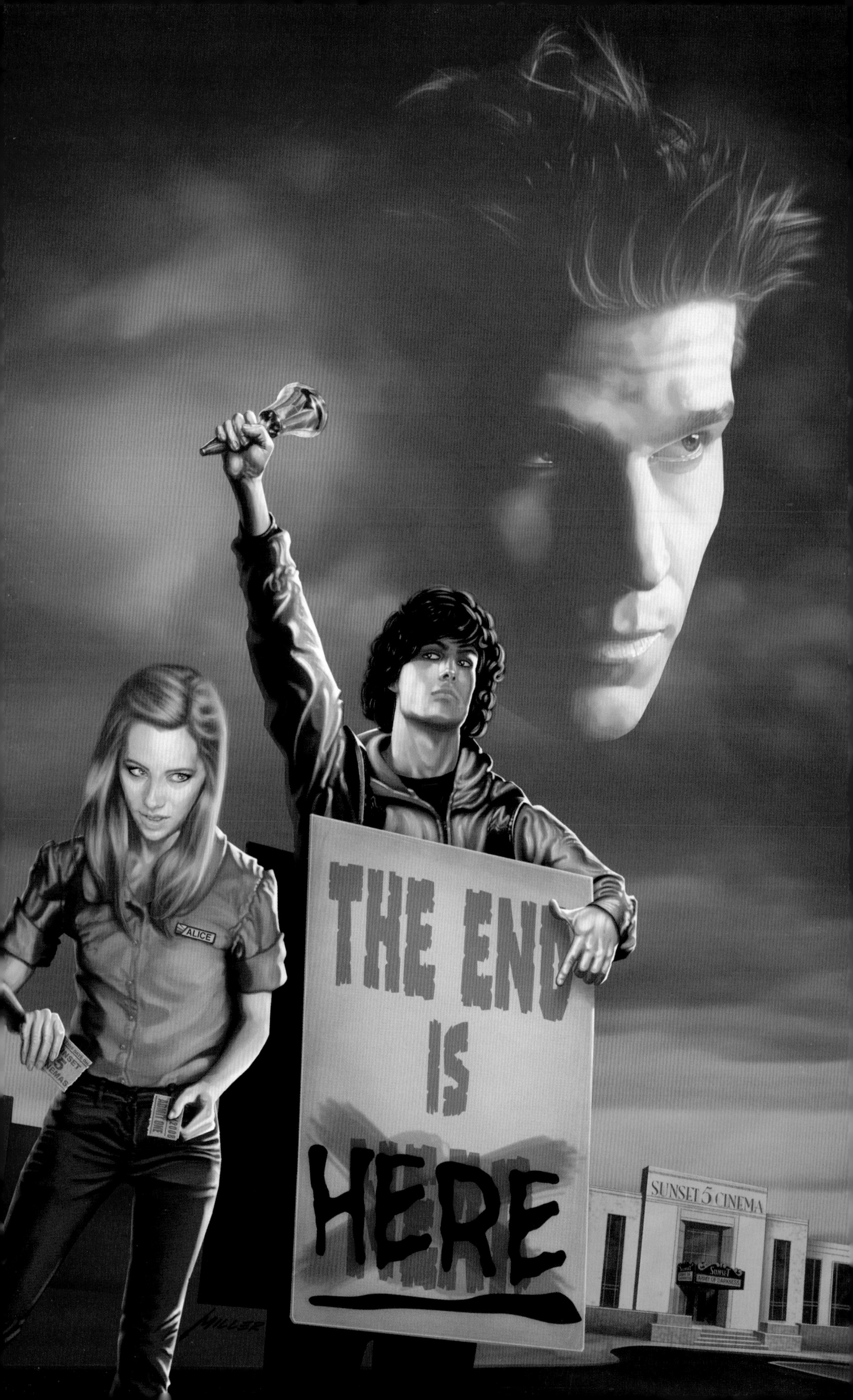
ALICE
THE END IS HERE
SUNSET 5 CINEMA
MILLER

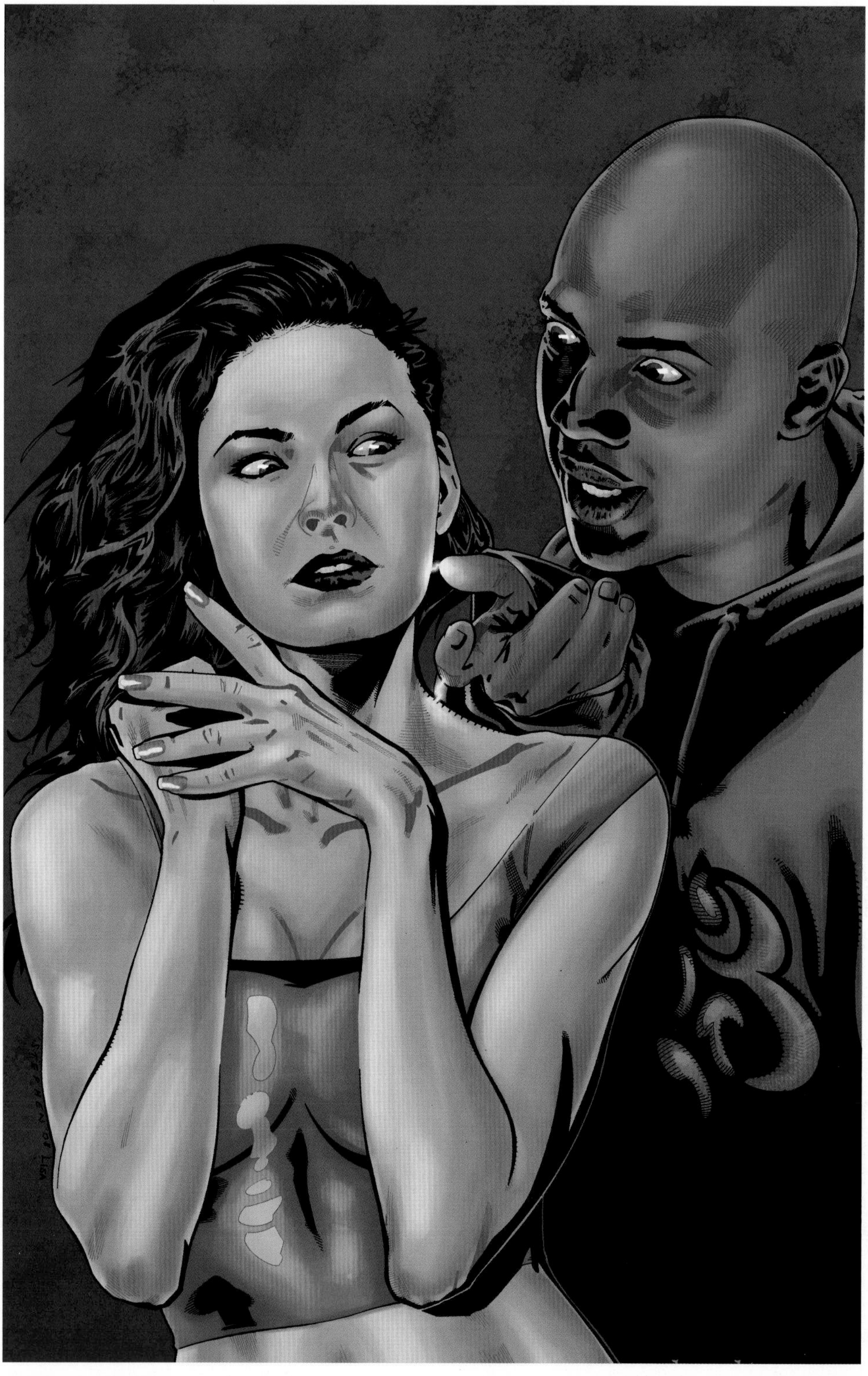

Opposite Page: Art by Brian Miller

This Page: Art by Stephen Mooney
Colors by Lisa Jackson

first night strikes back!

the forgotten stories from angel: after the fall: first night
by brian lynch

We have a lot of characters in *First Night*. Some may say too many. To those people I say, "I'd argue with you, but I'm really trying to finish this scene involving that one dude who Angel passed on the street in season three who didn't say anything but who really looked like he had a killer backstory." So, not every character got a *First Night* tale. But it wasn't for lack of trying. I tried to write everyone's. I'm serious. Everyone's. I leave no stone un-flashbacked. The following is a list of abandoned stories.

THE DRAGON

This was the big one. I tried it a thousand different ways. Why does the Dragon switch teams (not in that way, *slash-fictioneers*)? How does Angel win him over? I wanted Dragon's story to be told with big full-page panels. Dream artist: Arthur Adams.

I wrote one tale that began on Dragon's homeworld, where Wolfram & Hart laid waste to Dragon's little Dragon-babies before swiping him. Threw it out. Dragon doesn't have that maudlin of a backstory.

Next attempt was narrated by The Dragon, and we learn about how Dragon was trained to kill Angel since he was a little baby Dragon himself (shedding light on the fact that Wolfram & Hart had been planning this whole thing long before Angel tried to rise up), only to question it when Angel didn't seem like the angry villain Wolfram & Hart was making him out to be. That didn't feel right, and the narration definitely didn't work.

The final and best attempt (if I do say so myself) was Wolfram & Hart snatching Dragon from a heavenly dimension (the Dragon was the alpha dog) and using millions of shapeshifters to morph into Angel and beat him every day. It was harsh, and dark, and the visual of a legion of evil Angels would have been neat.

The problem with it, and with all of these stories actually, is they aren't about the Dragon's *First Night*, they're backstories. They didn't seem to fit with the rest of the tales. And then when we wrote Gunn's story, I realized it contained more than enough Dragon-info. So out came a Dragon origin!

SPIKE

Even though his story was told in *First Night*, originally there was more to it. It begins the same way as the one that made it into the book, with Spike happy and retiring, but then Spike hurries back to his apartment (from *Spike: Shadow Puppets*) to check on his elderly neighbor Miss Konikoff (also from *Spike: Shadow Puppets*), only to find she's dead, having suffered a heart attack from the helling of Los Angeles. This makes him pick up arms and want to defend those that are left. He actively seeks out Fred/Illyria.

This was taken out because you would have had to have *Spike: Shadow Puppets* to understand Spike's "second home" and just who Miss Konikoff was. Also, Spike didn't need THAT MUCH incentive to be a hero—he's proven himself at this point. But most importantly, it became a plot point that Spike and Fred were placed close together in hell, so out came the old lady!

Plus, I wasn't about to kill Mrs. Konikoff. No way.

NINA

Nina deserved a *First Night*, but the story was mostly her racing to get out of LA, failing, and then wolfing out. There wasn't much to it, and certainly nothing we didn't already know. Her story REALLY began when she found Connor, and that didn't happen for a few weeks in the *After The Fall* timeline.

BETTA GEORGE

George had a longer story. Making his way home from Universal Studios, he promptly got in the first Lord gang fight and swiped by Kr'ph (which is, of course, where we first saw him in *First Night*). It was fun to write Kr'ph again, but the whole thing just didn't feel necessary, even with a cameo from Loan Shark (who knew George from "way back").

LINDSEY/EVE

Chris Ryall and I were going to write this story. It featured Eve getting called by Wolfram & Hart because they were looking for the perfect go-between for them and Angel. Eve was called in, excited she was getting a second chance…

…only to discover a resurrected Lindsey, who promptly killed her. He had to prove himself to Wolfram & Hart to convince them he was on their side, and they demanded a sacrifice. He wanted to know when he could get back to Angel (and Lorne). They replied simply with an ominous "…wait."

This would have been a great, *Twilight Zone*-ish story, but it was discarded for a few reasons. First of all, I'm not entirely convinced Lindsey would kill Eve like that. Second, it would lead the audience to think that Lindsey was more important to the story than he was (in fact, Wesley handled everything Lindsey was going to do in issue 12, and the whole scene plays more powerful coming from a friend). Third, this story would kinda negate Lindsey's brilliantly frustrating and surprising ending on the TV show.

So out came Lindsey and Eve.

GROOSALUGG

Making a living posing for romance novel covers (which explains the return to his Pylea garb and hairdo), Groo is bored with his LA life and decides to leave when suddenly everything goes to hell. He is, of course, very excited by this prospect. This could have been great, and I still may use pieces of this in a future Angel story, but it was cut for space.

CORDELIA CHASE

The crown jewel! The one that got away! Sadly, this one never made it past the planning stages. The story of Cordelia unsuccessfully convincing The Powers That Be to let her go to hell and help Angel. They, of course, tell her what we learn in issue 9. She can't go because they don't have the power to send her there.

Even with Cordelia's desperation, the story didn't feel powerful enough. If Cordy was coming back she deserved a great reason and entrance (and I think we found one in issue 12). Plus, the ending of "we can't send you" "aw nuts, well Angel I hope you're okay" would have been disappointingly anti-climatic.

And thus concludes my tales of what-might-have-been. Ah, memories.

first night notes from brian lynch

It all started with a girl.

That sparked an Internet debate the moment Cartoon Network posted the preview images. People argued over who specifically Rachel was talking about ... she says it includes Puffy, Freezed, Cody.

Ryall insisted it was Steven Ward's mother, which made me question that he actually reads my scripts.

The first episode draft reads differently: it starts right in with a television set in the window of the electronics store. In the second panel a trashcan is thrown through

it so the looters could enter and steal supplies. The TV was destroyed,

not—at—all—subtly acknowledging we

Allow me to ramble about *Angel: After The Fall: First Night: Curse of the Black Pearl* for a bit.

When Joss Whedon first asked me to be a part of *Angel: After The Fall*, I assumed the first issue would take place mere seconds after the finale of the TV show. It was an exciting thought: I would get to flesh out the battle between our heroes and the endless hordes of evil. I would get to write just HOW Angel kills that Dragon. It was going to be the ***greatest comic book fight of all time!***

And then when the smoke cleared, we could drop them all in hell, one by one, and see their reactions. That part was even more exciting to me than the alley fight. Angel realizing he's human, Wesley being told he couldn't move on, Spike surviving yet ANOTHER series finale, Gunn's turn, this was going to be momentous.

I mapped it out in my head: Issue 1 of *Angel: After The Fall*, fight in the alleyway. Ending with a big white flash and everyone going to hell. Issue 2, each character dealing with their first night in hell.

Okay, great, we're all set, a clear plan for how the beginning of this story was forming.

But.

Joss wanted to begin *Angel: After The Fall* months after that alleyway fight. Let the audience catch up to the characters, long after they went off on their own and established their new lives. No alleyway fight! No dragon slaying! NO FIRST NIGHT IN HELL!

But the more I thought about it, the more I realized that it was absolutely the right move. People have already seen Angel fight monsters. Joss' plan would throw the reader right into the fray (no pun intended) and deal with the characters' new lives. Better for drama, more interesting all around, the perfect jumping off point.

So the characters' first night stories were shelved.

But.

We got to talking about the book, and our plans for the month-to-month of it all. Editor-in-Chief/co-conspirator/best pal Chris Ryall pointed out that our amazing artist Franco Urru would need a break at some point. I had an idea: in between issues 5 and 6, we could suspend *After The Fall* for one month (giving Franco a moment to relax) and put out a one-shot special (entitled *Angel: First Night*).

Angel's "First Night" was already seen as a flashback in issue 3, but there are so many other characters to deal with.

Maybe too many.

More and more characters kept warranting their own stories, the book got bigger and bigger and bigger, to the point that it was very obvious that it wouldn't be a one-shot so much as a phone book. The one-shot became a mini-series, which IDW wanted to fold into *After The Fall*.

We were worried that people might be really annoyed that they'd have to wait a really long time to find out what happened to Angel and company in "present day." Plus we'd have three entire issues of a book called *Angel: After The Fall* with no Angel in it (save for a few fleeting appearances in flashbacks).

To solve the first problem, Ryall came up with the idea of putting out the last issue of *Angel: After The Fall: First Night: Prince Caspian* and the return of *Angel: After The Fall* proper in the same month, to cut down on the wait. That is why Chris Ryall is Editor-in-Chief.

As for the second problem… no, Angel's not in *Angel: After The Fall: First Night: The Undiscovered Country* all that much. But as I wrote the stories, it became more and more clear that most of the stories are, in some way, about Angel. How he's influenced who they are, be it directly or indirectly: Lorne is dealing with the repercussions of carrying out Angel's orders, all the while stepping up and becoming a reluctant leader (which, of course, he also learned from Angel). Connor is, through an exchange with a beautiful stranger, inspired by Angel. And of course, Gunn's story is almost completely about Gunn's feelings for our lead character.

He's not walking around and leading the charge (in fact, considering when most of these stories were taking place, he can't walk at all), but he's a part of every story.

And thus, *Angel: After The Fall: First Night: Citizens On Patrol* was born. It was a long birthing process but the resulting baby should look pretty, huh?

Let's take a closer look at some of the stories, shall we? Sweet!

ISSUE ONE

BETTA GEORGE

Like all epic tales, ours begins with a fish laying on a bed and a bored guy in a chair guarding him.

Boring? Oh absolutely.

When the Betta George pages were written, I was well aware *First Night* was being folded into the regular series, and I anticipated people being all sorts of up in arms as we cut away from a battle royale featuring THE RETURN OF FRED and over to something resembling a fish taking a cat-nap. So, we acknowledge that this cutaway is indeed frustrating as George mentions that something way cooler is probably going on somewhere else.

And then we move onto George's first night in hell. All of two panels. George liked to hang out at the *Jaws* section of the Universal Studios ride and freak people out. This would be the first of two "Universal Studios" references, the other being in *Spike: After The Fall #1* (with a Dicky Duck ride replacing the since-destroyed King Kong). Am I allowed to reference Universal Studios in this book? I hope so.

SPIKE

A solo *Spike* story written by me that doesn't feature Franco Urru on art. That is just not right. Yet, looking at David Messina's pages, it doesn't get any more *rightier*. Mr. Messina has had much practice drawing William the Bloody in *Angel: Auld Lang Syne* (now available in paperback!), and in real life he and Franco are friends, so it all fits in the circle of life.

PAGE THREE

Spike's initial reaction to being sent to hell was written to be the polar opposite of Angel's. Angel is mangled and depressed, Spike laughs it off and celebrates the fact that he's survived another battle to the death.

PAGE FOUR

As soon as I wrote the panel featuring "Screw you, Dawn" I knew it would be made into many-an-avatar. For those of you without action figures on your desk, an avatar is a little picture that appears directly below people's names on webboards.

For instance, on my webboard at angrynakedpat.com, I have a little picture of Spike Puppet from *Spike: Shadow Puppets* under my name. Other people have pictures of themselves, a Transformer, or a photo of Angel and Spike photoshopped so they're doing something gay. These are literally the only three avatars you are allowed to use by law.

Anyway, once it occurred to me that "Screw You, Dawn" could be taken out of context, I had Spike beat people to the punch and verbally worry about it. Breaking a fourth wall? Kinda. I am not the biggest fan of this kind of joke, and I certainly didn't want to do it a lot in the *Angel* books, but Spike is very, very happy at this point so a celebratory shout-out to the fans would be something he could get behind.

PAGE FIVE

Another difference between Angel and Spike. Angel saw someone in need of help and he LEAPT from the top of the building to get to them (which he soon realized was a mistake). Spike sees someone in need of help, and he takes the elevator. Spike just survived his SECOND certain-death series finale, you can't expect him to go along risking his neck immediately.

You'll notice the elevator, despite being all "hell-ed out," still plays Muzak. The fact that it's "The Girl From Ipanema" is a shout-out to *The Blues Brothers*.

PAGE SIX

Fred's "return" was seen at the very end of issue 5 of *Angel: After The Fall*, but we get a little more into it here. Notice that she and Spike were teleported away from everyone else when Los Angeles went to hell. BUT they were teleported right near each other. It makes one think…

PAGE SEVEN

Spike tries to retire, he makes a real attempt to stop rescuing humans, but it lasts all of five seconds. Oh Spike, you tried!

CONNOR

Art by the amazing Stephen Mooney. Stephen not only tackled Connor's tale, but Kate's in the next issue.

Kate was definitely one of our more successful surprises in the book. People knew there was going to be an older character returning (it was mentioned in *Previews* and I think Ryall and I dropped a few hints), but *Internetians* weren't certain just **who** would be coming back.

Connor's new role in *Angel* proved popular with the fans. It originated, as most awesome ideas often do, in the *geniusy* mind of Mr. Whedon. He wanted Connor to step up and actually enjoy himself a bit. Be a real hero. Certainly a change from the Connor we saw on the TV show. And it really clicked.

If someone told me that Connor would be among my favorite characters to write in an *Angel* book, I would've called them crazy, and then maybe apologized for jumping to conclusions about their sanity but then I'd mutter "but you are crazy" under my breath as I walked away. But sure enough, a well-adjusted character among a bunch of not-so-well-adjusted characters definitely stands out.

First Night sheds some light on just why Connor is a changed man when we meet him in issue 1 of *After The Fall*. The answer: he's inspired by his father. In a roundabout way of course, but there you go.

PAGE TEN

Connor's story takes place moments after we saw him leave Angel's side in "Not Fade Away." Angel told him to leave, but Connor's having second thoughts. Being a teenage boy, he's also having impure thoughts about a lady he's passing by.

PAGE ELEVEN

Stephen Mooney is awesome. Connor is very Peter Parker on this page, and that's exactly what we wanted. Also notice that Connor, like his father, wants to slay a dragon.

PAGE TWELVE

A new wrinkle to the character: Connor remembers everything that's happened to him since conception. How? Why? It'll be explained soon, but it would appear to be freaking our boy out, especially when…

PAGE FOURTEEN

…he remembers his first sexual experience was actually with someone who helped take care of him when he was a baby. That would mess a boy up pretty severely. Even if it is Charisma Carpenter.

PAGE EIGHTEEN

And now the bad guys know he's Angel's son! Oh MAN who is torturing our heroes like this?

I like the demon army. I mean, sure they're awful and evil and want to kill our heroes, but at the same time, they're not really that organized and missed the big alleyway fight. I can identify. Many a battle to the death has been avoided accidentally because I lost track of time.

LORNE

When we last saw Lorne on the hit TV show *Angel*, he was troubled (to the say the least) over the fact that he shot someone in cold blood. But then, BUT THEN, dear reader, when we see him in the hit comic book *Angel: After The Fall*, he's well-adjusted and in charge of Silverlake, the ONE LIVABLE SECTION OF HELL! How did this happen?!

The answer is easy: Much like Angel spends his life making amends for his bad deeds, Lorne is helping people to make up for what he's done.

I thought it would be fun to tell the story in a style suited to the character. So we tried it entirely in verse.

When Ryall told me that John Byrne had agreed to draw the *Lorne* story, I was shocked and elated and felt undeserving. Byrne is, to say the least, one of my favorite comic writers/artists. His epic run on *Fantastic Four* is what got me into comics years ago. *Man of Steel, Action, Superman, Legends, She-Hulk, Next Men,* hell, his *Doom Patrol Secret Origins Annual*—I have it all. I felt very honored that he took the time to play in our sandbox.

And he played with the verses a little bit, to make it flow better. He's not only a brilliant writer and artist, he can collaborate on a tune! I'm willing to bet the man can choreograph the heck outta a dance number as well. He's a quadruple threat, this one.

The whole thing was done perfectly. Illyria crawling out of the FRED grave, Angel's "neat plans," the taxicab's face, Byrne made it playful and light until it needed to go dark. Coupled with Len's amazing colors, the whole thing pops.

If *Angel: After The Fall* is the last comic I ever do, I had a story illustrated by John Byrne. THAT is amazing.

ISSUE TWO

BETTA GEORGE

A few people were a bit confused as to what is going on in the third panel. After all, George was stuck in a hotel room, and then suddenly he's at a carnival with Spike. And Spike bats around a vampire-punching bag. Simply put, Betta George is using his impressive mental abilities to force the vampire into thinking that THAT is exactly what's going on.

The old "telepathic fish tricks a vampire into thinking he's a punching bag" trick. Sometimes comic writing can be fun.

Oh, and I should point out an error that was made on my part. The fact that George declares, "help!" was supposed to directly lead into Kate's story. Makes more sense now, doesn't it? Fish needs help, Connor needs help. Yeah, I got confused on the order of the stories. I'm not perfect, people. Adorable, tall, charming, YES… perfect, oh no.

WESLEY

One look at Nick Runge's art and you can see why we wanted him to stay in the world of *Angel: After The Fall* a little while longer. Nick went on to grace us with his pencils for issues 9, 10 and 11, and a slew of covers when Franco lent a hand over at *Spike: After The Fall.*

Wesley's death on the television show was an insanely sad moment. Heart-wrenching. And this story takes place mere moments after he died. We twist the knife even further, letting Wesley (and maybe, just maybe the reader… if they didn't read the first five issues) think he's getting his happy ending but then ripping it from him.

PAGE FIVE

Here's why Wesley is a cool character. He gets a moment of perfect bliss. He's lying in bed with his true love… he could very easily stay in this moment, but he doesn't want to. It's not real, and he won't accept it.

Also, dig how great Runge is with reactions. That last panel still looks like Fred, but now there's a sense of evil to the previously angelic face.

A lot of people asked me just WHO is posing as Fred. They figure it might be Wolfram & Hart's pencil pusher Eve from season five of the show. Certainly the "Adam & Eve" symbolism in later pages could be taken as a hint. Still others thought maybe it was Lilah. Truth is, it's neither (certainly not Lilah, who wouldn't take such glee in Wesley's torture). The identity of Wesley's tormentor isn't important. The message, and Wesley's reaction to it, most definitely is.

PAGE SEVEN

The second panel was originally supposed to have Wesley's Wolfram & Hart contract scribbled all over Fred's body.

PAGE EIGHT

It was previously stated that Fred's soul was destroyed. The person that said that was a bad man. Now it's stated that a piece of Fred is somewhere. The person that said that is a bad woman. Who to believe? Wesley doesn't know, but the smallest glimmer of hope that Fred is out there and that he can be with her is enough for him to play their game.

PAGE TEN

Look at Runge's drawing of Amy Acker. Can he and I do a series called *The Further Adventures of Amy Acker*? *Acker The Fall*? Something? Hello? People?

KATE

Connor's narration really made me wish that I could play more with his inner dialog in other books. So much fun to write this kid. And Stephen Mooney's facial expressions added so much to it. The Connor/Kate stories are among my favorite *Angel/Spike* comics that I've had a hand in. I think they came out really nice.

PAGE THIRTEEN

Kate's reveal. And she gets a logo. I've never gotten a logo. Believe me I've tried.

We needed someone to kinda nudge Connor to become the hero we've seen in *Angel: Ater The Fall's* first five issues. We wanted a character who had been directly inspired by Angel so Angel could indirectly inspire Connor. Kate seemed like the perfect fit. Second choice was introducing Connor to Nina at this point, but (A) Nina would be in no mood to inspire anyone, (B) I didn't want Connor to KNOW this person had a direct link to Angel, and (C) I love Kate, wanted her back, and she was someone who literally received a pep talk from Angel right before our eyes on the show.

PAGE SEVENTEEN

Kate's dealer was also the topic of conversation on the Internet. Some thought it was Gwen. I don't think the identity of the dealer is important, but if it increases someone's enjoyment, it can be whoever they want. If Kate ever gets a spin-off (AND SHE SHOULD) maybe we'll meet the dealer.

PAGE EIGHTTEEN

Kate is quoting Angel while making a bomb out of car parts. I can do that first part ("Personally, I kinda want to slay the Dragon!"…see?) but not the other. Maybe that's why I don't have a logo. I do have an avatar though.

PAGE NINETEEN

This is the moment Connor becomes a hero. I hope he didn't take Kate's two favorite weapons in that last panel. That would suck for her.

We should've cut back to her later, being attacked by a monster, reaching for those weapons because they're enchanted or some nonsense, only to see Connor has taken them. She would die cursing the little moppet.

BETTA GEORGE

I liked giving Betta George such a huge reveal. "Oh you didn't bother reading the fish page? Nah, you didn't miss anything, just SLAYERS!" And then that fish-avoider cries and cries. And then reaches for enchanted weapons but Connor has stolen those as well.

ISSUE THREE

BETTA GEORGE

George only gets one page this time out. To go back to the slightly lighter telepathic fish moments after seeing Gunn's *First Night* would lessen the impact of Gunn's tale.

Though I was very happy we were able to get in an AIR SUPPLY reference before we left George. My Mom was a big fan. I mean, I think she still is, but much like that vamp, she's too embarrassed to admit it.

GWEN

Gwen's story pays off big-time later in the series. The emotional state she's in by the end of this tale, and her overwhelming need to get back to how things were, might lead one to worry about her. I mean, she could touch people for the first time in forever and then suddenly she's accidentally killing people. She needs help. I just hope she doesn't fall in with the wrong crowd.

On a happier note, congrats to Gwen for getting her own logo. I knew she could do it!

In the script for this story, I asked the artist to make "Nate" look like Nathan Fillion. Nathan Fillion, for those that don't know, was in a VERY popular TV show called *Two Guys, A Girl And A Pizza Place*. I think he retired from acting immediately after that show, but he really truly should get back in the game. Just a hunch, but I do believe he'd mesh with Joss' style of writing very well. Mark my words, if Whedon and Fillion ever get together, there is going to be FIREWORKS I tell you.

Please forgive Gwen's cleavage, everyone. She was in the middle of a heavy petting session or else she would have been more demure.

CIVILIANS

This was a bit of a risk, telling a story that didn't star the *Angel* characters in the middle of the *Angel* book. But I thought it might be fun to see how someone who doesn't know *Angel* from *Bones* would react to his or her city going right to hell.

The art for *Civilians* is by Kevyn Schmidt, a good friend of mine who was working on an online comic featuring himself and his girlfriend Alice as the leads. I loved how great Kevyn was with facial expressions and wrote this story with him in mind. I even wrote Kevyn and Alice as the lead characters (though Kevyn was called "Curly" in the script).

I didn't know that one of the covers actually featured these characters (a full-on painted cover by the extremely talented Brian Miller) until a week or so before the comic came out. It was thrilling to see my friends drawn as full-on heroic comic characters. I was worried that people wouldn't like the cover because it didn't feature any *Angel* characters (save for Angel's head looming in the sky in the background, a la the Baby Sun on *Teletubbies*). I shan't have worried, people really dug the cover. And now Kevyn and Alice had an avatar for life. And as you all know by now, that's the most important thing. Next to a logo. A logo is the coolest, followed by an avatar. Third place is reserved for a famous haircut. Like "The Rachel" from *Friends*. I think eventually "the Brian Lynch" will catch on, and thousands upon thousands of people will walk around with sideburns and a bald spot.

PAGE NINE

When "Curly" is changing the letters on the marquee during the flashback, please notice that all the movies playing star (or at least feature appearances by) Angel and Buffy actors. They are, as follows:

Valentine (starring David Boreanaz)
Chance (written by/directed by/starring Amber Benson,
        co-starring James Marsters and Andy Hallett)
House On Haunted Hill (with an appearance by James Marsters)
My Bodyguard (starring Adam Baldwin)
Good Burger (the greatest movie of all time, and co-starring J August Richards)
The Indian In The Cupboard (with Vincent Kartheiser)
First Knight (with Alexis Desinof)
Catch Me If You Can (with Amy Acker)

The movie poster on the side of the marquee is for *The Room*, a cult movie written/directed and starring Tommy Wiseau (the inspiration for one of the villains in *Spike: Asylum*). The Sunset 5 (location of this story) is the only theater where *The Room* plays, so that poster is LOCATION ACCURATE!

The other poster is for *Culted*, a short film by Gary Gretsky, a friend of Kevyn's. And mine, but a better friend of Kevyn. I mean, I know Gary and I like him, but he's closer to Kevyn. That's not to say Gary and I couldn't become close in time, but we're on opposite coasts so we're really going to have to work at it if we want this to happen. My point is, I don't think Gary and I are going to be best friends but it was nice to give his movie a shout-out. And also that Gary should move to LA if he truly loves me.

PAGE THIRTEEN

Please notice that Audrey 2 from *Little Shop Of Horrors* is alive and well in hell.

Grace Is Gone is on the marquee. Yes, this comic takes place a little while ago, and yes, *Grace Is Gone* is fairly recent, but let's assume this theater got the movie early. Like, before it was shot. Shut up, I don't point out continuity errors in YOUR comic books.

People have asked what happens to the lead characters after this story ends. I don't want to say—it's fun to leave it up in the air. What do you think happened? Is Alice okay? Why did she never come back? What about the Homeless Guy? The last panel has him drawing a sword as what looks to be a giant Bull-Man is heading for him. And begin your fanfiction…

…nooooow!

GUNN

This is what's known as "the main event" in *First Night*. Everyone's been waiting for the specifics of Gunn's turning. Many people guessed it was Harmony who did it. Not quite sure where we could go with that. Still others thought Angel or Spike were the culprits (which neither would do, knowing full-well he'd rather die).

The answer: it doesn't matter who turned Gunn. Whoever did it—in Gunn's eyes—Angel is to blame.

Scott Tipton collaborated on the plot and dialog for the *Gunn* storyline, because (A) I'm a fan of Scott's previous work on the Angel comics, and (B) Scott is a friend who knows and loves these characters and deserves a story in official *Angel* canon. It was fun emailing back and forth with him, laying out beats and coming up with specifics.

Fun fact about the vamp who turned Gunn: his name was Matthius. I took his name out at zero hour because the mere introduction of his name seemed to suggest that we should know more about him.

Another fun fact about the vamp who turned Gunn: we asked Mirco, the artist on Gunn's story, to draw the vamp to slightly resemble Angel. We wanted a square-jawed all-American looking guy to try and be the leader, so Gunn could cut him down quickly.

This is also the most we've seen of the alleyway fight, to date. So, if you think about it, I kinda sorta got to have a hand in the **greatest comic book fight of all time!**

And thus concludes my insane scribbling about *First Night*. If you've made it this far, you are to be congratulated. You deserve a prize. So here we go, and don't share this with anyone who didn't read this entire thing, we're a secret society (handshakes to follow). So here we go, the official *Angel: After The Fall: First Night: Jason Goes To Hell: The Final Friday* drinking game. It goes a little something like this:

1. Take a sip of your drink whenever you see tentacles coming out of the ground (be it streets or manholes). WARNING: If you are drinking alcohol, you might get very drunk. Try it first with apple juice and see how it goes.

2. Finish your drink whenever you see a giant spider. You'd be surprised.

That's it for me, guys. I do hope you enjoyed yourselves. See you for volume 3!

Brian Lynch
Proud owner of many avatars but no logos
07-17-08

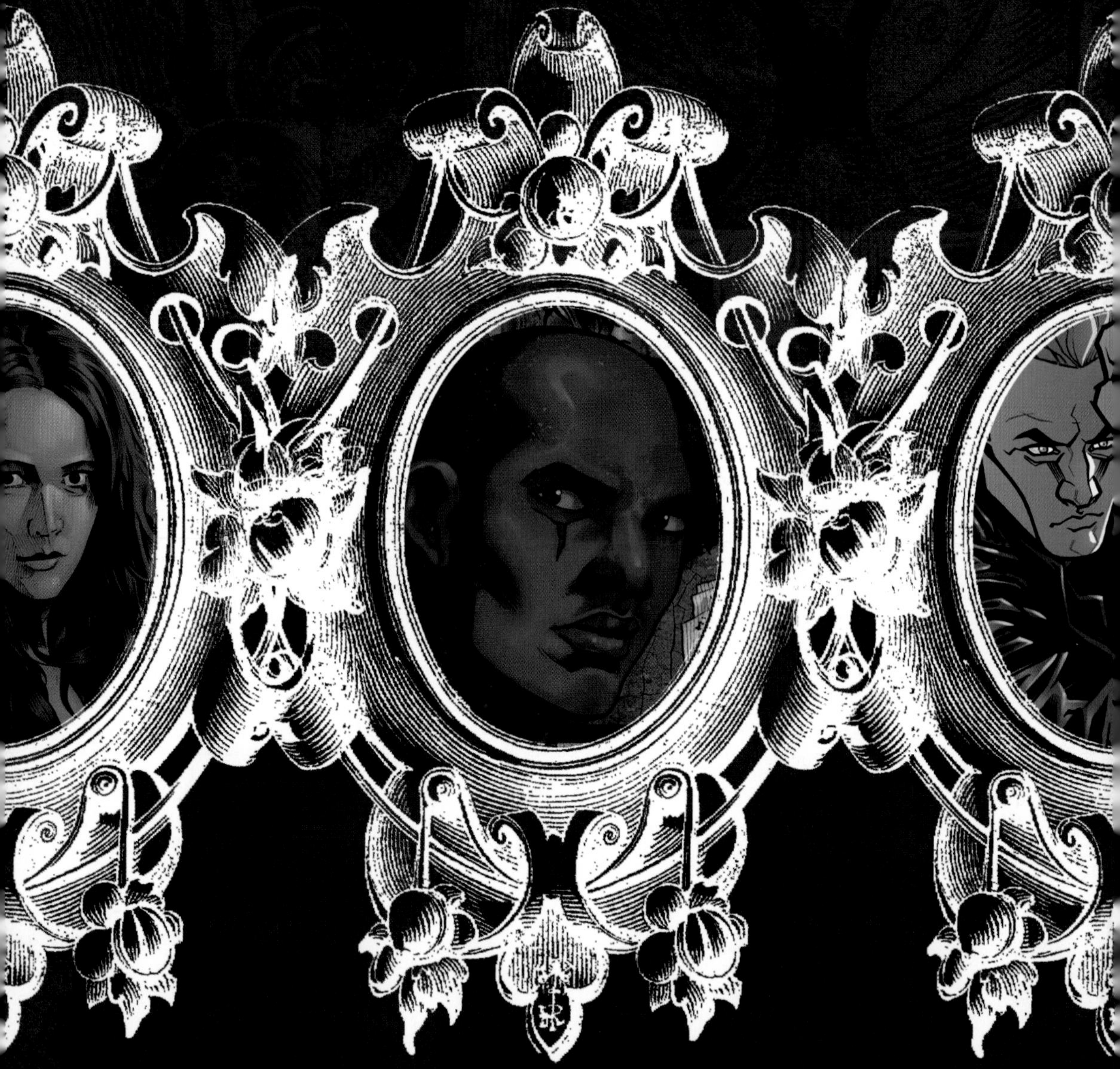

ANGEL™

—AFTER THE FALL—

VOLUME 2

F I R S T N I G H T